NOT THE WHOLE STORY

Not the Whole Story

A Memoir

Angela Huth

Constable • London

CONSTABLE

First published in Great Britain in 2018 by Constable

1 3 5 7 9 10 8 6 4 2

Copyright © Angela Huth, 2018

A CIP catalogue record for this book
is available from the British Library.

ISBN: 978-1-47212-706-8

Typeset in Bembo by SX Composing DTP, Rayleigh, Essex
Printed and bound in Great Britain by Clays Ltd, St Ives plc

Papers used by Constable are from well-managed forests
and other responsible sources.

Constable
An imprint of
Little, Brown Book Group
Carmelite House
50 Victoria Embankment
London EC4Y 0DZ

An Hachette UK Company
www.hachette.co.uk

www.littlebrown.co.uk

For my grandsons:

Erskine, Caspar and Conor,

and Otis and Elvin.

Contents

	Prologue	1
1	America to Farnham Royal	5
2	Dolls	33
3	Boarding School	50
4	The Grandmother	67
5	Lawnside	81
6	Paris and Florence	112
7	Debutante Interlude	135
8	Advertising and America	156
9	Work	174
10	Synaesthesia	196
11	Television	209
12	Wootton	234
13	Change	251
14	Pullens End	268
15	Forty Years On	290
	Appendix	301

Prologue

Suddenly, I am old. My grandsons say I am *very* old. They look in puzzlement at my shortness (well, one of them is over six feet), my glasses, my struggle with hearing. They can't understand the changes, and nor can I. Old age is a state of being that for decades has been a distant hazy horizon. It did not threaten. It was something to envisage merely with mild curiosity – a state to sympathise with, not to think about too much. Then, some immeasurable years ahead, to encounter.

Naturally, in the last decade, I've observed a few of the minor ailments that some contemporaries, once so energetic and healthy, would describe with a hesitant laugh: arthritic thumbs, puckering neck, wayward aches and pains. Many of us have confessed to not being able to remember why we have gone to the fridge, or where we have put glasses, keys, and the list we have made to counteract forgetfulness. There have also been, among these friends, disasters of a different order – strokes, heart attacks and a too-long list of cancers. I have been lucky enough to avoid most of those troubles, and energy, that most enjoyable of sensations, was still intact. When we moved from Oxford to the country ten years ago I found that unpacking 137 boxes, and putting the stuff away over three floors, was a trifle more tiring than all the other moves we had made, and then remembered I was seventy. But once everything was in place, I returned to the work routine I have followed since I was nineteen, and have no intention, ever, of retiring.

I have been lucky. I realised this very acutely in 2014 when six of my old friends died. My chief anxiety now is that time is running out. I've not yet written a book that I am proud of – will I be capable of that in the short years left? I doubt it. Will my slightly fading energy be enough to keep me writing till I die? And, indeed, will anyone want to read what I write in my dotage? I doubt that, too. This could be my last book, though I hope that is not the case, and it is not the whole story, but it's all I'm prepared to tell. I am against writing about entirely private matters, be they triumphs or disasters. I believe in indication, and evocation, but not in exposing events whose very privacy makes them precious.

These were my thoughts before I began writing this small memoir, but I had no idea of how many pitfalls I would come across. Memory was no problem: I remember very clearly disparate things since I was a small child. What to leave out was more difficult. I decided, with some reluctance, not to write much about friends. Although I would have loved to describe many of them as I see them, I had no wish to cause offence by subjective descriptions, even if they could be amusing. Many a wise autobiographer advised me to be wary of name-dropping, and I was. But in the arts world in which I have always hovered, inevitably I have become friends with artists, writers, musicians and actors whose work has made them famous. It would be a pity to leave them all out, I thought, as many of them provided stories worth telling. But I decided to include a few of them only if there was a specific reason. I have tried to keep to that. The balance between loyalty and honesty has been a precarious one.

This short volume has turned out to be merely a handful of recollections of well-remembered times and stories – some probably misremembered, too – and a few people who have played a crucial part in my life. And some confessions: I have never before tried to write about my doll phobia, for instance, or about the effect synaesthesia has had over the years. I can only hope that this collection of stories from times past might give some idea of a mostly happy life that has gone, and is going, much too fast.

1
America to Farnham Royal

I was in a basket.

It was one of those upright wicker baskets with a handle like a walking stick relied on by elderly shoppers. I'm not sure who was pushing me – my mother? My nanny? I was only aware of streams of very bright colour on each side of our path. Later I learnt we were moving between long stalls of fruit and vegetables at the Farmers' Market, Santa Monica, California. It was 1941.

Blank, then.

A year later I was standing at the stern of some enormous ship, fascinated by the huge fan of white water jumping behind us. There were other ships nearby: we were returning home in convoy. Beside me was a sailor, kneeling. He held up a strange, bent yellow fruit. Suddenly he unzipped the skin, offered me the pale curve and asked me to try it. 'It's called a banana,' he said. I loved it.

Then, blank again.

* * *

Memory is full of shavings that become hopelessly dislodged from their sequence. Very early memory, when it exists, often appears in the form of small, brighter-than-life shards. In conversations in which grown-ups tax each other about their earliest recollections, I've often been derided when offering my two exiguous memories. To remember things at two years old is unbelievable, they say. But it isn't: there are a good many people who retain snippets of inconsequential pictures that never fade. Some time after the Atlantic banana, I'm not sure when, the pictures clumped together more closely, more frequently. Well, I was older: almost four.

Before the war, my parents bought a house near Windsor, in Burnham Beeches, Buckinghamshire – then an unwrecked forest of magnificent, ancient trees. East Burnham House was a Queen Anne house of grand proportions surrounded by different-level lawns, cedar and oak trees, a sunken rose garden and a huge vegetable garden. Woods and fields stretched in all directions. They loved EBH, as it was known, and were happy there for a time. But at the beginning of the war, the house was requisitioned by the Dutch government. The decision, later always regretted, was made for my sister Trish and me to go to California with our mother and Nanny. My father was by then directing films at Pinewood Studios. He rented a house at Farnham Royal, to be near work. Fir Trees was one of a clump of pre-war houses, architecturally identical to the dolls' houses of the time: mock beams and small dark windows. Gloomy fir trees guarded the garden from any hint of sun. My parents, who had been extraordinarily happy since their marriage in 1934, decided after only eighteen months of our stay in America that they could no longer bear to be apart. Hence the decision for us to return in the middle of the war. We docked at Liverpool in 1943.

'And Daddy,' said my mother, 'was the only father not to be there to meet us.'

At Farnham Royal, the war did not impede on our lives very much, but we were always aware that something disturbing was going on. The house had a cellar to which we repaired several nights a week when there was a bombing raid. I remember feeling reluctance, sharp as pain, when we were woken by the howl of the warning siren and had to leave the warmth of bed to creep downstairs till the raid was over. I don't think real alarm pierced our sleepiness, because Nanny was good at assuring us it would all be over in no time. 'They'll be gone in a minute,' she would say. Her prediction of time might not have been accurate, but we knew she was right: we just had to wait patiently for the all-clear siren which would definitely come. Once in the cellar, which smelt of coal dust and musty biscuits, we huddled together in a tense little threesome – I don't remember my parents joining us. Nanny always wore her pink quilted dressing gown from America, her long plait of black hair – by day made into a neat bun – snaking down her back. Not one to let standards slip, even during a raid, I could see she had managed to brighten her cheeks with a dab of Pond's face powder with its eternally comforting smell.

Under the stairs of the house was a large store cupboard, dauntingly crammed with tins of fruit salad brought back from California. Almost every meal ended with this lurid stuff

– cherries of an eccentric pink, and flabby wedges of dead pineapple floating in a syrup of vile sweetness. We were encouraged to appreciate how lucky we were, all this fruit salad, compared with some.

One day a woman came round and gave us each a gas mask. She also delivered great thick sheets of black rubber embossed with circles. These we were asked to cut out, and they would be collected. 'War work,' she explained. The huge scissors for this job hurt our fingers, and the horrible smell of the rubber permeated the whole house.

An ever-memorable part of our lives at that time were the soldiers – some dozen real soldiers all over the garden, every day. In their camouflage uniforms and berets, they crawled about on their stomachs, randomly aiming their rifles. They were friendly, and liked the two eider ducks that provided our eggs. But they were not prepared to explain why they were there and what they were doing.

It's always curious to trace back grown-up prejudices, likes or dislikes, to occasions in one's childhood, and it was in this house that two minor things made a lasting impression.

One was the wallflowers. They were the only flowers in the garden – masses of them crowding every bed with their horrible curry colours and fusty smell. I thought, for many years, they were *war* flowers, and grew in gardens where soldiers with guns crawled on their stomachs. This made it impossible for me, to this day, ever to see their charm. The next impact for life came from an occasion when I was ill in bed. To take away the taste of the medicine, Nanny would cut me a small slice off a Mars Bar which had been bought with our precious sweet rations. It would not have occurred to me to eat more than one thin, perfect sliver: I thought that *sliced* was the way Mars Bars had to be eaten. Years later, rationing long past, a friend bit off a huge hunk of a bar, and continued to eat until it was finished. I was shocked. And the shock of someone eating a whole Mars Bar has never quite worn off. I have tried to overcome my foolish prejudice, but have never entirely succeeded.

It was during our spell in Farnham Royal that I remember seeing a man with a bald head walking across a field with my mother, and a couple of wolfhounds. Later, two beautiful wooden pencil boxes from Switzerland came through the post, addressed to Trish and me. Their tops folded back with the typical delicacy of Swiss craftsmanship. But there was something about them we did not like, though we did not discuss this. *Alec* had sent them for us, our mother said. We never used them.

Alec was the bald-headed dog lover, a French diplomat. Our mother had always had a penchant for the French, and he had snared her. I have no memory of ever seeing him, apart from that day when I glimpsed the two of them walking side by side in the distance. They inspired not a feeling of grown-up suspicion, but a flicker of incomprehensible unease. Perhaps her affair with him was retaliation on her part. She had discovered our father, despite his declarations of loneliness while we were in California, had been having a merry time with various women, one of whom had plainly diverted him from meeting us in Liverpool.

I have seen photographs of the family at Fir Trees, so assume our mother was there from time to time. But after the war, when we moved back to EBH, I have no recollection of her presence, apart from very occasional short and turbulent visits.

She had definitely gone (to France to live with her diplomat). She was not ashamed of this particular decision; happy to confess she was an imperfect mother. Bored stiff by small children, she admitted she had no desire to amuse them or look after them.

She did claim to love us, but the love was not strong enough to inspire interest in our lives. So long as we had enough food (she was a skilful purchaser of black-market eggs), Nanny to look after us, and we went to decent schools, she felt she had done her bit. Never once did she read us a story, take us for a walk or put us to bed. Before we left for America, on Nanny's rare days off, a nursery maid was hired to take over.

My mother's chief concern for our wellbeing seemed to be the care she took over our clothes. Always beautifully dressed herself (Dior, Lachasse, Givenchy), there were occasional trips in a local taxi, with Nanny, to meet her in London at Fortnum and Mason. There, in the children's clothes department, we stood for hours being measured up for silk dresses with Peter Pan collars and smocked bodices. I don't know where she thought these dresses might be worn, for in post-war rural Bucks there were very few parties. But they were immortalised in studio photographs by the then acclaimed photographers Marcus Adams and Dorothy Wilding.

On these trips to London, our mother's voice (I've no memory of her face) caused some unease in Trish and me. As she stomped through the departments of Fortnum and Mason, she commented very loudly about almost everything. Trying to keep up with her, and holding our hands, was Nanny – Nanny in her London clothes that came with the job: Prince of Wales suit, down-turned black hat, black fox fur round her neck, its mouth clasped to its front paws.

'*Mummy!*' she sometimes shouted. 'Wait!' But our mother did not slow down. She was anxious to be off back to Paris, where she now lived with Alec. While our new dresses were good reason for a visit to England, Christmas was not. One year she invited Nanny to bring us to London to see her in Claridge's, where she was staying with her Frenchman. We took her a swan's-down powder puff. Appreciation for it was scant, but then she'd never been one for showing pleasure in childish presents. Over the years I remember dozens of calendars, embroidered bits of stuff and crocheted mats that were swiftly swept into the bin.

Trish and I have always assumed that our mother's lack of maternal feelings was because she had no example of motherly love to follow. Her childhood was materially well provided for, but bleak. The schools she went to were mostly abroad, hence her skill at languages – for which she had a definite talent. In the few conversations we had about her youth I can't ever remember her complaining about the loneliness that must often have accosted her. In various portraits she looks pathetically sad, certainly not cheered by the extravagant amount of beautiful clothes that her mother – a great believer in the power of material things – bought her. There are no pictures of her with either parent, though she often said how much she loved her very old father.

There she was, a lonely rich child, with nothing, it seemed, to scintillate her barren life. Her mother, an eccentric monster of materialism, sent her off to schools in Switzerland, Italy, Germany and France, claiming that the foreign air would be beneficial for the weak chest from which our mother always suffered. The result was she became bilingual in French, and spoke fluent German and Italian, but beyond that seemed to have had very little education. She had a native intelligence and a very quick, often caustic wit, but lacked curiosity about worldly matters, literature, history, art and so on. Her father, a Yorkshire land-owner, Harold Nickols, was evidently a mild and kindly man: good looking, with dazzling aquamarine eyes which his daughter inherited. Although not an alcoholic, he drank a great deal (perhaps to numb the impact of his ferocious and demanding wife) and died when my mother was fourteen. Rather than share a house with my grandmother, she spent as much time as possible abroad. She was sent to a finishing school in Paris, where she was befriended by the sympathetic woman who ran it, Madame Boissier. Bois, as she was known, became her surrogate mother, adviser, helper. The two of them kept in touch and visited each other for some forty years, until Bois died.

There is no record of exactly how Mum was introduced to an extraordinary admirer – Manuel II, the last King of Portugal, in 1931. (Manuel Maria Filipe Carlos Amélio Luís Miguel of Braganza-Saxe-Coburg and Gotha. He reigned from February 1908 to October 1910.) But it is assumed they met somewhere in Europe. He was forty-two, married to Augusta Victoria of Hohenzollern-Sigmaringen. Mum was twenty-one. It's likely that she introduced him to Bois that year. Certainly the old headmistress and the king kept in touch, exchanged letters.

Her relationship with Manuel was of a recognisable, rather sad kind. The king had become near-besotted by the young

Bridget, though he did his best to keep his feelings in check. My late brother-in-law Geoffrey Ellis, a distinguished Oxford historian, translated what remains of the twenty-four letters, cards and telegrams which he sent to our mother, and which she left to my sister Trish. The detective work concluded that the affair was platonic, though that did not stop the yearning on the king's side. For our mother, of course, it was all flattering and exciting: to be entertained by the king in grand hotels all over Europe, to have flowers and telegrams awaiting her wherever she went in her mysteriously peripatetic life at the time.

'A ray of sunshine' or '*rayon de soleil*' was what the king often called Mum in his letters – so often that it's hard not to assume he imagined he had come up with a good description. He was not a natural writer. But through the strangled, often banal and formal prose, the depth of his feelings for the young woman of 'immense qualities' are apparent. 'You are an extraordinary being, and apart from many other sentiments, you are entitled to my admiration ... I do not admire many people. You have assumed a big part of my life.'

The king often mentioned plans in his letters, but did not specify what they were. As for our mother's reaction to his wooing, we can only surmise. None of her replies survives. But there are clues that there were occasional rifts between them: once, the king mentioned he was sorry his criticism had made her angry. But soon, in their capricious way, they were to meet again. The guess is that Mum found the king to be a comforting support, a flattering admirer, an older father figure. Geoffrey Ellis concluded she was willing to meet and please him, on her terms, but not too frequently. She was flattered by the royal attention, but could be evasive.

Also, she was keen to marry and escape the remaining ties to her mother. Sam Allsopp, whom she met in 1931, was the rich bachelor who slipped carelessly into the role of her husband. By the time they married, in February 1932, he had become the 4th Baron Hindlip. This pleased my grandmother, for Sam was equipped with many material assets. But for the king it was an agonising development. 'Be happy, my darling,' he wrote, 'and sometimes spare a thought for the one who now kisses your hand and sends you, from the bottom of his heart, all his deepest and true faithful tenderness.'

Marriage did not stop the correspondence between them. Within just a few weeks of the wedding, she sent news to the king indicating that things were not going well. She had made a huge mistake, she realised, even on her honeymoon. It seems likely that the king had suggested some of the places they should stay in Portugal – Funchal in Madeira, Lisbon, Pena National Palace in Sintra. But no matter the grandeur of their honeymoon, they were imperfect weeks. And, on their return, Mum, strangely, invited the king round to their London house to meet her husband. She wanted royal support for her view that Sam was an alcoholic. In the most understated terms the king agreed, in a letter to Bois in April 1932, that this was the case. The meeting also confirmed his undying admiration (love, infatuation?) for our mother. 'I am sometimes astonished by the profundity of her ideas and her views,' he wrote in the same letter. It's hard not to feel that infatuation, or whatever it was, coloured this touching opinion. Profound our mother never was, and had no interest in that quality.

Once married, the Hindlips divided their time between Sam's estate in Worcestershire and their London house, and led what sounds like extraordinarily dull lives. I once asked my mother to describe her day.

'Sam would have his first drink at ten a.m.,' she said, 'then go off to his club to carry on drinking. The cook would bring up my breakfast in bed, and we'd go through the menus if we were having people to luncheon or dinner. Then I'd get up and go, perhaps, to Peggy Sage to have my nails done, and on to lunch with a girlfriend. In the afternoon I'd have fittings, then go home for cocktails and to change for dinner. Several times a week friends came to us, or we'd go to them, and then on to the Café de Paris or the Four Hundred to dance.'

It seemed she and Sam never had an evening in alone. They never talked about anything except arrangements and people. She wasn't interested in the theatre, cinema, the arts of any kind. Reading she avoided as much as possible, sightseeing she found boring. Luckily she was blessed with a lively sense of humour which meant that, for most of her life, people enjoyed her company. She was also extraordinarily energetic, and very generous to her mostly rather dull women friends. Parties were her lifeblood, and they produced reams of facts (and fiction) about their friends that apparently provided her adrenalin. In truth, they were not a stimulating group, but provided amuse-ment of a limited kind. They were at ease with each other's ways and often snide humour. Oddly, our mother was never bored by this type of rich young thing, and had among these people a great many devoted friends. I met some of them when they were very old. They still shared a love of gossip, and admiration for social so-called achievement – i.e. money, title, stately home. Our mother herself, it could be said, though embarrassingly snobbish, had a quality of generous friendship.

People remained loyal to her throughout her life. She was exceptionally vivacious and could be very funny, though outrageously politically incorrect, and she clung to rigid prejudices. But she was a sympathetic listener so long as the person was not what she deemed 'very dull'. She was also very pretty and had the kind of laugh that swept others up in its slipstream.

Once married to Sam, it seemed the king could be less cautious in his declarations. 'What I feel for you … is the great joy of my life, a beautiful and deep joy, created by you …' And at last he came up with a specific plan. In his last surviving letter to Mum, he says he is looking forward to meeting her again on 27 June 1932 when, in consultation with Bois, they will plan a suitable celebration for Mum's thirty-second birthday on 8 July. She had agreed to this: the idea was to meet for a weekend. But days before the rendezvous, on 2 July 1932, Manuel suddenly died of a tracheal oedema. His mother, in England for Wimbledon just shortly before the fatal Saturday, had found him looking unwell. In his own words, the king was a 'complicated' man, highly strung and pushed to the limits of his strength, 'by overwork and stress'.

Our mother often spoke of him nostalgically: he had obviously meant much to her, though perhaps more in retrospect than in reality. But, in the whirligig life of the Hindlips, there was little time for mourning. And marriage to Sam, for all its material security, did not last long. Mum filed for a divorce in March 1933, eleven months after their wedding. They were faced by the blare of publicity afforded to high society in those days. Curiously, my mother retained a distant affection for her first husband until he died. Every year, on their wedding anniversary, she would ring him with the same suggestion. 'Sam, dear boy, it's twenty years today … don't you think we should have dinner?' A polite man, the wretched Sam would agree, and find himself in the usual restaurant in Jermyn Street, drinking champagne on this weird annual date. Goodness knows what they talked about. It wasn't as if there was much food for reminiscence.

There was a long wait between the decree nisi and the decree absolute, during which Mum plainly had a good time. She thought of herself as glamorous when she was young, and there was some evidence of this. She had a crowd of admirers, whom she liked to call 'gentlemen friends'. Names were mentioned including Alfred Tennyson's nephew. She would speak of him with some pride, as if trying to assure us that a man from an artistic family was no impediment to attraction, though I think he was the only one in that bracket. He was one among six other eligible men wishing to be her husband. But none of them was what she had in mind. Enter my father.

At that time he was a famous actor, who had been in several films – *Rome Express* and *The Outsider* were the best known. When our mother met him she boasted she was 'the only person in England who had never heard of him'. As she never went to the theatre or a film, that was unsurprising. He was the one who, in a different category from other admirers, really loved her, and the love was reciprocated. Mum could not go so far as to become interested in his work, but she provided entertainment, lunches and dinners, though no actors were ever on the guest lists. They had a house in Sussex and a flat in London: I don't think they were ever bored.

Wonderfully handsome, with deep-set, dark mahogany eyes, which meant he was usually cast as the villain, he had the most beautiful voice of any man I have ever met, although when his films (still) appear on television the sound is so bad it bears no trace of the reality.

His family were German bankers who came to England in 1714 and set up the Huth Bank in the City. (It closed in 1934.) His father and uncles had settled in Yorkshire. Apparently they had not inherited bankerly instincts: they were not good judges concerning future investment. My grandfather was offered shares in either Schweppes, or a firm that made unbreakable inkpots. He chose the inkpots.

My father joined the Honorary Artillery Company to fight in the First World War. He was blown up soon after he had become a major and was unable to speak for six months. For the rest of his life he suffered agonising stomach ulcers which he tried to ignore. He never mentioned the pain but, grim faced and pale, he would pace up and down until the spasm had passed. It was terrifying to see him like that. On many occasions I secretly thought he was going to die, and whispered juvenile prayers to God to take the pain away. But mostly God ignored my pleas.

It was from his mother that he inherited his artistic talents. She was one of ten Moore sisters, every one of whom was a painter, singer, writer or actor. One of his cousins, the actress Jill Esmond, became Laurence Olivier's first wife. Another cousin was the writer Roland Pertwee, with whom – for a while – he shared a flat and a giddy London life. Roland wrote plays in which my father acted: the most famous, *Pink String and Sealing Wax*, was much celebrated at the time. For a while, with his great love of fast cars, Dad abandoned acting to work for the Ford Motor Company. But to act was his whole *raison d'être*, and he quickly returned to the stage and films.

As a father whom I loved profoundly, and the great inspiration in my life, it would be easy to produce a string of his virtues. So better perhaps to face his foibles. In some respects he was a weak man, preferring to blur the truth and avoid trouble, rather than face a scene – most especially with my mother. He was liberal with the blurred truth, invariably adding his own sparkling touches to an anecdote. This was not to boost his own part in the story, but to make it more entertaining for his listeners. (I don't care if his memory of singing a solo in Canterbury Cathedral as a young boy wasn't entirely accurate. He told it so well we were there with him, terrified, thrilled.) This talent for embroidery I could only think of as an asset: his powers of storytelling were marvellous. Roland Pertwee's autobiography was called *Master of None* – a title which, I sometimes think, perhaps also applied to my father. He had so many talents: he played the piano, he could draw, act, write. But how good was he at any of these things? I was not able to judge as a child, and even in retrospect it is difficult. Certainly he wasn't a great pianist, but he could sit down and instantly compose pieces, and play duets with me. He drew well – his sketches of horses were full of life and he was able to explain how their bones worked. As an actor, he was no Olivier, but had his career not been cut short, I think he would have continued successfully to act for the rest of his life. In 1934 he was awarded what would now be a BAFTA for his performance in *The Outsider*. His copious reading – he was a lifelong fan of Dickens – made its mark on his writing. When he had time to write letters, they were superb. He never resorted to being vague – a trait I have tried to emulate. He would suddenly, while composing in his near-illegible writing

– have a thought about the starlings fluttering about outside, and pass it on to me in a way that never failed to make me laugh. In a word, although far above average at several things, he was probably not completely exceptional at any one of them. His quest was always to do better, find out, look, learn. There were twenty volumes of Egyptian history in his dressing room, all of which he had read and taken in, though he encountered few people who were keen to join him in discussing Egyptology.

But the reason everyone was drawn to my father was his charm – that elusive, magic ingredient that is instantly recognisable. He was interested in everybody, and listened acutely, and smiled his wonderful smile. Like my mother, he had a very good sense of humour – it was their humour that kept them just about together for thirty-three years. No matter how scintillating their rows, they could still laugh frequently. His ability to get on with anybody, his good manners and beguiling voice, were called upon even by people he did not know but who had heard of his reputation. On many occasions when there was a strike in the film industry he was invited to come and talk to the men, which others had failed to do. He would stand up in front of a thousand strikers and reason quietly with them. Almost invariably they would return to work.

His life, when he met my mother, was completely taken up with his acting. His world was the theatrical and film world. His friends were mostly actors and writers. One day, he and Noël Coward had lunch together and then walked back to Noël's house. Noël opened the front door to find a letter on the floor. He picked it up, read it. Then turned to my father.

'Oh God,' he said, 'another of those tiresome women wanting help to put their daughter on the stage. A Mrs Worthington. Why don't you come back this evening for a drink, and see what I've managed to do with the answer.'

At six o'clock Noël sat down at the piano and treated my father to the first ever performance of 'Don't Put Your Daughter On The Stage, Mrs Worthington'.

For a while, during this phase of a glamorous but very hard-working life, my father shared a flat with his pretty leading lady, Joan Barry, who was not altogether pleased by his success. All this, to my mother, was horrifying. She loathed the very idea of actors (although Raymond Massey and Adrianne Allen were among her friends).

She agreed to marry him on condition he gave up acting. My father, foolishly, consented to this: part of his occasional feebleness was to give in rather than have a row. Instead, he became a director and producer. He made some good films – *The Trials of Oscar Wilde* was his last, and considered his best. His great joy was to seek out young talent and give it a chance: Nic Roeg and Ken Hughes were two of his discoveries. He worked incredibly hard, ignoring constant pain, and enjoyed himself, though he always regretted having given up performing. Sometimes he would slip himself into a part so small that his wife would not notice. That was not difficult because she never asked about his work. When he decided to play quite a large part in *Blackmailed*, starring Dirk Bogarde, in 1951, my mother was abroad and did not see the film. So the intense wrath it would have sparked was avoided.

His working hours were very long – we scarcely saw him,

except occasionally at weekends. Sometimes I would catch him for a moment before he left for the studio, shaving in the curious 1930s pink glass bathroom that led to the main bedroom in East Burnham House, to which we had returned after the war. It was then I would take my chance to pin him down for advice. In the play I was writing, I explained, there were elves who lived in a forest. What should they wear – camouflage, or green tunics? My father would turn slowly round to me, stop his razor in its track of soap-covered skin, and ponder. I felt he took this matter every bit as seriously as some problem with his own film. He would give his opinion and add some further advice, and I would feel very grown-up. We'd had a conference.

Despite the absence of a mother, and a father little seen, life at East Burnham House went on in a happy, orderly way. My mother had made sure we were well catered for, and the house was kept immaculate by several ladies from the village. Indeed it was rather over-staffed for two school children, one nanny and an occasional father. There was an old, bent butler, Welfare, who used to be my grandmother's footman, and a friendly cook who lived above the stables with her husband and children. Welfare spent most of the day, in striped trousers and green baize apron, cleaning the silver with his thumb, flattened from years of polishing. He seemed to have few requirements and no friends. The pantry was his proud domain – a silent, sterile room, cupboards covering every wall. They were filled with hoards of silver given by my grandmother, which Welfare kept to their maximum shine. I daresay the thought that all his work would be appreciated one day kept him going. But there were few post-war parties, and the lack of a hostess. This did not deter Welfare from his main duty. I often stood and watched him at work, mixing powder and water into a pink paste and applying it to the neck of a candlestick with the thumb which, because of the chemical reaction, had become indelibly blue as well as flat. I wondered vaguely – not specifically – if his life was *all right*. Could he be lonely, silent in his pantry all day, dressed in striped trousers and a stiff collar that bit into the wrinkles of his neck? I never dared to ask him. But I often asked myself. I enjoyed imagining what went on in his mind. He was one of the first people I secretly questioned to myself, and provided answers that were probably far from the truth. But guessing about people was a game I loved.

On buses or trains I would wonder about the man with red hair sitting opposite: what did he have for breakfast? What sort of a house did he live in? Such questions became a habit which is still with me. Wherever I go I wonder about people. What on earth made a certain woman in a queue think her very short skirt suited her? I have not abandoned this odd habit because often the made-up answers provide the beginnings of a story. When I'm invited to schools to give lessons in writing, now so pretentiously called creative writing, the question I'm always asked is how to get an idea? I suggest my secret questioning about unknown people, or people in pictures. Once I took a postcard of Van Gogh's postman along to a class, and asked the children many questions about his life. Eagerly they shouted the answers, and produced lively stories. So I like to think this somewhat unorthodox method is a help.

Of course I never told Welfare I was imagining an inner life for him. He was a gruff man, and would have considered a

question about his wellbeing and private thoughts to be imper-
tinent. On his day off he would sit in his very small bedroom
smoking his pipe, apparently not wanting for anything, silently
reflecting. Looking back, I imagine that although our loyal
butler's life was lacking in many ways, it was a great improvement on working for our tempestuous grandmother. Treats for
him were the few occasions when my father would brace himself to ask people to lunch, so there was a real point in doubling
his efforts with the silver. They were also times of great enjoyment for my father, who was a marvellous host.

His guests were mostly members of the cast of whichever
film was in production: Stewart Granger, Margaret Lockwood,
Patricia Roc and Fay Compton all came from time to time –
the names naturally meant nothing to me. Or to Trish who,
when invited to hand round chocolates after lunch, peered at a
handsome brooch pinned to Margaret Lockwood's bosom.
The film star gallantly unpinned it from her white silk shirt for
Trish to inspect. With no warning, Trish suddenly jammed the
pin back into the famous upright bosom, and blood streamed
down the pristine shirt. That was one of the rare occasions
we were allowed into the dining room – a room, just like the
drawing room opposite, that exuded a hostile atmosphere.

In contrast to the far end of the house, the nursery – the
centre of our lives – felt utterly safe. It was a large yellow room
with a huge bay window on to the front lawn, and an open
fire. There we had tea every day after school: Welfare would
come tottering in with an enormous tray of bread and butter
and cakes which we would eat listening to Uncle Mac on
Children's Hour. At weekends my father would join us for lunch
and tea in the nursery, and tell us stories. These were mostly of

his childhood in Devon. He was good at doing all the different West Country accents, and we were enchanted. Nanny was forever in the nursery, in her white crossover starched overall, sitting by the fire darning, sewing, knitting.

Nanny, in our mother's absence, was the person we loved, relied on: we knew she would always be there. She was a near-saintly character who, like many of her generation and background, devoted her all to others. One of six children, she was brought up in a two-bedroom house in Canterbury. Once, she said, she had a boyfriend. They sometimes went to the seaside and walked along the promenade listening to the band, holding hands. Once he took her to a farm and they rode round a field on a carthorse. That was the sum of nanny's pleasure with a man. He was called up and killed almost instantly. There were no others.

In common with many of her contemporaries who did not want to work in a factory or become a land girl, she took a job as a nursery maid, and eventually rose to being nanny to Tommy Sopwith, the future racing-driver, born in 1933, whose father was the aviation pioneer and yachtsman Sir Tommy Sopwith. The rich and grand life must have been surprising after her own threadbare upbringing, but she took to it easily – waited on, and helped by a nursery maid. While EBH was extremely comfortable, it was not in the same league as her previous Sopwith house. But she was totally dedicated to us, supported us, was interested in everything that interested us. She only had one friend, nanny to our nearby neighbour Catherine, but she did not complain. She had few days off, when she would always go to London in her fox fur – lunch at D. H. Evans – and stock up with knitting and sewing things. Her salary was £60 a year. Out of that she bought me, every birthday and Christmas, an Oxford University edition of the complete works of some thirty or forty poets, thus leaving me with a collection for life. And she was the one who kept in touch while we were away at school. While my father managed one (marvellous) letter a term, and my mother two (in banal prose, declaring she was missing us), Nanny wrote every week. In her fat round writing she told of Canterbury news – 'went to W. H. Smith on Friday, rained again' and she always ended the same way: 'lots of love, yours faithfully A. E. Turner'. They were important, these letters: not because of their content, but because of their constancy. We were away, but she was always thinking of us. We would never have survived so well without her.

I have been asked many times what it was like not to have had a mother in our formative years. The answer is, genuinely, it was fine: not ever having had one that I could remember, I had no idea what I was missing. Nanny was a permanent, comforting fixture, who took care of all practicalities and read to us every night. Our father was an extraordinarily loving and imaginative man, and Trish and I had each other to play and quarrel with. On the rare occasions my mother paid a twenty-four-hour visit, the whole house was shaken, the peace broken. She was a heavy drinker, though not an alcoholic, and on return to EBH went straight for the gin, perhaps for courage on her brief visit to the family she had abandoned. 'Oh dear,' Nanny would say mildly, 'poor Mummy fell down the stairs last night.' I have no recollection of what my mother looked like at that time. I remember only a vivid tension in the air, shouting behind a closed door, my father's troubled face, and the feeling of infinite relief when she had gone.

In the summer she organised, from whatever far-off place she was, our holidays: Westgate-on-Sea, or Frinton, with Nanny, Catherine and her nanny. A boarding house was chosen – always damp, with cracked china and over-boiled cabbage, and for me the longing to return to our grim bedroom and get on with *Black Beauty*. But the nannies, believers in fresh air no matter the weather, insisted that part of the day should be at the beach. We wore hand-knitted bathing suits, scratchy with sand, and made sand stables for a collection of miniature horses. We were allowed one heavenly sixpenny vanilla ice cream in a cornet a day, and eked it out shivering in the bathing hut, looking at the thick line of solid grey made from cloud and sea clamped together.

One year there was the luxury of staying in a hotel, where we met other children, all with their parents. We were allowed to stay up for early supper and listen to the band. When one night the conductor asked if I would like to sing, I agreed to try the only song in my repertoire: ''Tis the Last Rose of Summer'. It was my first taste of the thrill of being on stage, performing. Ideas of being an actress came to mind. (I realised very quickly I would never be a singer.) Nanny was thrilled. My mother would have been furious and would have forbidden me to perform. Nanny gamely kept the secret.

In the holidays at EBH there was not much to do: we had riding lessons three times a week – wearing beautiful handmade jodhpurs and jackets from the local tailor – and sometimes were put in for shows. We got to know one or two more local children who Nanny gallantly sometimes asked to tea in case we were bored. I was never bored because I spent the greater part of my day in an imaginary world, writing stories, painting pictures in rich detail, braving the drawing room to make up songs on the piano. I also read constantly – mostly Dickens. Trish had a much bleaker time. Her chief occupation was to chase the heifers in the field in front of the house, and see how many she could get to jump over the fence. When this pastime was forbidden, she flew into incandescent rages, usually with me. Once she stamped on my toy farmyard, crushing it to dust. On another occasion she pinned a notice to my back saying 'You Are A Pig'. The pin was rusty. My back became infected. There was a gruesome fortnight of medication, but Trish was unrepentant. She always had great spirit.

EBH was the first of five houses I have been in love with, despite its alien parts. When I was taken into my father's study, at the age of one, apparently I screamed so searingly that I was never taken there again. And there was an archway on the first floor beyond which Trish and I only went together. As you climbed a small flight of stairs to the two guest bedrooms, a tingling down the spine began. There was a weird echo in the spare bathroom. Beneath this part of the house were the dining room, outer hall and the drawing room. They, too, had a powerful atmosphere that was not like the inner part of the house. The drawing room was usually kept under cover – dustsheets thrown over the elaborate sofas and chairs covered in eau-de-nil raised damask. The walls were hung with sub-Gainsborough snooty ladies looking down on us. The fire there was rarely lighted, so it was cold. But it was the place where, with a few friends, we had dancing lessons. The renowned Miss Vacani would come from Windsor, to instruct a group of small girls in silk, frilled socks and bronze dancing shoes with cross-over elastic straps, to be swans on a lake, or willows in a wind. It was all pure Joyce Grenfell, but I liked it because on those occasions it cheered up the drawing room. But I often had to go there by myself, as it was where the grand piano lived, and I liked to play long before I had lessons. When my father joined me, played to me, the room stirred happily again. On my own, there was always the slight shiver of unease.

Many years later, I was asked by a newspaper to contribute to a series on revisiting the house of one's childhood. With some anticipation I set off for Farnham Royal, which by then had joined Farnham Common, but eventually found the front gate – no longer the wonderful old white wooden structure, but an electronic replacement. I drove up the avenue to the front door, the well-remembered limes on each side, saw the old tennis court repaired – and round the corner to the front door. It wasn't there. The house had gone. In its place was a modern redbrick building of absolutely no charm, a swimming pool just a foot or so from the house built into the lawn. From various windows I looked on to the vast sentinel trees, the oak I had planted on my first birthday, the rose garden: the views of the garden, at least, were unchanged. Then I went to the part of the house that had replaced the spine-tingling wing. It was by now a dazzle of bright Laura Ashley rooms, and whatever dark spirit had haunted the original house had obviously flown, appalled by the new habitat. The singer Jenny Lind had lived at EBH for some time: maybe her restless spirit was accountable for the disturbing atmosphere. It was lucky our end of the house had been all light and comfort and security. EBH was our refuge, the place I loved and to which, when we went away, I always pined to return.

It was in the nursery that, at the age of five, I began my serious writing. Enid Blyton brought out a weekly magazine called *Sunny Stories*. I decided to produce a similar magazine called *Sunnier Stories*, for the sole entertainment of my sister, from whom I demanded just one old penny a copy (Enid Blyton's sold for twopence). I would make a list of titles, then fill in the stories – a habit I still have, though for the last forty years I have had to decide whether the title should be for a novel, story, play for radio or television – whatever. I would illustrate each story – it all took up a great deal of time, but the reward was the finished magazines (four sides of folded paper) week after week. I once asked Nanny how people like postmen and butchers and train drivers had time to write stories. She explained that they didn't – most people weren't writers, she said. That was probably my first moment of disillusion, having assumed everybody's heads were full of stories. I also wrote a good many plays for three actors – my sister, our only nearby friend Catherine, and myself. We would rehearse hard and then perform in the drawing room to the faithful audience of two – Daddy and Nanny, whose encouragement was a huge reward for all our efforts.

The acres of gardens at EBH were managed by a team of four gardeners. At their head was the Italian Trelani, whose job it was to take Trish and me to school in the cumbersome Wolseley, with its cracked leather seats and sagging dashboard. He was an agreeable man, but had an Italian sense of time. Although he managed to deliver us on time, punctual collection in the afternoon defeated him. It was his unpunctuality that is the single memory of that school. Every day I dreaded the time to go home, when I knew I would be left, alone, waiting in the large, empty, cold and echoing front hall. A grumpy groundsman would come in and out, rattling his keys, complaining he couldn't lock up, and what did I think I was doing? Trelani's non-appearance brought all sorts of terrifying visions to my mind – a car crash, illness: how would I get home? Sometimes I waited for as much as an hour till he arrived with his daily apology, but no promises to try to do better. It was during one of those long, bleak times alone in the school hall that I swore to myself that, never, if I could help it, would I be late for anyone. So this was another childhood experience that affected the whole of my life: I'm never late, I hate the idea of keeping anyone waiting. My acute punctuality is acknowledged by many – infuriating, no doubt. But I think waiting is an appalling waste of time. Do unpunctual people enjoy waiting for each other? I have often wondered.

In 1950 the French diplomat committed suicide and my mother returned to my father, who was totally forgiving, overjoyed. They settled for a new pattern of life, founded on an old and deep affection, and their sense of humour. My mother was keen to move to London: she had never liked the country. My father was anxious to do whatever would best please his wife now she was back. She ignored his own reluctance to leave, and decided he should be the one to break the news to Trish and me. We were to leave EBH and move to London, he said. *London* … I could not think of anything more devastating – that great noisy, foggy, dirty city, where doubtless there would be more visits to Fortnum and Mason. The prospect of leaving was totally desolating. Night after night I cried myself to sleep. EBH was the house that inspired my passionate love of certain houses. It was the place where the different music of every door and the shafts of sun on the carpets were ingrained in my soul. Some sixty years later I can remember every curtain, the feel of the hump-backed mahogany banister beneath my hand, the creak of the linoleum floor in the nursery bathroom. They are all printed indelibly in my mind. EBH was home. We should not be moved.

I said this to my father over and over again, and of course he agreed. We shared our sadness, but there was nothing he could do. We were to live in a large flat in Eaton Square, my mother said, in the belief that would cheer us up. But Eaton Square meant nothing to us, and while we waited to leave there was the terrible sense of something very strong being wilfully broken: the comfort of the huge trees, the nursery fire, the lily-of-the-valley chintz that covered the twin beds in the room Trish and I shared. The safety of a much-loved place would die. It could not possibly be replaced in a London flat.

But some bad memories, too, were held within EBH: the strange atmosphere in various parts of the house, the vibrating rows when our mother returned, and the acute fear that came upon me one day in the nursery – a phobia which was to last for life.

2

Dolls

It lay on my knee, this rigid, heavy 'baby' made of icy china. Its painted eyelids were at half-mast. Its open rosebud mouth exposed two horrible little teeth. Where its head was screwed to its body there was a ridge like thick wire round its neck. Stiff arms reached upwards. It was obscenely dead.

This was no ordinary doll. My grandmother, who practised excess in many areas, had bought it from The White House in Bond Street – in those days a very grand and expensive shop for baby clothes. She had chosen it from several life-size dolls that sat in the window modelling extravagant dresses. She had also bought several of those, with the idea that I would enjoy dressing it. And finally, outrageously, she had bought a real baby's pram in which, I suppose, she envisaged her grand-daughter taking this life-size doll for walks.

From the moment I received the doll 'asleep' in its pram I avoided it, though I could not explain to myself, or to others, why. The pram sat in the corner of the nursery, ignored. The sleeping doll became dustier, therefore even less desirable.

I suppose I was encouraged by Nanny one day to take a look at it, change its clothes. I remember the feeling of acute distaste as I lifted it from the pram, laid it on my knee, and watched the eyelids crank down from some mechanism in its head. I suppose I must have taken off its clothes, for it was its horrific naked state that caused me to scream as I'd never screamed. Nanny quickly snatched it from me, tried to calm my hysteria. I begged her to take it away and never let me see it again. It was the moment my doll phobia struck and was recognised: I must have been about six.

There had been earlier, puzzling intimations. My sister and I had an appealing collection of bears and soft animals, but not many dolls. Those we did have were pushed around in (ordinary) dolls' prams, but we did not play with them often. I was given a wax doll dressed as a jockey. This Jock I particularly disliked: the slimy shine of the wax skin, its staring eyes. I took it one day to school and dropped it by mistake. Someone asked if I was going to pick it up, and I realised I was unable to do so. I was paralysed. I didn't even try to bend down, for I knew I could not touch it. I assured the child who picked it up for me that she could keep it, and never saw it again.

In those days, at children's parties, there were frequent puppet shows and, worse, ventriloquists for entertainment. Their ghastly dolls – with huge heads, floppy legs and insane grins full of chunky teeth – terrified me. I dreaded being invited up to 'talk to Archie' – many children regarded this as a great treat – and always chose to sit in a hidden place at the back. I also became cunning at avoiding puppets, though on occasions

I was caught out when a friend came into the classroom swinging one of them, with its dabbing hands and broken neck, and I would have to flee with some excuse. From a very young age I was constantly secretly plotting how to avoid contact with dolls of all kinds. The irrational fears I kept to myself, though obviously Nanny knew something traumatic had happened on the day of The Scream. After that, our other dolls seemed to disappear as a result of her instinct to protect me. Trish and I then played mostly with the animals.

But one day my mother, who considered my attitude ridiculous, bought us two identical dolls on one of her visits to Paris: wax, again, with hair permed like Hedy Lamarr and an assortment of superior dresses. They had eyes that opened and shut, and stiff lashes. But there was something wrong with mine: instead of shutting just when it was laid down, the eyes constantly fluttered open and shut whenever it was moved even slightly. It was horrific, but a useful weapon for Trish. If she wanted something I was reluctant to give, she simply chased me with the doll till she got her way. Once this happened at a lunch party for some near neighbours. The grown-ups laughed. 'Afraid of a *doll*?' they scoffed. My father simply put a hand on my shoulder and led me away. He didn't laugh, or jeer.

Despite the fact that I've become pretty skilled at sensing approaching danger, there have inevitably been many embarrassing doll moments. On one occasion recently, in my seventieth year, we went to a large Sunday lunch party where, to avoid being thirteen, someone had put a Victorian doll in a high chair on our host's right. Victorian dolls are some of the worst, with their pea-sized eyes and rouged cheeks, their coarse hair, and then the way chamois leather switches to china for the hands. On many occasions I've been shown into bedrooms where there are shelves of such prize dolls, much admired by their collectors. Fearing one of them might fall on me, or be handed over to admire, I've had to escape very fast. On the occasion of the lunch, I told myself to be calm, think rationally, and make no fuss. But I was on our host's left, just a yard from the doll. Could I eat, think, talk normally with it staring at me? I couldn't. Very apologetic, I asked for it to be moved, which it was at once. It so happened that our hostess was a friend of the only friend I had who shared my phobia: she was used to dealing with doll crises.

Embarrassing and terrifying moments are part of a phobic's life. Others' stories inspire deep sympathy. Bernard Levin, who had a phobia about spiders, suffered a traumatic experience staying with friends in the South of France. He was to be not in the main house, but in the guesthouse. He returned there late one night after dinner only to confront a spider in his room. In a word, he trashed the place – very hard to imagine, this, Bernard in his impeccable suit and waistcoat and tie: but he set about it like a manic builder in an act of demolition. It cost him a great deal of money and much shame. But, as another writer who often tried to convey the nature of a phobic's fear, he was happy to recount this story

I've had many a nasty moment, when the daughters were small, in other people's playrooms: sofas were dangerous places. I would sit down only to find the arm or leg of a Barbie doll sticking into me, and being unable to remove it. On those occasions I would leap up with some excuse, trying to conceal my battering heart, shaking hands, general terror. Those wizened Barbie dolls with their yellow nylon hair which, on some models, *can be pulled out of their scalps to make it longer*, were a particular dread. By good luck, and some skill, I've always managed to avoid dolls that cry, have bottles of water pushed down their throats and then, oh the joy for a child, have to have their nappies changed. Perhaps worst of all would be those dolls that actually walk by themselves. If ever a doll walked towards me, I would simply pass out.

When my elder daughter was born I was faced with the major problem of what to do. There were those who I consulted who suggested, in the gentlest possible way, that it would be mean, even cruel, to deny Candida dolls. But as far as I could see there was no option. I simply could not survive in my own house knowing that at any moment I might run into a doll, and that if I did, Candida ran the risk of being subjected to her mother's terror. So I provided the most endearing toy animals I could find, and explained to her at a very young age that I hated dolls, could not touch them or go near them. It was stupid, daft, ridiculous, I said, but it was a fact.

The amazing thing was, Candida seemed not only to understand, but not to mind at all. I don't remember her ever asking for a doll, and she did not seem much interested in playing with her friends' dolls. Most fortunate of all was that she took it upon herself to protect me. Whenever we went to a house where there were young doll-inclined children, she would survey all the rooms and warn me not to go into whichever ones were doll-infested. If a child came near me holding a doll, Candida would manage to get it from her and take it away, thus avoiding my embarrassed explanations. When she was older she herself had a mild fear of birds (a common phobia), so could understand that people have different fears about different things.

I went through the no-doll guilt thing again sixteen years later, when Eugenie was born. But, amazingly, she approached the inconvenient problem in exactly the same way as her sister. If she felt she was being deprived of dolls, she never let me know. And now my grandsons have taken my peculiarity on board: much less risk with boys, of course, though there are some Action Men, with limbs that terrifyingly bend every which-way, in their house. But they shout touching commands: 'Get rid of the Action Man!' should I chance upon one that has not been hidden.

The phobia naturally extends to waxworks and shop mannequins. In my mid-twenties, when I lived in London, having done copious, cautious research, I could journey through Harrods without ever bumping into some ghastly life-size man with nylon hair. It was only when the layout of such monsters was changed I was caught unawares and often had to flee, too shaken to complete some purchase. There were certain shops, where the owners chose to put mannequins each side of the door, that I could not go into at all, and others, where the models had no head, where I felt infinitely relieved. As with dolls, there were several mannequin moments that make my heart beat faster even remembering. One was in a part of Harrods I had not recced: the children's clothes department. I took the two-year-old Eugenie there to find the place littered with life-size models of all ages. While I was paying the bill she dashed over to befriend a fibreglass contemporary. It fell over. Several beady assistants looked angrily at me, expecting me – not unreasonably – to pick it up.

Of course that was not a possibility, nor could I begin to explain. I simply grabbed Eugenie's hand and dashed away, shaking. On another occasion, in Salisbury, I was in a run-down general clothes shop, whose models in the window were way past their prime. But as far as I could see they were safely gathered only in the window, none casually standing about to surprise. Then I turned a corner to find a *smiling* man. To me, a smiling mannequin, with its exposure of the teeth, is a great deal more petrifying than a closed mouth. What's more, this particular figure was slightly tottery on its base. His upturned shoes (why do they always have upturned shoes, these male models?) were not firm on the ground. As I began to move away, the old floor of the shop juddered, the man swayed. His terrible teeth, crowding out of his mouth on to his painted brown lips, clattered. He was all but alive. I was all but dead.

Frights, on my own, I can usually deal with. When they occur with others, who have no knowledge of my phobia, they are more of a problem.

There was an occasion in Florida, in the late 1950s. I was staying with a couple who were anxious to show me 'the oldest house in America'. We walked a long way through some town, eventually coming to a very small cottage. Famous for its age, it was open to the public. Payment was required to look inside. My far from well-off friends bought me a ticket which, as a penniless student travelling the States in a Greyhound bus, I could not afford.

We went into a very small room. It was inhabited only by a waxwork of an old crone rocking back and forth in an automated chair. Her yellowy wax fingers grasped the arms. It seemed to me she cast her rheumy glass eyes at us visitors. She was only a few feet from us: stiff, dusty, horrendous. I screamed. I ran from the cottage, alarming the kind American couple. Goodness knows where I went: I ran till I could run no more, shaking with sobs. An hour or so later I was found on a park bench, unable to explain what had happened since I raced away. My chief concern was that I'd wasted an expensive ticket. So I made my apologies, and attempted the difficult explanation of my horror, which luckily seemed rather to intrigue them.

Over the years, on the occasions my phobia is discussed, I've often tried to make people understand the horror of these lifeless things, and mostly fail. Several people say they are completely spooked by films featuring dolls: curiously, these have little effect on me. I would never choose to go and see one. But on the occasions I've chanced on a filmed horror-doll, although I'm repelled, I'm not traumatised as I am when confronting one in real life. The answer is, I find dolls on film nasty as they are meant to be, but they don't endanger me. A doll on film can't touch me. It's the idea of the feel of the rigidity, that rigor-mortis-corpse thing that I find unbearable. I once saw a picture in a paper of a waxwork of Queen Victoria seated in an aeroplane. Presumably some passenger was going to have to cross the Atlantic beside the rigid, silent queen. Had I been unlucky enough to board that plane, pass that seat ... Well, it would not have happened. I would have fled screaming with not a thought of the waste of the expensive ticket.

It occurred to me that at some time I should try to convey my phobia in a novel. I set about this, with some trepidation, in *Wanting*. In the opening, an old shopkeeper, who is closing down his shop, takes his five ancient mannequins to a Norfolk beach early one morning. The tide is out. He drives them to the remains of an old wreck, leaves them. Later, my heroine, Viola, walking across the beach, sees the group of women with fluttery scarves gathered for what seems to be a picnic. Their absolute stillness, apart from the wind tampering with their clothes, is the only clue they are not real. Viola is disturbed, intrigued, puzzled. Finally, when she realises the picnickers are not alive, she flees terrified from the gross reality, just as I would have done in the same situation. As I wrote the scene, I remember feeling acutely fearful just choosing the words, conjuring the picture. I wanted to convey my own strange fears; I wanted others to see what I saw. But I think I failed absolutely. Nobody ever mentioned the chilling beginning of the book, because to ninety-nine per cent of the population, a few models sitting on a beach is not a matter of horror.

I have only met one other person who had a phobia about dolls: Princess Margaret. She was the only one who ever understood: we were bound in our agreement about the dangers, the terrors, and she was more endangered than I ever was. For when her daughter Sarah was a child she was often presented with a magnificent doll along with a bouquet of roses. Unable to touch it, she relied on the swift response of one of her ladies-in-waiting to snatch it away. On one occasion we were going to some charity ball at the Pump Rooms in Bath. To get to the ballroom, we had to walk along a passage between glass windows full of waxworks in period costume. Princess Margaret was supposed to walk tranquilly beside whoever was the host. I was to follow a little behind. We were both terrified. But, before setting off, she turned to me, took my hand, and said if we walked with our free hands sheltering our eyes we would be able to make it ... Somehow we did, and were able to laugh once the ordeal was over. Goodness knows what the officials thought, but we were in no state to care. In fact, to me, if waxworks and models are behind glass, they are slightly less bad in that – the old safety thing, again – I know they can't get me, fall on me. I'm shaken, but safe.

Due to my own life with a phobia, I naturally feel particularly sympathetic to others who suffer terror of disparate things. So when I worked for the BBC's *Man Alive* programme in the 1960s, I suggested making a programme about people suffering from phobias. Good idea, said Desmond Wilcox, the producer. He was gleeful at the thought of subjects being *confronted* by their phobias. Bound to make good footage, he thought.

The idea was advertised: hundreds of phobics wrote in offering to take part in the programme. Many of their fears were well known – spiders, birds, snakes, heights, the sea, dogs, cats, leaving the house, flying, and so on. Many I had never heard of: ambulances, pearl buttons, visitors, leaves. Eventually a bird phobic was chosen, to represent one of the most common phobias. A wretched woman gallantly agreed to be scared witless walking across Waterloo Station, in those days more densely inhabited by pigeons than passengers. The birds hovered and fluttered everywhere. The woman's progress, as she hesitated out from a hiding place behind W. H. Smith, was terror personified, and the cameras greedily kept turning.

In Corby, Northamptonshire, I interviewed a young man whose love life was impeded by the fact that if he saw an approaching dog, even a Pekinese, he was obliged to shin up a lamppost. It was decided that I should be the one, on camera, to tell him that his parents were planning to get a dog. His appalled reaction was to decide to emigrate to New Zealand, 'where they have almost no dogs,' he said. Then there was the sad lady traumatised by a knock on the door, or a ring of her bell: visitors induced paralysing fear. She was used to hiding under the kitchen table if anyone came to call. The director's 'inspiration' was to get her to approach her own house, as if she was the visitor. We watched, agonised, as she crept across a field: twenty yards from the house she stopped, unable to go a step further. I can't remember how she managed to get back into the house: I suppose she let some time pass to calm down, then went back to being herself as she unlocked the front door, rather than pretending to be a visitor.

But the most extraordinary subject of all was the man who was terrified of leaves. Such was his fear that he could never drive less than 40 m.p.h. round the roads of Stanmore because, if he went more slowly, leaves would come into focus. I interviewed him in his vegetable patch where he was digging up sprouts. How come he didn't mind their leaves? He explained it was fine when the sprouts were still young and their leaves very small. As soon as they reached full growth, he could not go anywhere near them. His fear kept him a prisoner in his own house for a great deal of the time, but even there he was not safe. I was alerted by the researcher to one of his worst experiences. This inspired my question, which subsequently went into the BBC archives as one of the oddest ever asked on television: had he ever had any frights with rhubarb?

'I certainly have,' he said. 'Once, I was in a room on the first floor, my daughter came in with a bunch ... I had to jump out of the window.'

The programme, which had set out with serious intention,

did not entirely receive the serious contemplation it deserved. Ken Russell said it was the funniest film he had ever seen. And it's hard not to admit that seeing people traumatised by things that most of the population considers to be normal has a certain humorous appeal.

Desmond Wilcox insisted we had a psychiatrist on the programme to explain what a phobia is. He was hardly enlightening. 'An irrational fear of harmless objects,' he said, though most phobias concern living things. It was then suggested I myself should get some treatment to rid me of my weird condition. I'm not much of a believer in the remedial powers of digging up one's childhood, but I agreed to try. The psychiatrist came to our flat in London, insisted on drawing the curtains in my study, and asked me such boring, banal questions in a soupy voice, that I suggested we cut short the encounter. He agreed willingly, having found me uncooperative. He also said that if he had been able to rid me of my fear of dolls, the phobia might remain, but in a less convenient form, such as milk bottles. So I stuck with dolls.

When I was at my boarding school in Great Malvern, we were taken several times a term to Stratford to see a play. On one occasion, having arrived early, we walked round a park where there was a gathering of statues of Shakespeare's characters. It was my first experience of proximity to statues, and somehow I reasoned to myself that they were different. But they weren't. Lady Macbeth's eyes, staring down at me from her bronze face, set off all the usual manifestations of fear. I was scolded for 'leaving the crocodile without permission', but not asked why I had done so.

The realisation that statues were almost as much of a problem as all other models of humans was upsetting news, for as an art student I was keen to see as much sculpture as possible. In Paris I had a very scary time trying to study Rodin's crowds of melancholy figures. I remember my knees shaking so hard I had to find somewhere to sit down. In Italy, at school in Florence, we pupils were taken all over the country to see hundreds of works of art at a wonderfully tourist-free time. I was always on the alert, and kept at the back of the group, cursing myself for being unable to go near a pietà, or a bust, to observe it closely.

In Florence itself I discovered I was able to get within about two feet of a small but charming Donatello bronze, and thereafter found myself quite bold when it came to statues of not more than eighteen inches high. But the most curious thing, in Florence, was my relationship with Michelangelo's *David*.

In those empty days of the mid-1950s, the Galleria dell'Accademia, where he stood, was not much visited compared with now, when there are constant queues to see him. I was astonished by my first visit, and just wanted to keep on looking, pondering. Goodness knows how many times I revisited David by myself, alone for two or three hours in the gallery, trying to work out if his head was too big for his body, and how Michelangelo had set about sculpting the giant body, and how he had endowed it with such frightening vitality. Sometimes I moved to the place at which the blank stone eyes seemed to be looking, but could never catch his eye. And always I kept my distance. I felt reasonably safe as he stood on such a high plinth, but the imagination sometimes took charge. I could see him stepping down, approaching and, for some bizarre reason, putting on a yellow T-shirt. I often had nightmares that in this T-shirt he chased me round the Piazza della Signoria. But although I scared myself, I kept going, trying to fathom why David was so powerful, so terrifying, a creation of such genius. After several months of keeping to the back of the gallery, I sometimes dared myself to go nearer. Step by slow step, like someone playing grandmother's footsteps, I would creep forward. With every step there was something new to contemplate. Progress was very slow. Often I felt dizzy with fear. By the time I left Florence, I had managed to get within thirty feet of David, an achievement that naturally I kept to myself. And he still haunts me.

I keep thinking that I'm getting better with statues – after all, as art, they should overcome irrational fear. But the power of art is not, sadly, quite enough in my case: I've had bad moments in France, Italy, Greece, and recently in San Francisco, where a marvellous Rodin exhibition left me very shaky. Much to my regret I was unable to go to see the Chinese Army, when some of it was shown at the British Museum. I heard that, in a small space, it was necessary to be very close to the statues. For me, hopeless.

My kind of phobia inevitably leaves me with a sense of wonder and admiration for the many people who do what is to them a perfectly normal job. I look with awe and admiration at shop assistants who unscrew arms and legs of mannequins and carry them about as if they were no more alarming than a bunch of coat hangers. How can they pick up those decapitated heads and try on a variety of nylon wigs? How can employees at Madame Tussauds fix glass eyes into wax sockets without a tremor? How can those people, nobly learning about first aid, put their lips to the mouth of a dummy and breathe into it? How could the actors, in a marvellous production of *A Midsummer Night's Dream* a few years ago, handle the robotic changeling doll (it cost a fortune, the director told me) – which twitched and moved in a repellently lifelike way? Watching it, from a few rows back in the stalls, I was ready to flee, in case by some accident it took off and came sailing towards our seats ... How can removal men carry those terrifyingly near-human figures made by Ron Mueck, each hair stuck separately into flesh-like skin, into galleries? Such acts are mystifying to me, but I know that is ridiculous.

Very occasionally I come across people who are mildly, puzzlingly disturbed by the human inanimate form, though they are not fully fledged phobics, and they have my sympathy. Recently there was a documentary about a particularly dreadful kind of doll that is a bestseller in America, and does well here, too. It's a very expensive, bespoke doll – you can order the colour of the hair, skin and eyes so that it looks 'related', and is made to appear as realistic as possible. Such dolls are mainly sold to childless women. The idea is that the 'mothers' are comforted by the fact that, pushing the pram, people peer into it and think the 'baby' is real. This apparently boosts some kind of low-esteem among women whose children have left home, or who never had a baby. The baby paraphernalia is bought (one 'mother' spent thousands at Harrods) and then the whole charade of the baby's routine acted out in the house. One woman, at the end of a long day tending to her doll, handed it to her husband. 'No thanks,' he said. 'It's really spooky.' I felt for him.

A doll phobia, for me, extends a little over the edges beyond man-made mannequins, waxworks and so on. It extends, partially, to babies. I can't cope with very small ones. When a friend tried to hand me her newborn four-pound son, I made some feeble excuse and backed away. They don't induce the total horror of dolls, but I have a powerful feeling of not wanting to touch or hold them. Luckily, my own daughters both weighed over eight pounds when they were born, which was fine, and a great relief.

Death, too, is touched by the phobia. I know I could never deal with it appropriately. I have never seen anyone dead, and never want to. I was with my father when he was dying, but I slipped away before, I think, his last breath. I also refused the opportunity to see my mother when she died, and Quentin Crewe, my first husband, who died at home. His children sat all day round his bed: I couldn't look into the room. I want to remember people as they are alive, and can't help thinking the image of a newly deceased face would be hard to erase from one's mind. As for touching a corpse: for me, impossible. Those who do, whether for love or duty, include all the people whose courage I so admire.

I've never picked up a dead bird, rabbit, lamb; even a mouse. Often I wonder, as a grandson swings off with a rabbit he has proudly shot, and rigor mortis is setting in, just what it is about these inanimate or dead things that fills me with such horror. Stiffness, rigidity, sightless eyes; open mouths, teeth, coarse, dead-looking hair. Those are elements, but not the whole. What *that* is, I suppose I will never know. My children, thank goodness, have not inherited this weird trait, which I imagine will be with me for the rest of my life. I'm used to being on the alert, and I'm better than I was as a child at dealing with unexpected situations. Perhaps, one day, I shall give up asking others if they, too, cannot see the horror of an icy china baby, or a sweating waxwork, or a decapitated plastic head on a stand. It would be comforting and interesting if they could, but that, I think, is a thin hope.

3

Boarding School

I was to go to boarding school, it was decided, at the age of eight. There are many who are outraged by this so-called cruel British practice of sending very young children away from home, and while it is upsetting for some, it is absolutely fine for others. I was one of those. Not for one moment was I homesick.

The school, Guilsborough Lodge, was a cosy old hunting lodge half a mile from a village in Northamptonshire, surrounded by fields over which the Pytchley Hunt regularly clattered. There were some fifty pupils and a very small staff – the fierce matron, the spectral headmistress and the gallant Miss Derby, whose permanent hairnet was bound by a ribbon of corn-coloured velvet.

Miss Watson, the headmistress, was a hoodie before her time. Her daily uniform was a long grey cloak, which billowed against her skeletal frame as she filtered about: from the depths of the hood you could catch a glimpse of a blade face, forced askew by a minuscule but grim smile. Her feet, narrow as knives, flashed in well-polished shoes fastened with several skinny straps. She was a taciturn woman: frightening, but not unfriendly.

For my first two terms, like everyone else, I gave her little thought. Except at prayers, we hardly saw her. She was not the sort of figure to fire curiosity. Then, my first summer term, she decided we would do some scenes from Shakespeare at the end-of-term concert. She chose *A Midsummer Night's Dream*, and quickly it became apparent that the single love in her life was Shakespeare.

Every evening, after prep, cloak discarded, she would take us into the garden and, Jean Brodie-like, impart her understanding of the magical play. The scene she chose for a friend and me was the one between Puck and the fairy – I was the fairy. There were weeks of blissful learning. But, just as I'd got the words, the girl playing Puck resigned from the part for reasons she never explained. So I was quickly switched to taking her place. I was thrilled. Puck, it seemed to me, was a far greater challenge.

By the next term Miss Watson had retired again to the protection of her grey hood, and it was hard to remember the summer vitality fired in her by Shakespeare. But her one talent was an inspiration. Looking back, I realise that – despite the fact that my education lacked a great deal in many ways – I was incredibly lucky to be taught by some people brilliant in the subjects I loved.

Miss Derby was one of them. She, it seemed, was knowledgeable about everything. She taught us all subjects, including the piano. But what I most loved was a subject I'd never heard of: history of art. Every week she would bring in a postcard of some famous painting, and urge us to study it – really study it.

'*Look* at it,' she would urge us. 'Really look. Find things in it … Make people see what you've found. You've no idea how hopeless most people are at looking at pictures.' Subsequently, going round galleries, her point has been proved dozens of times. Once I was in the Mauritshuis in The Hague with my husband, the observant James. We came upon a picture of a life-size cow. I thought I'd test him.

'Notice anything odd?' I asked. He contemplated the cow for a long time.

'No,' he said eventually.

'Its hooves are back to front.'

'So they are …'

I loved Fridays, the day for new postcards. There was Fragonard's *Girl on a Swing*, Watteau's genteel ladies in the Champs-Elysées, Corot's silver mist landscapes ('always look for the red dot, the scarlet beret'), Van Gogh's wondrous chair, blazing out even in miniature – dozens of others, unforgettable. We would learn about the artists, reflect deeply on the picture we'd been shown, then write an essay.

During the horrendous winter of 1947, the school was completely cut off by such vast drifts of snow that food had to be delivered by tractor. Most of us had measles and were in bed, rather enjoying being waited on by the overworked staff. Never had such white light flared through the bedroom windows, lighting up the chipped paint of the iron bedsteads.

When at last spring broke through, we found ourselves learning about sex. This part of our education came from watching the conscientious ram serving his flock in the nearby fields. Sex education rarely came from parents, or indeed teachers. But the ram and his harem furnished us with amazing, giggle-making facts.

Further help in our sex education came from the pet rabbits that some girls brought to school. We would sneak down to the damp stable before breakfast and watch, astonished by their antics. One among us, Jane, was a rabbit expert. She brought a whole team of rabbits in hutches. She would get up early every morning and exercise them in specially made harnesses and leads, proud of their obedience: they acted like well-trained dogs. Thinking this ability enviable, I brought back a pretty silver doe one winter term. Not only did it lack the talents of Jane's rabbits, it did not seem to have any desire even to try to obey my commands and become a performing rabbit. Instead, it died very quickly. I found it one icy, foggy morning, stiff as an old glove in its hutch. My embarrassment was that, terrified of dead things, I was unable to pick it up. Jane buried it for me, and nobly kept my secret.

Parents made infrequent visits to see their children – my parents never came. Northamptonshire, apparently, was a very long way from where parents lived. But we had our weekend treats. Best among them was being allowed to follow the hunt on Saturday mornings. The orchestra of hooves as dozens of horses clattered to the first covert sent a thrill down many a nine-year-old spine. Then came the melancholy note of the huntsman's horn. The excitement of it all kept us struggling across winter plough as we tried to keep up with the field, and the scarlet coats, ever more distant. We fell over, became muddy, exhausted, but were exhilarated by the chase. We never saw a fox killed, but for some of us it was the beginning of a love of hunting.

By the time we left Guilsborough, we were not only knowledgeable about procreation, but were also pretty skilled in the long jump and the high jump, both much practised in the summer term. Also, we could recognise dozens of birds: this was because I had started a Bird Club, chiefly because I thought the idea of *meetings* was appealing – an idea that soon foundered. Enthusiastic members used to vie for how many different species they had seen each week and they were then urged, bossily by me, to describe these birds in detail to make sure they were not cheating.

We left Guilsborough with little academic prowess, though some of us had been inspiringly introduced to art, music, Shakespeare, hunting, and the point of Girl Guides. It had been a happy time, and we were in some dread of the next step. Everyone but me was to go on to a more senior boarding school. My mother, in her quest for her daughters to learn French, had found, via the au pair, a convent in a small town in Switzerland. That was to provide the next part of my education.

Eaton Square, in 1949, was not the glamorous part of London that it was later to become. The huge houses – some had just started to be converted into flats – were shabby, war-scarred, unappealing. Many of them were occupied by refugees. But my mother had the feeling that one day it would all be repaired, painted, desirable. In that she was prescient.

While we waited for renovations to the flat to be completed, holidays were spent in various rented houses near EBH, and our mother felt it necessary to employ an au pair, a nice Swiss woman, Henriette, in her late twenties. Welfare had been sent to some unknown place until he could be accommodated in London, and Nanny had gone back to Canterbury until she, too, could join us. The wrench of parting from her was as searing as leaving EBH.

Living in the same environs, albeit in a different house, meant we could continue some of our old life in the holidays. We still went riding two or three times a week, immaculate in our Wetherill jodhpurs and jackets and black velvet jockey caps. One Sunday morning, the day for hacking rather than dressage, we were galloping up a hill. Trish's pony, in front of me, suddenly stumbled and fell to the ground, throwing her off. The pony died instantly. Trish was bruised, shaken, crying. There was a long wait in the alien field, the pony horribly still, until someone with a car arrived to take us home.

Back at the rented house, we hurried to the sitting room to explain what had happened. There, our mother, cross-legged in an armchair, was radiating something very powerful that we didn't understand. She was not much interested in the equestrian disaster. My father, at his most courteous and affable, was handing a drink to a large, ruddy-face man of German descent – an important figure in the City, we were later assured.

'This is Uncle Fred,' our mother said. 'Catherine's father.' *Uncle?* Catherine! Our only nearby friend ... He was agreeable, and sympathetic to Trish's bad morning. What we could not have guessed was that he was going to be part of our lives until he died.

Once we moved to Eaton Square, my mother's new attachment flourished, made easier by both parties being in London. Her affair with Fred must be one of the dullest liaisons on record. It was hard to know how they kept up such rigorous, daily communication without tarnishing the love, excitement, or whatever it was. This was the pattern they kept to:

8.30 a.m., Slough Station. Fred rings to say good morning.

9.30 a.m. Fred rings from the Stock Exchange to say good morning again.

1 p.m. Fred rings to find out how the day is going. Though on Tuesdays and Fridays they lunched at their favourite restaurant Au Jardin des Gourmets. These were immovable feasts. Should Trish, or I, or anyone require our mother for anything at lunchtime on those two days, she was unable to oblige. They were her absolute priority. After lunch Fred would see her into a taxi back to Eaton Square.

4.30 p.m. Fred rings to say he is on his way.

5.30 p.m. Fred arrives at Eaton Square. He is given three very large whiskies while she gets through five lethal martinis. Sometimes our father is there. Husband and lover get on well, talk about the politics of the day – a subject that never comes up with my mother. (Goodness knows what she and Fred do talk about.) Sometimes he plays the piano, thunderously. My mother leans up against the Steinway Grand in imitation of Marlene Dietrich (whom she once saw at the Café de Paris) and sings along: 'Heaven, I'm in heaven' … completely out of tune. It's so bad it's faintly endearing. Fred takes a puff on his pipe and is encouraged not to stop. He can play *anything* you ask, Mum says proudly, and often. Trish and I sometimes come in and listen. Sometimes Fred, a generous man, gives us a fiver. My father pours his own whisky, my mother pours Fred's.

6.30 p.m. Fred leaves for Paddington in a taxi. Sometimes Mum goes with him.

7.30 p.m. Fred rings from Slough to say goodnight.

This schedule went on, almost without interruption, *for twenty-five years.*

After Fred had gone, my mother would have her sixth martini, which was her undoing. She had an extraordinarily strong head, and claimed she had never had a hangover in her life. But five martinis were all she could accommodate before sliding into a tottering wooziness which we hated to witness. Plates were dropped, supper took an age. My father, hungry after his very long day, would be in trouble for requesting a biscuit. Conversation at supper was impossible. Once it was over, Mum would go to her bedroom and ring Fred's sister, a real-life Widow Twankey, also drunk, and they would enjoy their endless inebriated conversations.

Our mother, Trish and I reckoned, was not an actual alcoholic: with the greatest of ease she gave up drinking entirely for the forty days of Lent. But her enormous consumption of gin and champagne meant that we could never rely on her to be sober at crucial moments, so we lived in constant fear of embarrassment. I often longed to ask Fred if he could 'do anything' about her drinking, but I never dared. Besides, she was mostly clever enough not to go over the top in his presence. She always waited till he had gone before having the sixth martini.

Fred's wife and children, like us, were all aware of the long affair, but nonetheless Fred took certain honourable precautions. When he went away on business, he would write her dry little notes devoid of all declarations of love, 'just in case anyone came across them one day'. (We did come across them not long ago. He would have been pleased to know how boring we found them.) He gave her a beautiful aquamarine ring and a collection of antique silver boxes, but I don't think they had much fun. There was little chance to get away. As an old member of Balliol, Fred sometimes returned to Oxford for a gaudy, and took our mother with him. They stayed in the Randolph, but as Fred had to have dinner in his old college, Mum was abandoned till midnight. They went to Lausanne a couple of times, and Paris. But married restrictions meant few overnight outings. My father was extraordinarily generous about Fred's constant presence: his wife was adamant that vice versa was not a possibility. And Fred was certainly compelled (or was it habit?) to keep up the visitations. When for a while we had a cottage in Berkshire, he would make the three-quarters of an hour drive from Farnham Common just to have a pre-Sunday lunch drink before 'getting back'. If he wasn't coming one Sunday, he would, of course, ring. Often my father would answer the telephone.

'Hello?'

'Ah, Harold. It's Fred.'

'Fred! My dear fellow. Shall I get Bridget?'

'Thank you.' That snippet of communication must have been played a thousand times.

Over the years, Trish and I grew fond of Fred. He was highly intelligent and had a dry sense of humour. He never interfered, was interested but not over-interested in our lives, and helpful if we asked for advice. His use was to keep our mother feeling glamorous, desirable, busy – for she had an unconstructed life, its emptiness only excited by the gossip of numerous friends. When Fred became too ill to come to London, and was rarely able to telephone, there was misery on both sides. Somehow, a final meeting was agreed to by his wife. My then brother-in-law arranged for Mum to be taken to the house near Farnham Common in his firm's chauffeur-driven Rolls. The door was opened by Fred's wife.

'Up the stairs and first on the left,' she said.

'I know,' said my mother.

Shortly after that I went with her to his memorial service in London. When it was over, hundreds of friends queued up to say a word to his widow. I took Mum out to lunch.

'It's not easy, going to a married lover's memorial service,' she said with a brave smile. 'No one dares to queue to offer consolation to the mistress.'

Having left Guilsborough Lodge, the plan for me to spend some time in Switzerland materialised. The nice au pair Henriette lived with her elderly parents in the small town of Sierre; a town where, as far as I could discover, not a single person spoke English.

My mother did not bother to visit what was to be my home for six months: she trusted the au pair, and luckily she was right. The small house was of the cleanliness that the Swiss are famous for, and its wooden walls smelt like cigar boxes. My room looked out on to mountains, and roofs. The bed was comfortable. There was a large desk. Henriette's parents were kindly, and the food excellent. Once again, I did not feel homesick, though sensed an unnerving distance from England.

The frightening aspect was the convent to which I went

daily: crowds of very noisy children shrieking in a language I could barely understand, the nuns' huge faces clamped between the stiff edges of their starched headdresses. I was given a uniform pinafore, put in a class, introduced, and no concession was made to my not being able to understand French. I had to do every subject that was being taught, and much of it was taught very boringly. We spent six months on the geography of the small region of Sion. But at least, being just eleven, I picked up French very quickly. This meant that my initial struggle with homework was reduced, and the ensuing emptiness left each evening was hard to fill. I would sit at my desk, contemplating the evening sun colouring the snow on the mountains, reflecting deeply – I thought – on my life. I came to the conclusion that I was perfectly happy to be on my own, and to read, but what I wanted to do was to write more, as I used to before going to school. So I began a book, dedicated to Trish. Inspired somewhat by Enid Blyton, it was the story of a budgerigar, copiously illustrated.

I made a few friends at the convent, but invitations to their houses were rare. One girl did ask me to lunch at her house one Friday: she explained that as her family could not afford fish, their custom was to eat kitten. Would I mind? I made my excuses.

Henriette did her best to entertain me. We went to Milan to see *The Last Supper*: it was thrilling to confront a life-size original painting at last. An essay Miss Derby would never see sprang to mind. We skied several times at Montana. But what I most enjoyed was the approach to Christmas in Sierre. The smell of thousands of gingerbread St Nicholases came from every *boulangerie* in the main street, while the deep snow creaked under our feet. At the convent we sang beautiful French carols:

> *C'était la vieille de Noël,*
> *La nuit sereine était sans voiles:*
> *Et sur le chemin bleu du ciel,*
> *On pouvait compter les étoiles …*

At the end of every day I would walk back along the *chemin bleu du ciel* knowing there would be a delicious supper waiting, then I would have several hours in my room to carry on with the book. I would look forward to the weekly letter from Nanny, who never let me down, and occasional funny letters from Trish, who did not like my being away. (Shortly after my stay in Switzerland, she was sent to a horrendous convent in the South of France.) It was neither a happy time, nor an unhappy one, but it went very slowly. I left with – finally – an enamel star for 'trying' to pin on my pinafore, a finished book for my sister, and a fluency in French which, had she ever heard me speak, would have pleased my mother. But I refused ever to speak to her in French lest she scoffed that I was not nearly as good as her. So I never gave her the chance to judge. By the time I returned home from Switzerland she had chosen a boarding school, far from London, to which I was to go.

She had also, thankfully, found a cottage in Norfolk for the holidays. This was a great relief, because the London flat, for all its elegance, was claustrophobic. Neither Trish, my father nor I liked London: we longed to return to the country.

Oxnead Mill House was a cottage by the huge white mill that erratically provided our electricity. (Our lights dipped up and down choppily as a rough sea. You could never make a plan to read after dark.) It was yards from the river Bure, which made 'a whispery and watery Norfolk sound, Telling of all the moonlit reeds around', as Betjeman described it. The gush of water into the millpond was constant music. A five-minute walk through the fields brought you to the big house. This had been built especially to accommodate Charles II on a visit. Once he had gone, the bankrupt hosts pulled it down, leaving only the servants' quarters. There must have been a lot of them: it was a very large wing, built of mellowed brick, a faintly Dutch air in its design, set among terraces that meandered down to a marsh.

Oxnead Hall, as it was called, was owned by our mother's friends the Mosleys. John was Oswald's brother and looked just like him: he was witty, funny, good company but feeble. His wife Anne, a Romanian with wild hair of unlikely red, who may once have been good looking, seemed to have only two interests: men, and mayonnaise. This she made every day. It's hard to remember her without a bowl between her knees, whisking, pouring oil, manoeuvring her large mouth of dazzling lipstick into shapes of disapproval as she mentioned dozens of names of friends in Paris.

The Mosleys – like the previous owners of the house, bankrupted by Charles II – had no money. The house inside was cold, bleak, damp; altogether dispiriting. I frequently thought, with its views of terraces, marsh and vast skies, how wonderful it could be inside: but it never was. I went there often by myself, when Anne and John were away, to practise the piano – a gloomy instrument of ochre keys, completely out of tune. This was always a somewhat spine-tingling experience, the hour in the stygian drawing room, for it was supposedly haunted by a raven which was said to peck at the window. I kept looking over my shoulder, expecting to see the ghostly bird, but never did.

There was a stable block at one end of the house, in no better shape than the house itself. But we were allowed to keep our hired ponies there in the holidays. And it has to be admitted that our mother, now she was 'back' and rather enjoying the primitive cottage, decided she should make up for all the years she had not been with us, and try to be a better mother. She succeeded in many ways: became something of a gymkhana junkie, driving us miles to far-off horse shows, where she produced mammoth picnics. She would go early into Aylsham to buy the first hot doughnuts for us, and she became a seriously good cook (cooking, but not asking us to help with the washing up seemed to be her way to our hearts). Her small repertoire included too much butter and cream, but her variations on a chicken, and English puddings, were wonderful.

Sometimes we went to Overstrand to swim. Invariably, by the time we arrived the sky had become overcast and a nasty wind was chafing at the sea. But we would huddle on the shingle beach, enjoying the sandwiches packed with Anne Mosley's leftover mayonnaise. I remember the scratchiness of the bathing suits made of that ruffled and elasticated cotton, so prevalent in the 1950s, and the sandy feel of a damp bathing towel round my shoulders, hopeless at providing warmth. What made these outings bearable was our parents' shared humour. Somehow they managed to make very good jokes about the grimness of it all, which meant we resisted asking to return to the cottage as soon as possible. I secretly longed to return to get back to writing my 'novel' – a Florence Nightingale-inspired story set in the Korean War, about which I knew nothing, but enjoyed imagining. I also wrote dozens of essays there, in the tiny 'study', half taken up by the old nursery table. These were short pieces of very purple prose mostly about Nature. (I had just become a keen reader of Wordsworth.) I showed some of them to my father, who had them typed out for me. He always encouraged, but never went overboard in his praise and gave useful criticism. Then my mother found one of these essays: she read it out loud, she later told me, at one of her 'girls' lunches'. All her friends found it simply wonderful, amazing. So did she.

I had never been so furious. It was the first time I could ever remember losing my temper. I alarmed even myself.

'Never, ever again will you see anything I write,' I screamed. 'You and your friends know nothing about writing. I don't want your stupid praise ...' I kept my word, vowed never to tell her I intended to be a writer, and she never read another word till I began working as a journalist.

The cottage, like the big house, was haunted. Trish and I had adjoining rooms, and they both opened on to a small landing. Often in the night we would wake to hear footsteps rhythmically going round and round. We thought nothing of this, for to soothe his endless stomach ulcer pain, our father often paced about in the night. But then came the time that he was in London, and the footsteps continued. And there were often occasions that we heard voices downstairs, outside, talking to someone at the front door, though Mum was asleep. She scoffed at such claims, until one bright afternoon we were all in the sitting room. Overhead we heard very heavy, regular footsteps. My mother admitted there was 'something'. She sent Dad upstairs to see. He saw nothing. We were all a bit shaken.

Gradually we made friends in Norfolk. There were some fanciable boys we met at Pony Club dances, some of whom were at Dartmouth College and wore their glorious naval evening uniforms. It was at one of the dances, aged twelve, I was kissed for the first time, having been pushed with some haste deep into a laurel bush. Years later I saw a picture of a famous opera singer and realised it was he – purveyor of my first kiss.

By day we were occupied attending to Joey, a fat and sluggish pony whose scant enthusiasm for jumping was a daily disappointment. And always, no matter how we spent our time outside, I was longing to get back to the peace of my so-called study. Despite its air of faint unease, I loved the cottage and that part of Norfolk. I loved sitting in the garden writing beside the buddleia tree, a confetti of butterflies fluttering about my head. I loved the quiet brown waters of the river, so slow it was impossible to see the flow. But then there were the sudden shrieks of watery surprise as they crashed into the millpond and were whirled for a while before rejoining the further stretch of calm water.

Oxnead Mill House was only rented for a few years. But luckily my friend Felicity's parents had taken a cottage in Brancaster, on the coast some way north. We stayed there often. Now such a popular village, seething with uninspired new houses, in those days Brancaster had little more to offer than a golf course, and dunes of restless marram grass, bending towards a beach so vast its distances exercise the eyes. It was a place scarcely discovered by those who did not live there. No car park, no kiosk of balloons and ice creams. The very few walkers and swimmers are now replaced by hundreds of people, much of the year.

The immensity of Norfolk sky, which hints at the curve of the globe, is what it is impossible ever to take for granted. In the thirty years I lived in Oxford, that is what I most missed: sky. And glorious though Norfolk is under sun, when it rains it is no less magical: showers fall in visible lace folds across the marshes and the flighting duck. It's perfection of a rare kind.

I've been returning to Brancaster for some sixty years, now: family summer holidays, silent winter weeks writing in my sister-in-law's barn. Several of my novels are either set in Norfolk, or the county plays a walk-on part in them. It's the place I would most like to be able to evoke precisely, but that remains a constant challenge, not yet achieved.

4

The Grandmother

The dislike of a close relation is an uneasy sensation, fraught with guilt. Our maternal grandmother, Isabella Nickols, was not a likeable character – the most materialistic woman I have ever met; haughty, imperious, interested in so few things. In her favour she gave a great deal of work to master craftsmen, for whom she had considerable respect. She was not kind to her wretched spinster daughter, on whom she relied for the practicalities of life. The only person she seemed genuinely fond of was my father.

Isabella had been born in Ireland in 1874. As I have little natural interest in my antecedents, perhaps because what I have heard of them does not sound very gripping, I have never bothered to research her background. My mother claimed her grandfather owned a shipping line in Dublin. My father said no, he owned a couple of old sardine smacks. My sister, who enjoys the new fashionable pastime of digging up families, says Isabella McConnell, as she was born, was the daughter of a labourer. Whatever the truth, for some unknown reason she moved to Scotland when she reached marriageable age.

According to photographs, and a portrait by Philip de László, she was very good looking, with auburn hair and wide-set eyes. She was certainly lively, flirtatious, and deeply ambitious. In no time she found a rich Scottish husband. They had a son, James who, even as a schoolboy at Eton, was a drinker. One day he was relieving himself in the Thames when a gust of wind caught his coat, casting him in. He drowned. His sister Jenny lived with my grandmother for the rest of her life, the epitome of a sad 'old maid'.

When the rich Scotsman died, leaving Granny very nicely off, the idea came to her that the South of France might be a good place to search for a replacement. It was there she met my grandfather, the widower Harold Nickols, a Yorkshire land-owner. He had eight grown-up children, who were not overjoyed at the sudden presence of a stepmother younger than themselves. My mother was born fourteen years before her father – whom she loved – died. The stepsisters were kind to her, but she rarely lived at home in the vast house in Seymour Place in London, or in Yorkshire. She was educated abroad, which meant Granny could lead her own life unencumbered by the presence of a young child.

After her second husband had died, judging by the amount of furniture and pictures she left behind, Isabella Nickols must have indulged in a great deal of therapeutic shopping. Curiously, for one distinctly lacking in fine education, she had a keen eye. She would go to sales at Sotheby's and Christie's and acquire good Victorian pictures, Dutch still lifes, and even modern art of the time – she loved Brangwyn, for instance. She was equally enthusiastic about furniture, china and glass, though it seems she was not always clear as to whether the things she wanted were for sale.

One day she went to the Victoria and Albert Museum and found a magnificent collection of glasses, plates, bowls, decanters and jugs – dozens of pieces in all, elaborate hand-cut glass that slightly pricks your fingers. Each piece was engraved with a VR: it had been made to celebrate Queen Victoria's Silver Jubilee.

'I'll take all that,' said my grandmother, presumably thinking she was in a large department store. When her offer to buy the unique glass was turned down, she was undaunted. As a determined woman who nearly always got her way, she somehow managed to persuade the museum to let her have the set copied. The only difference from the original was that her initials replaced the queen's. And she left this eccentric purchase to me.

Many years later, when I lived in London, Liberace happened to come to dinner. I did my best to make him feel at home, putting a candelabra with lighted candles on the grand piano. He arrived in a dazzling suit. On one lapel was pinned a brooch that would make a talking point lively enough to break any ice: a diamond octave with a scale of diamond and sapphire notes. The open piano he ignored, but when he entered the dining room he gasped as his eyes skittered over the twinkling glass.

'I'll take the lot,' he said, with a huge wave of his shiny pink hand, unknowingly echoing my grandmother's earlier desire.

'Oh no you won't,' I said, like the man in the museum. Ever since then it's been known as the Liberace glass, only used on special occasions because it's no fun to wash up.

The triumph of the glass was not my grandmother's first venture into the pastime of having things copied. Well able to afford all the original furniture and silver she wanted, she preferred to have copied whatever piece she fancied, thus providing copious work for master craftsmen. Often she went to Versailles to see what caught her eye in the palace. Months later, pieces of very French furniture, more suited to their provenance than to her own overcrowded drawing room, would appear. There was an elaborate dressing table of beautifully inlaid wood, with enamel cupids flying across the doors, as well as side tables with marble tops supported by golden eagles, hefty cupboards and chests of dark mahogany. The best thing was a magnificent desk she found in Versailles: with intricate leather top edged with brass, and brass rams' heads on the legs. She had a copy made which she gave to my father who passed it on to me – my writing place for the last forty years. Much of the dottier stuff my mother, sister and I sold in difficult moments over the last decades, but I am left with a magisterial dining-room table and six Chippendale chairs – six original, six copies. I also have a bespoke grand piano, still with its very fine tone, that she had made by Steinway in 1912.

I have no recollection of my grandmother before the age of twelve, by which time my mother had returned home from her years in France and we were living in London. The impression was alarming. She was a small, solidly built woman, her auburn hair dyed to an unsubtle red. Long before her time she had indulged in face-lifts, which meant her eyes were tilted at an uneasy slant, and the bottom of her face appeared larger than it should. She wore bright red lipstick and a jacket of 'the finest' mink – each animal chosen in consultation with her furrier. On every possible occasion this jacket would have an outing, and certainly passers-by would reward her with a second glance. She was as proud of her deportment as she was of the jacket, and it was extraordinary: ramrod back, shoulders down and walking like a guardsman, perhaps to give an illusion of height she did not have. A crocodile handbag and crocodile shoes were part of her uniform, and always the three rows of pearls – oh, those pearls.

The story was that the centre one was known to be the most valuable pearl in the world, though where this judgement came from, I never discovered. It had been stolen in the middle of the nineteenth century, but found in a matchbox in a gutter in the City in 1914. My grandfather bought it for some astronomical price, and then went on to find dozens of suitably pedigree companions to make a magnificent necklace, which can be seen in the de László portrait. My grandmother wore it every day, but it was a hazard. It would always have to be covered by a scarf if she was out, lest some robber pounced on her. When it was cleaned at Cartier, they insisted she had to sit and chaperone the pearl cleaner to make sure the trusted man did not stuff the necklace into his pocket and nip out at the back. My grandmother put up with these inconveniences because she was very proud of her necklace. On the occasions when she was assured of absolute safety, such as at our flat, she would pull back the chiffon scarf and demand our admiration for the hundredth time.

While hunting for the perfect place to live in London, a very long hunt, Granny and her spinster daughter Jenny lived at The Ritz. When we were children, some of the worst nightmare occasions for Trish and me were lunches with the two of them in the Ritz restaurant. Granny ate the same thing every day: Irish stew and rice pudding. Although these simple dishes had never caused her any reason to complain, or an upset stomach, her suspicion of what the chef *might* one day put in them never left her. She would beckon a waiter, hand him a chunk of lamb and pearl barley on a fork, and insist he try it. Rather than face a scene, the waiter would oblige, and invariably declare it was fine. So Granny was happy till the rice pudding arrived, when the same procedure was repeated. Trish and I could see a group of waiters in the corner arguing about which one should go and do her bidding. We were scarlet and sick with embarrassment. Occasionally, she felt like a change of location: lunch at Claridge's. That was even worse than The Ritz, because the waiters were less accustomed to her peculiar ways. Wherever we were, my mother persisted in shouting at her, but the loud attempts at conversation could not penetrate Granny's acute deafness. We could not fail to be aware of other people in the restaurant turning to look curiously at our table.

Perhaps my first vivid memory of our grandmother was the night she came to a 'dance', as she called it, that my mother had decided to give in our flat in Eaton Square. There may have been a few of our own friends but, to spare them, we claimed most of them were unable to come. So there were some twenty children of my mother's friends, young and shy in their first long dresses and dinner jackets. One of them, who later became a senior figure in the Bank of England, my forward-planning mother had in mind as a perfect husband for me. I was twelve, but she liked to think ahead.

The sofas in the modest drawing room were pushed back. The three-piece band took up much of the floor space, and played sloomy music with an air of insurmountable fatigue. The awkward young clustered close to the walls in dread of the parquet floor that beckoned them to dance. Poor old Welfare, the butler, hovered around with fruit cup and cider. My father, who had stood firm about not wearing a white tie – which my mother, curiously, had thought appropriate – took up a position by the fire looking utterly miserable. Enter Granny, followed – like Dame Edna Everage's bridesmaid – by Aunt Jenny.

I suppose Granny was no longer besieged with the kind of invitations that required grand clothes, so she had taken this rare opportunity to dress up. She wore a crimson velvet coat with a six-foot train; the pearls, of course; long diamond earrings and a huge diamond brooch. I don't know what was under the coat for she never took it off. She sashayed into the room with – I have to admit – her very impressive deportment, swooshing the velvet train about so that the astonished guests had to jump out of the way. She glided towards my father.

'Harold,' she said, 'let us dance.'

There was nothing he could do but oblige. A good dancer, he cantered around with her for what seemed like for ever, while the onlookers developed skills in avoiding them. Each time a tune came to an end, she clutched at him and begged for more. In the end my mother guided her to the dining room, where she sat in her vast pool of red velvet and picked at the food. The young, at last free to giggle, made an effort to dance. Aunt Jenny sat silent as always in a corner.

She was a tragic creature. Her only joys in life were music and cats. She was not often free to go to a concert, and was not allowed a cat. Nor had she inherited her mother's looks or sparkle, though when she was in her twenties she found a man she wanted to marry.

'Never,' said my grandmother, when she learnt who the suitor was. 'I'd rather you put your head in a gas oven.'

Aunt Jenny acted upon this advice almost immediately. She was pulled from the oven unconscious but not quite dead. From that day she suffered from a slowness, a kind of incomprehension about everything, except how to play the piano or to stroke a rare cat. Her place, she grimly realised, was to be my grandmother's constant companion for life, a job it would be hard to beat for horror. Her downturned watery eyes hid goodness knows what depths of unhappiness, but she had neither the energy nor the competence to escape from her position as the grateful spinster daughter.

The most pathetic thing about her was her desperate need for declarations of love. Every time she came to visit us she would ask my sister and me the same question:

'Do you love your aunt?'

'Yes,' we would chorus with the eye-rolling, sneering voices of eleven- and thirteen-year-olds who can't be bothered to disguise their opinion that she was a stupid old bag, and we certainly did not love her. But the answer never failed to please her.

In the 1950s my grandmother, for some mysterious reason, was the only woman with a private account at the Bank of England. To keep this account afloat she was obliged to make sure the balance never dropped below £10,000. She had a ritual way of doing this and invited me, one day, to accompany her on a topping-up procedure. I would be interested, she said, to see the inside of the bank. It was not among my prime ambitions, at the age of thirteen, but I agreed to go.

We walked, very slowly, from her flat in Half-Moon Street to the Regent Street branch of the Westminster Bank. In charge there was a charming old-fashioned bank manager, Mr Perry, grey curls blurring his pink bald head, who always wore striped trousers and a black jacket. The frequent visits from Granny, I imagine, put him into a terrible dither, causing him to be less than efficient. On this particular afternoon, after acting out an over-the-top rapturous greeting, he led us into his husky office where his mahogany desk was cleared of all traces of work. I cannot recall precisely the delay while my grandmother wrote a cheque to be delivered in the City, but she accused Mr Perry of being too slow in checking her current account (which, due to the many transactions, he must have known by heart). She suddenly picked up her folded umbrella and whacked him hard on the backside. He smiled, saw us out with a small bow and a smaller smile. He was a bank manager who would gallantly put up with anything to keep her account.

Next, we had to catch a bus, taxis being Granny's area of acute meanness. She had no idea what number bus was needed, but hailed the first one she saw approaching the bus stop. I had to heave her up on to the platform as she only had one free hand to help herself. The other was clutching the perennial scarf over the pearls.

'Take me to the Bank of England,' she demanded of the conductor when he approached. By some miraculous chance the bus happened to be going to the City, so he overlooked her lordly demand and nodded agreeably. She opened her vast crocodile bag, and purse, and held up a threepenny piece.

'There,' she said.

Others on the bus were enjoying the scene, making no attempt to hide their smiles. I wanted to die.

Several alternatives visibly crashed across the conductor's face. Either he had to make a fuss, demand the right fare, turn her off the bus if she refused to pay – or he could opt for peace and accept the dotty old bat's offering. That's what he wisely chose. Doubt contorted his face as he accepted the threepenny piece, but never have I been so grateful to a bus conductor.

At the Bank of England, Granny stalked her way down the great marble halls, inclining her head slightly, like a bride, to a great many clerks in morning suits who proffered well-trained bows. Her top-up cheque was received with extravagant gratitude, and we were bowed out to find another bus. There was the same performance with another threepenny bit and, by some million-to-one chance, another conductor who reckoned it was just not worth battling with so daft a passenger. Never again did I agree to accompany my grandmother on one of these financial adventures.

But I could not escape, on one occasion, a trip to Harrods to buy a dustbin. They had the very best dustbins, she declared. On the way there she confessed she liked to be served by men. I knew I was in for a bad afternoon.

After ambling straight-backed through many a department, whose assistants received the benefit of her loud, unasked-for opinion of their merchandise, we at last came to a floor that housed stuff for outdoor life – garden furniture, wheelbarrows, and so on. Granny declared this was just where she wanted to be, but was suddenly unsure of the exact location of the dustbins. She needed help. Help was nearby.

On a stretch of artificial grass was a large a man in striped trousers (which were almost ubiquitous in my grandmother's world) and a bowler hat. He was bending over a mowing machine. My grandmother sidled up to him, raised her weapon of the folded umbrella, whacked him on the behind no less hard than she had whacked the bank manager.

'Can you help me, my man?' she asked.

The portly figure jumped up and spun round to her, scarlet in the face, eyes exploding.

'No, madam, I cannot,' he shouted. 'I'm a *customer*, not an assistant.'

My grandmother was not one to apologise. By this time I had moved several yards away, but could see her give a small, balletic spin on her heels and move towards me, no word of apology offered to the outraged customer. Due to her acute deafness, she had probably not heard what he said. But perhaps she felt that a man in a bowler hat, abandoning his scrutiny of a mowing machine to jump round and pay her some attention, represented a considerable form of flattery.

A further visit to Mr Perry was necessary when she decided to set Trish and me up with an annual allowance of £60, for which we had to write very grateful thank-you letters. But that allowance came at a high price: it felt like a bribe to make us do whatever she wanted. Should we demur, hints that the allowance would stop would be made. In some ways she was a generous old thing (she bought far more handmade shirts and Savile Row bespoke suits for my father than he could possibly accommodate), but her method was always to pay for what she considered we needed rather than for what we might have wanted. And it was payment, of course, for company. 'Come and see me and I will give you something.' Sometimes she forgot to hand over a reward; sometimes it was one of those huge white paper £5 notes.

Clothes were her passion, the house of Worth her favourite couturier. When I was fifteen she declared I needed a winter coat. Off to the warm, scented House of Worth we went. The *vendeuses* there knew her well and did not even try to conceal the looks that passed between them. We sat on a silken sofa while bolts of material were brought in for our inspection. At that time I had just got my first pair of jeans (though I was not allowed to wear them in London, except at weekends) and found it hard to summon interest in the exquisitely soft grey flannel which was eventually chosen. Next came the linings, and there I got my own way: emerald satin. Finally, fur for the collar. Persian lamb was the unanimous choice. My faint opinion that I didn't want a fur collar at all was passed over. This initial planning meeting took three hours.

I dreaded the next appointment with Worth, for I knew that by then the wretched coat would be cut out and there would be no going back. That was the case. A couple of months had brought it to the stage of tacking stitches, chalk marks, and no lining or collar. It was hard to visualise the finished thing. There were several more fittings, each one more depressing. Finally, the coat was ready.

I stood looking at myself in a long mirror. Behind me, reflections of the *vendeuses* cooed their admiration. It was, indeed, a beautifully *made* coat. It hung in thick gathers from a smock-like yoke, over which was placed the Persian lamb collar. The sleeves puffed out from the yoke at the top, narrowed down at the wrists. The main body of it drooped almost to my ankles. The satin lining did feel soft, and I was able to agree it was a marvellous, wondrous coat ... for someone of sixty, I privately thought: it would have suited Queen Mary very well. But I was still not sixteen.

My grandmother got out her Bank of England chequebook, and the coat was swathed in tissue paper, where it lived unworn till the day I took it to a smart second-hand shop. It fetched about two per cent of its worth.

Once I had left home, I gave up any pretence of being a dutiful granddaughter. There had been too many ghastly public incidents, and visits – once she was completely deaf – seemed pointless: a strain for both of us. At the age of ninety-four she was finally persuaded to have a nurse to look after her. The afternoon the woman arrived, there was a knock on the door. In rushed two men with stockings over their faces. They tied the nurse up with flexes, hit her on the head with a small steak hammer from Selfridges, its price tag still intact. The terrified nurse was warned that should she try to escape, she would be electrocuted. Then they went into my grandmother's bedroom, where she was sitting up in bed.

She was thrilled to find she had visitors: two 'nice young men', as she later told reporters. They said they'd love to see her jewellery. She said she would be delighted to show it to them. Out came the pearls, the earrings and brooch, smiles all round. Then they scarpered.

I remember seeing the story on the news that night. Airports and ports were on alert. But the robbers were never found, nor the jewellery. There was the insurance, of course – a few hundred pounds, about a hundredth of the value of the stolen stuff, which went straight into her current account. After that little incident, my mother quickly put her into a home, where she died at the age of ninety-nine. As she had never believed in consulting financial advisers and making arrangements for after her death, her entire fortune went to the government. Trish and I did not go to her funeral, and remember her with little fondness but a certain smile. She was a genuine eccentric who afforded – in retrospect – some amusement. But she was not the grandmother of childish dreams, and she was the only one we knew.

5

Lawnside

Lawnside, Great Malvern, Worcestershire was to be my boarding school. I don't know why my mother chose it. Perhaps she
heard from other mothers of her acquaintance that it was a
suitable establishment. Perhaps, knowing it was 130 miles
from London, she appreciated that it would be very inconvenient
to pay many visits.

One foggy day in November 1950, she and I made the long
train journey to Great Malvern – a grim town on the side of a
steep hill, as far as I could see. We took a taxi to the 'best'
hotel, the Mount Pleasant, where we were met by Miss
Winifred Barrows, the headmistress. The interview was conducted at a very white-clothed table; the food was lukewarm,
but the conversation lively, in that Miss Barrows, to put us at
our ease, told a multitude of stories illuminated with famous
names connected with Lawnside. Lunches at the Mount
Pleasant were her favourite form of interviewing potential
pupils. She paid for them herself. Before we left to take a taxi
back to the school (again, she paid), she gave me a small animal

made out of a pipe cleaner and admitted to being a keen collector of miniature ornaments.

At Lawnside, the main house of the school, we were greeted by the butler, whose duty it was to offer sherry to visitors before lunch. For us he suggested a glimpse of the drawing room with its two grand pianos. On one of them, Bernard Shaw and Edward Elgar had famously played a duet. Then we were taken to Miss Barrows' study, a much cosier room, the round central table alight with winter roses, the desk hectic with chaotic papers. Its French windows overlooked a sloping lawn edged with vast and mournful trees. Longfellow's dog, we learnt, was buried under one of them. Miss Barrows scurried about as she described the nature of the school, frequently scratching at the mottled skin of her arms. She pointed out the two hundred ornaments on the mantelpiece, and informed us it was some girl's Public Work, for a week, to dust every one of them every day. Another of the most dreaded Public Works was 'brushing Marco', the oldest spaniel that ever stank into decrepitude – flea-ridden, blind, bad tempered. There were dozens of other character-building Public Works of a similarly puzzling nature. Luckily, in my four years at the school, I escaped ever having to dust the wretched ornaments or attend to the beautifying of Marco.

Miss Barrows was a woman of some means, as was indicated by her generous paying for lunch and, as I later discovered, footing the bill for a party every term for the whole school. One of her forebears was William Murdoch, inventor of gas lighting in 1792. Her grandfather had founded a well-known and prosperous engineering company. In 1925, searching for 'an outlet for his daughter's tremendous energy and talent', he bought Lawnside for her. She was twenty-seven at the time, and presumed to be the youngest head teacher in the country. But she knew the school well, having gone there as a pupil in 1910, and been a housemistress during the First World War. She had very firm ideas of the sort of school she wanted to make it, and indeed had the energy to accomplish this.

Her own talents were concentrated in the arts. She painted, and she wrote poetry, which was published by the Poetry Society magazine. At seventeen she had various articles published on subjects such as 'Stray Thoughts on Wartime Art', and 'Thoughts of Dante'. Travel and history of art were also her passions. Although she did not play an instrument herself, she was musical and somehow – goodness knows how – befriended many an eminent musician of the day, frequently managing to persuade them to give concerts to the girls. As head teacher she naturally had to provide lessons in maths, biology and geography, but for her there was no magic in such subjects. (Once there was no geography teacher for a year, but no one complained.) She had no academic qualifications or teacher training, but she was one of those rare creatures whose own joy in life and enthusiasm for the arts was infectious, inspiring. For those of us whose interests coincided with hers, therefore, Lawnside was an ideal school.

One glance at Miss Barrows today and she would be judged as a spinster with very definite ways that verged on the eccentric. Rossetti might well have fancied painting her portrait – she had an 'illuminated-from-within' countenance, with wide arched brows, huge, unmade-up eyes, and long grey hair that lodged in unruly coils over each ear. (Once a year, for the Hallowe'en party, she let them loose, the better to look like a witch. Freed, the coils came down to her waist.) She had her own uniform: variations on the navy dress but never, ever, a skirt. Her hats were inspired by those of the then queen – a turned-back brim, often in shiny navy straw, that haloed the vitality of her features. Her shoes were of the kind that, since my love of vintage began thirty years ago, I aspire to but can rarely find: double straps, Louis heels, leather punched with intricate holes. She was a small, trim woman who moved fast and jauntily. Progressing down a passage, her presence went before her. We could thus be warned of her mood. Naturally good natured, warm, full of Christian love, she was also always on the lookout for any misdemeanour she felt could become a habit and would hamper a girl in her grown-up life. Her temper would suddenly flare. '*Why* is your shoe undone/your hair unbrushed/your tie not pulled up?' Her screech was terrifying. She would stomp off, outraged, but never sulk. Revelling in an audience, she was magnificent on the stage at Prayers every morning, and on the huge stage at the Winter Gardens for Prize Giving. But she would become slightly flustered if there was some crisis, and very definitely flustered if some Very Important Parent was coming to see the school. (When Monsieur Massigli, then our ambassador in Paris, came to inspect the school for his daughter, not only were all the rose beds outside her study window replanted, but 138 summer dresses were especially ironed lest he should catch sight of a crease. His daughter did become a pupil.) One of Miss Barrows' foibles, it was generally admitted, was an element of snobbism.

Brag, as she was always known, had three main supporters in the staff, for whom Lawnside was their life for some forty years. They, too, were spinsters. Two of them, Miss Gwendoline Parke (Music) and Mademoiselle Courcou (French), like Brag, were totally unqualified to teach, but brilliant at conveying a love of learning their subject. The chief matron and third faithful prop, known as Nannie P, was a cousin of Benjamin Britten, whom she naturally persuaded to visit the school and give a concert. She joined the school in 1925. An inspector from the Board of Education deemed there was 'abundant proof that Nurse Painter ... could take every possible care of the moral and physical welfare of the girls'. She certainly seemed adept in this: one moment beaming her sweet old-fashioned smile, the next being very strict, most particularly about running in the corridors. Besides that, she had a certain genius for managing peculiar events. There was a time when she considered that a lot of middle-school girls should progress to brassieres, particularly for games. We were all duly measured. A week later Nannie P summoned us to the gym, where she had laid out rows of very stiff pink cotton bras on the floor. We were urged to find one of our own size, and to try it on then and there. Nannie P kept a completely straight face as we lumbered about in our thick brown knickers, jostling our bosoms of various sizes into the stern pink cups. It was said the gardeners were ordered to stay away from the roses near the gym that day.

Miss Parke, the senior music teacher, was a figure who could inspire total terror, but all of us who learnt the piano wanted to be taught by her because she was a musician of considerable talent. I was lucky enough, in my last two years, to be her pupil – yes, I learnt on the Shaw/Elgar duet piano with its silver plaque that reminded generations of the famous occasion.

When Miss Parke wasn't targeting one of her plum-coloured screams at me for mistiming a crotchet, she talked to me of blue tits in her cottage garden on the other side of the Malvern Hills. I knew nothing about her – and would never have dared to question her past. Only recently I read a volume compiled by old girls called *The History of a Malvern School*. There I discovered she had won a scholarship to the Royal College of Music, but, as an impecunious orphan, found herself playing in nightclubs and restaurants to earn the required money: very hard to imagine. What did she play? The 1930 song 'Dancing on the Ceiling'? Her concert debut was at the Wigmore Hall, and she made a number of concert tours. But, of a somewhat feeble disposition, she didn't much like travelling and performing and was delighted to be offered the quieter life of a teacher at Lawnside in 1925.

In the two years of learning the piano with Miss Parke, I had a fantasy about becoming a concert pianist myself. To this end I would practise for four hours a day – two hours before breakfast, two hours in the evening, leaving scant time for prep. When I dared confess one day – she was in an unusually good mood – my ambition, she gave a sympathetic smile, and a nod of her head, which always unlatched the roll of hair round her neck, but made no comment. I took this to mean there was some hope. Besides, she always supported my ideas of what pieces to learn. Although she did not share my love of Liszt, she agreed to my trying 'The Hungarian Rhapsody'. It took me six months to play very inadequately, but I got good marks for 'trying'.

The weekly music lesson was always preceded by a thumping heart as I stood in the hall of deep and silent carpet, knocked on the drawing-room door, crept into the almost hallowed room, moved to the famous piano, sat down on the leather stool still warm from the last pupil who was so much more skilled than I. In a brief glance at Miss Parke, her sharpened pencil at the ready to point out some mistake, I could read her mood from the depth of her complexion. Sometimes, within minutes, her exasperation at my inadequacy flared. A purple flush would spread across her features. On other occasions she would simply take her place on the stool and play four or five pieces to me from which I should choose what to learn next. Those were the times that made her bad days worth surviving. The semicircle of upright chairs in the room would fade as the winter sky outside whittled down to a single streak of dim light, and here was pure music, played with all her might and sad, amorphous yearning. It was a good start to a life of loving music but, even at fourteen, I could see the foolish ambition to be a concert pianist fade along with various other daft plans. It's hard, but fun for a while, to fool oneself.

Singing was an important part of the school curriculum. If you were a 'special singer' (goodness knows how I passed that audition), you learnt with Sir Ivor Atkins, reputedly Elgar's best friend. He looked just like Elgar: white hair, white moustache; a gentle, rather handsome face. He always dressed like Elgar, too: striped trousers, black jacket, stiff white collar, fob watch slung across his waistcoat – an intimidating figure but someone who, with a flick of his hand, could make you understand how a musical phrase should be executed. Miss Parke, a trifle nervous, judging by her high colour, would accompany on the piano the sort of songs Sir Ivor liked us to sing:

Pack clouds away, And welcome day …

But he also coached us in the *St Matthew Passion* until we were good enough to sing at a concert in Tewksbury Abbey, and he conducted us several times in Worcester Cathedral. When Sir Ivor retired, he was replaced by David Willcocks, many years before he took over at King's College, Cambridge. So it could be said we were fortunate in our singing masters.

We were also lucky in our French teacher, Mademoiselle Courcou, who came to the school in 1923 and stayed till she retired in 1978. Mammy, as she was known, was always old but never older. She had a clump of unbrushed white curls, flat sandals in all weathers, and an all-season overcoat whose hem sagged to various depths. Apparently impervious to the sort of deportment we were encouraged to practise (head up, straight backs), Mammy slopped along the roads between the houses, constantly weighed down by two heavy bags of exercise books which balanced her like old-fashioned weighing scales. Her private domain was a small room at the top of Lawnside Grove. Here she burrowed every evening among stalagmites of unmarked work. To be sent there to fetch something was not a job anyone fancied, the smell in this dark-eaved room being almost overpowering, but it was impossible to guess its source.

Mammy, in common with many of the older teachers, had a twinkling smile but could turn to incandescent rage if she judged some girl was not concentrating. She would lumber up and down between the desks, slop-slop went the sandals, insisting on the repetition of verbs in a way that would be considered cruelty by education experts today. Yes, it was boring. But it was only ever for ten minutes of the lesson, and the subjunctive of irregular verbs was pounded into us for ever.

Then we would leap to La Fontaine and chant, altogether: *Maître Corbeau, sur un arbre perché, Tenait dans son bec un fromage …* Many of those fables remain with me, seventy years later. But even more enjoyable was being allowed, at the age of twelve, to read Victor Hugo's *Les Misérables*. Each one of us read a page out loud, and if a word was mispronounced it would have to be repeated after Mammy several times till the sound was correct. I daresay such teaching would be considered too hard and too boring for twelve year olds today, but it didn't seem like that. It felt thrilling.

I became very fond of Mammy, and her occasionally scribbled *bien* meant much. But my initial encounter with her was unforgettably agonising.

There was a French dining room in which some thirty girls were required to speak nothing but French at every meal. Mammy presided. Somehow her beady ear managed to zoom in on the smallest utterance in English and the offender was publicly scolded. On my first morning at the school I was put into the French dining room: having come from school in Switzerland, Brag thought I would feel at home there. What did not occur to her was that the thing most fatal to the happiness of an English schoolgirl was to speak good French.

I was put to sit next to Mammy. She beamed, kindly. Even before we had started our cereal, she tapped her mug for silence.

'Angela Huth, here, has been at school in Switzerland for three months, where she spoke not a word of English,' she said. 'So she is very good at French. I would like you all to hear how French can be spoken. She and I will have a conversation.'

Long silence. My cheeks turned hot scarlet as I felt hostile stares from all round the room, and not a few sniggers. I knew none of these girls. I only knew that I would now be the most unpopular girl in the school, and never dare open my mouth in a French lesson.

'*Alors, Angela, est-ce que vous êtes contente d'être revenue en Angleterre?*'

Mammy was off, but not taking me with her. I answered her in monosyllables, head down, appalled. By the time that horrific breakfast was over, I noticed a few sympathetic looks, and I think Mammy felt her idea had been a bit rough, for she never suggested another public conversation. In class, when it was my turn to read, I toned down my accent so far that Mammy accused me of 'going backwards'.

Not all our teachers were blessed with Mammy's flair and exuberance. The history teacher's idea of instructing us was simply to dictate to us reams of facts – kings, Acts of Parliament, prime ministers and so on, with dates – that we have to learn by heart. So, although I will forever know the date of the repeal pf the Corn Laws, or the Unification of Italy, I have no idea what those *times* were like, what motivated the characters in power. The teacher did not like to be asked those questions, and seemed to have no answers. Sadly, I was put off history for life. The geography teacher was known for her transparent blouses and boring voice. Nothing seemed to shake her from her dull understanding of dairy farming in Denmark. One day, a senior form decided to surprise her. The stunt was brilliantly organised by Sally Churchill, later to become my sister-in-law. All very good at gym, the senior pupils made a human pyramid that reached the ceiling of their classroom. Mrs Southall, as she was called, came in and looked up in the kind of amazement she might have regarded Everest, and with one beautifully executed movement the girls tumbled to the ground. A few moments later they were back with the dairy farming, no word of condemnation from the shocked teacher.

Maths, algebra and geometry were subjects for which I had a passionate, burning loathing, chiefly because the miniature, pernickety teacher who wandered about with her little finger crooked as if she was about to pick up a prissy cup of tea, did not seem able to answer my questions. Could she explain *exactly* what 'a − b' was, I kept asking? No, she couldn't. Finally, her patience (and mine) ran out. At the age of twelve I was 'released' from all maths lessons on the grounds that my lack of understanding was 'detrimental to the others in the class'. With huge relief I was able to spend these lessons reading in the library and have never for a moment regretted the abandoning of mathematics.

Latin, which I enjoyed, for some reason ceased to exist for all of us at about the same time. That was an eternal regret. As for biology (there was no science of any kind), there was a primitive lab, but I seem to remember that the uneventful life of the amoeba was as far as we went.

But what we lacked in core subjects was certainly made up for in poetry and public speaking. Brag herself, in the hall after Saturday Prayers, guided us through the Romantics. Shelley was her particular love. She had a very distinct way of reciting – laughable, perhaps, now, in its undulating cadences. But we all had to chant in unison, in exactly the same way as she did: (gaily) *O wild West Wind! Thou* **breath** *of Autumn's being/Thou (pianissimo) from whose unseen presence the leaves dead/ Are driven …*

And the final shriek: **Pestilence**-*stricken multitudes …!*

Even now, when the words come back to me, it's hard not to hear them as we learnt them from Brag. But we did get through a great many poems, and besides reciting them in unison, we were made to take individual exams – bronze, silver and gold medals. We were obliged to recite one obligatory poem, one of our own choosing. The set poem was always rather a curious choice:

Oh blackbird, what a boy you are!

Again, Brag conscientiously coached each one of us to say the poem in her own inimitable manner. She taught us to smile, to keep our ankles together, not to let our fingers fidget, to hold ourselves upright. It was hard not to feel sorry for the examiner 'from London' – a description designed to enhance her importance – who had to listen to forty girls reciting the same poem in the same way, but it resulted in a good many medals.

I chose Walter de la Mare's 'Silver' for the silver medal and when the moment came, alone on the stage, I suddenly decided to caricature Brag's advice. I slurped through *Slowly, silently, now the moon* outrageously slowly. At the end I saw a small jerk of the examiner's head as she stirred from a well-earned sleep. My silver medal was for a performance she had not heard.

Brag was just as keen on public speaking as she was on poetry, firmly believing it was a skill that we should all acquire. So another woman from London, this one in a hairnet, came each week to inculcate the art of speech-making. She gave us helpful tips about voice production, and breathing, and taxed us with various tests. She would give us some object – a hammer, a waste-paper basket – and get us, one by one, to speak on this subject for two whole minutes. We had to be witty, informative and, above all, fluent. No stopping to think. Many years later, auditioning to be a television presenter at ATV, I was handed a ruler and asked to speak about it to camera for a minute. Some old Lawnsidian training came to my rescue ... how practised I was talking about disparate objects on the hoof.

In public speaking, as in poetry, there were nerve-racking exams. But we were well practised. For every day, at Prayers in the hall, three different girls were challenged. (We were often reminded how many distinguished guests had performed in the hall: among others, G. K. Chesterton had read poems and Laura Knight had painted a portrait of Shaw. In my day Léon Goossens, Vladimir Horovitz and Alfred Cortot had all given concerts.) Each girl had to stand and deliver in front of the whole school and the intimidating gathering of staff on the stage. The first one gave a Newsflash. Material was frantically gleaned from the wireless the night before, and from scouring the papers before breakfast. It all had to be learnt by heart. Not a note allowed. Three minutes at least. Some of the sixth form managed twice that. This was followed by a girl standing to read a Great Thought plucked from a calendar, and a third girl giving a brief, learnt-by-heart biography of the writer. By the end of our schooldays, dozens of scraps of unmemorable information about poets and writers had cluttered our ears. And gradually the speakers, who were often found to be shaking with nerves, grew less nervous. It could be said public speaking almost came to be natural to Lawnsidians. When, as a bold senior, I once asked Brag why it was so important, she replied that we would all be asked to open fetes.

I had to wait eleven years to open my first fete. And in 1972

I was the speaker at Prize Giving in the Winter Gardens, packed with parents and, behind me, banks of Lawnsidians who much more recently had been studying the art. I knew it was vital that I spoke for the allotted half-hour without a note. Brag, by then retired, was there: I like to think she observed I had remembered the rules. And I don't scoff at her insistence on all the practice we had to do: it's been very useful on many occasions.

The hall was the setting for another weekly ritual – the public confession of our weekly sins and successes. It was difficult to get through a day at Lawnside without being aware of the elements of reward and punishment that quivered in the air. There was a bizarre, original form of making these things manifest: stars and stripes.

Stars were for excellence, or outstanding effort, in work, though sometimes they were given for obscure virtues such as 'showing courage in the face of temptation'. Stripes were generously handed out by many members of the staff for myriad minor acts of wickedness: talking after lights, forgetting to wear blue knickers for Greek dancing, and so on. On Saturday mornings at Prayers, everyone who had been donated stars or stripes had to stand up and declare them. Four stripes or more meant punishment. Four stars or more, and you were rewarded.

Brag would stand at the edge of the stage looking down on the mass of saints and sinners, and as the confessions were made her expression flicked from praise to shock. Not many of us escaped her ire: I was always a high-stripe earner. But at least you could take comfort from the 137 sympathisers all around you.

The punishments were no punishment at all to some of us: forbidden to watch a hockey match, perhaps, or the learning of many lines. This was a great pleasure, being given time to read and learn poetry that, because it was devoured at an age when things learnt are retained, has mostly been remembered for life. Rewards were another matter, always the same. A small group of star girls, in Sunday coats and hats, were allowed to walk unescorted to the teashop in the town. There was a standard tea of scones with solid jam, and a singular sponge cake topped with grated coconut – one of the most disgusting cakes I have ever eaten. (The identical cakes were sent to the school many times every term for girls' birthdays, and presented to them at Prayers. Brag herself paid for these cakes, as she did for the star teas.) There was also the problem of the star company. Certain goody-goodies were frequently rewarded with teas, and some of us had little in common with them. So communication was not much fun. Tea in the town was not a reward to be looked forward to with any great enthusiasm. In fact, some of us managed to hold a fourth star over to the next week in order to avoid the threat of a coconut cake.

God was much amongst us at Lawnside: Prayers every morning, Matins every Sunday. The long crocodile of us – in stockings as thick as carpets, Sunday dresses of turgid brown and velour hats – would trudge to the magnificent priory church, wondering who would faint (and escape some of the service) that week. When a bishop was invited to speak, the temperature of the sermon would rise. But for the most part the services were endurance tests. God seemed closer on winter Sunday evenings, when groups of us would gather in the drawing room to listen to Brag's reflections on life, many of which made good sense. In summer these talks would take place on the lawn, where she was able to lift her eyes up unto the hills with great frequency.

One piece of advice she gave that many of us would never forget was 'never to kick against the pricks'.

We were as innocent as she as to the darker meaning of this, but there was no chance of kicking against any kind of prick, as boys were totally off limits. If anyone received a letter with an Eton postmark, it had to be opened and read to Brag. My boyfriend, when I was thirteen, was the brother of one of my friends and the Master of the Beagles at Eton. He wrote to me every week and sent the letter, hidden in the pages of *Horse and Hound*, to his sister. This was a secret plan that gave a frisson to the arrival of the post on Thursdays. The trouble was, fierce in my youthful criticism, I was so appalled by both his green-lined writing paper, his handwriting and his banal declarations, that reading the letter in the stationery cupboard was a weekly disappointment. Came the moment when he wrote that he loved me. I pondered on this for some time. Eventually I responded with a phrase I had been mulling over, and thought rather good. 'Your letter has *confirmed my suspicions*,' I wrote. 'I love you too.'

This was a shaming lie: I'd just wanted to make use of my phrase. Soon after that, our correspondence petered out, as did our occasional meetings in London, where we were allowed to go to a newsreel provided we were back in time for tea. Years later, I wrote a piece about 'First Love' for some newspaper that tracked down the old Master of the Beagles: he had only the vaguest recollection of my existence.

Any communication with our neighbours at the Malvern Boys' College was unthinkable. But then, to contribute to the celebrations of the Coronation, Brag came up with a surprising idea: girls would meet boys. A 'dance' was arranged. This meant endless meetings of the essential committee, who found it hard to agree on procedure. Brag insisted on the dress code: summer dresses for us, shorts for the boys. *Shorts?* Luckily the headmaster put his foot down there: the boys would come in long trousers.

Girls and boys met one summer evening in the gym. Long benches had been arranged at both ends, trestle tables in between. Drink was orangeade. Food was bridge rolls smeared with fish paste. Students stood glaring and blushing at each other across the empty floor. Then a man, reputed to be the second-best folk dancer in England, mounted a bench and urged us with a small laugh to 'mingle, mingle'. He threaded and unthreaded his fingers, to show us how. There was an embarrassed shuffling as the two camps headed towards each other. We were urged to take partners for the Lambeth Walk and a barn dance. There wasn't much mingling.

But, despite the restrictions on any kind of instant attraction, signals were exchanged. Letters arrived with Malvern postmarks. A reckless boy and girl were found in a cellar – not *in flagrante*, the rumour went, but there was volcanic trouble. Punishments: great chunks of the Bible to be learnt, no more attending netball matches. And never again were we to be exposed to the danger of a party with the boys' college.

However, there was plenty of other dancing. Once a week there was Reel Club in the gym. Those of us who were of even vaguely Scottish descent wore our swanky kilts, and the complicated intricacies of reeling were drummed into us as diligently as the declensions of French verbs. There was ballroom dancing, naturally, where we became expert at the reverse turn in the fast waltz, and there was Greek dancing. I wondered many times if our version was anything like the dances the Greeks had – possibly – enjoyed. We wore blue tunics, flitted barefooted about, with waving arms and rigorous smiles, and sometimes wondered how useful this gallivanting would be in the grown-up world. There would be a display on the lawn to parents (never mine) after Prize Giving. A piano would be lugged under the trees so that Miss Parke could provide great torrents of Chopin to accompany our well-rehearsed dance. Despite being one of a large troupe, I remember the feeling of acute nerves waiting for the first chord, the signal to swoop out from under the trees to bob up and down in imitation of the sea, or a wind, or the lumpen boat.

The dancing teacher was another who stayed faithful to Lawnside for many years. Miss Parsons had the smallest feet I'd ever seen, always in stilettos, a large head and a lantern jaw. But due to the shoes and the thickness of her make-up (no other members of the senior staff wore any at all), she exuded a certain glamour. She was another character who switched from encouragement to terrifying fury in a flash. Today, she would be sued by rhythm-less pupils for being insulting. But she managed to coax impressive performances from most of the girls, and was annually congratulated for her co-direction, with Brag, of the Nativity play.

This was a major theatrical event, looked forward to every Christmas term. We rehearsed several evenings a week, and certainly learnt the meaning of striving for perfection. As a junior, one played a minor part: a 'child at the manger' which required nothing more than to slump on the stage round the manger trying to look asleep. Non-sleeping juniors were called upon to dance to 'The Holly and the Ivy'. This meant skipping in circles through the many verses, brandishing a branch of ivy. Some of the skippers, fed up with adhering to perfection, were occasionally known to lash out with their whip of ivy and earn a public rebuke.

A year later we might be promoted to 'dancing angel'. As the dancing angels waited to make their entrance, the tension in the Green Room, which led on to the stage, was palpable. Our nervous, sweaty feet left imprints on the icy linoleum floor. We had to keep dabbing something called Odorono under our arms, where melon shapes of sweat had appeared on our silk tunics. We were allowed a glimmer of lipstick, a smudge of blue eyeshadow. With a quick straightening of our halos, a final check of our gold cardboard trumpets, we awaited our cue. It came: the voice of a senior verse-speaker from the back of the hall as we scrambled into position.

'And suddenly, there were with the angels, a heavenly host …'

The curtain snapped back and there indeed we were, the heavenly host, praying we would not fall from the crowd of very wobbly ladders.

One year I was called upon to recite a poem that Brag had come across, which she felt conveyed perfectly the Christmas message. I had many rehearsals in her study, mimicking her usual, very particular way of reciting the lines to (in her opinion) best effect. I stood alone on the steps in front of the stage, and went for it.

The star that shone on **Beth***lehem,*
Its bright, ethereal ray, (smile)
To guide **three** *kings and show to them*
The place where Jesus **lay** (deep breath)

Shine (pause) *on* **your** (pause) *path,* **all** *through the year,*
To guide, to comfort, and to cheer (big smile) *and bless you*
On (pause) *your* (pause) *way.* (Count two, three, stop.)

Another year I was the Madonna, a part which called for an unmoving hand, one finger up, as I sat staring down into the rays of a bicycle lamp – luckily there was no doll Jesus. A dancing angel was more fun.

By my last year, as a 'special singer', I was part of the choir who stood at the back of the hall for the whole performance, singing those carols with their descants that we had learnt so thoroughly all through the term. And it was as a singing spectator we could finally see that the many hours of rehearsal, often boring, were all worth it. In darkness torn only by a light over Miss Parke's music at the piano, out of absolute silence a single voice would begin:

Three Kings from Persian lands afar ...

An hour later, after all the skipping, trumpet-blowing, carols, and snatches of the Bible beautifully recited, the lights came up to show that hefty fathers really were dabbing their eyes. The spirit of Christmas had somehow yet again been summoned, had touched people and been seared into our memories. To this day I can only think of snatches of the story in the way that Brag had taught us. '... *and there* were, *in the same country, shepherds abiding in the fields, keeping watch over their flocks by night.*' For years I've been saddened to hear these familiar words torn apart by readers in churches who had no feeling for their rhythm.

Of course, as the school curriculum lacked several essentials, there was plenty of time to concentrate on theatricals, and having seen, now, dozens of Nativity plays over the decades, I'm still of the belief that those produced at Lawnside were outstandingly good and moving.

There were several opportunities to be playwrights, the best being for the Midsummer Party on Midsummer Night on Midsummer Hill. That was always an extraordinary occasion. Brag, but no other members of staff, took the whole school in buses to the foot of the hill. We carried our picnics up through the woods to the top, walking waist-deep through young bracken. Various 'poets' recited their works to us as we ate, watching the sun going down over the tail of the Malvern Hills. It was possible to see why Elgar had been so taken by this corner of England: North Hill and the Beacon, which towered over the town itself, had far less charm than these more minor hills. Several plays were performed in the crepuscular light – again they had been practised endlessly, and I think – even in retrospect – the standard was high. We walked back in the light of a summer moon, a few of us taking it in turns to talk to Brag who, on such occasions, for all her warmth, seemed an isolated figure. It was the kind of situation that made some of us reflect that Lawnside was Brag's *whole life*. Was that enough for her? Back at the buses there would be copious prizes for poems, plays and games: and the night smell of woodland beyond the buses' headlights. They were good occasions, those parties.

A regular treat was going to Stratford for a Shakespeare play, always studied beforehand, at least twice a term: so by the time we left school some of us had seen at least twenty productions. Sometimes we were taken, too, to the Birmingham Repertory Theatre. Once, it was to see Molière's *Tartuffe*. Sir Barry

Jackson, who had founded the theatre, was another of Brag's friends. He offered a prize to the girl who wrote the best review of the play. I didn't win: the prize went to Phyllida Barstow, later Hart-Davis, who was to write many bestselling historical novels. I came second. Our reward was to have dinner with Sir Barry, in Brag's sitting room, waited upon by Ardiff, the impenetrable butler. That was an evening of high life. We sat listening, enchanted, to the wise and fascinating Sir Barry. I can't remember exactly what he said, but I came away shrouded in some amorphous longing, and determination, to do something in the theatre one far-off day. This fantasy, I felt, was slightly more likely to be fulfilled than my previous one to be a concert pianist.

Health and exercise were a vivid part of Lawnside life. Hockey and netball were the winter games: I was useless at both, though was once picked to play in a hockey match when the choice was between me and a girl who had polio. But there was a belief (shocking, I suppose, these days) that if you were no good at something, you should give it up and concentrate on your strengths. So many an afternoon I was let off hockey in order to work in the art room, or read French books in the library. There was no getting out of gym, though: those dreaded afternoons when girls of various degrees of spryness heaved themselves over a leather vaulting horse – to what end? I so often wondered. Sporting girls were much admired, so you had to make a show of trying. I tried in tennis and eventually played for the school in the third couple. Team players had the great privilege of being coached by the Wimbledon star Dan Maskell. How Brag provided us with so distinguished a coach, we never discovered.

The dreaded part of our exercise regime was the constant walks up the steep pavements, in crocodile, to the unappealing hills. There, we were allowed to break ranks, but always had to be two or more. This rule might have been made for no particular reason, but how wise it was. For on numerous occasions we encountered the Man of the Hill, as he came to be known. He took up various posts behind trees, and flashed a piece of mirror in the sun to get our attention. His upper body was always hidden by greenery, below which moved the flashing white handkerchief he employed for his business. He kept his distance, was probably harmless. But he inspired many concerned meetings: should we tell Brag? Yes, of course we should. The juniors had to be protected. But the question was, what should we tell her? We were unsure of exactly what it was he was up to, though instinct told us it wasn't altogether wholesome. And none of us could find the right words – feared we might giggle long before we were able to suggest that perhaps the police should be notified about this nameless offence. On many occasions we passed trios of girls from the Malvern Girls' College, moving towards his sightline, and were in an agony of indecision. Should we warn them? And if so, what of? In the end, due to our embarrassed and inarticulate state, the Man of the Hill's antics went unreported, and he was able to carry on with his chosen habit undisturbed.

The only good thing about all those crocodiles was that you had a chance really to talk to just one girl, undisturbed. Friendships were made. Decisions not to be friends were made. You often learnt interesting things. For instance, a girl called Gillian told me one day that her parents had bought a television. A *television?* What did it look like, I wanted to know? She stopped, picked up a stick and did a childlike drawing in the dusty path: screen, two knobs. I was fascinated, and not a little envious. We had no television at home. *I've NEVER HAD TG ,*

Just as we were taken regularly to concerts in the Winter Gardens, Tewkesbury Abbey and Worcester Cathedral, so were we also taken to art exhibitions. Malvern was nicely placed for Birmingham, and it was at an exhibition there that I discovered Van Gogh. Previously all I had seen was a postcard of his *Chair*, at Guilsborough Lodge. Now, faced with the real thing, with its thick, blazing, tragic colours, I was embarrassingly overcome and had to hide till the tears disappeared. Thus began my passion for Van Gogh, which has never ceased, and it was about then the thought occurred to me that I should be a painter.

I was reasonably good, and indulged in a great deal of extra art, mostly in order to avoid hockey. We had a charming old art mistress who flitted among the easels in her artist's smock, and spoke so quietly it was impossible to hear exactly what she said, though somehow she managed to convey her opinion. I appreciated her encouragement, but on reflection knew that I was no more an artist than I was a pianist or a dancer. But I carried on pretending that I wanted to be a painter, because I never quite dared admit to anyone but my father that I intended to write for the rest of my life.

For the first two years at Lawnside I was a rotten pupil, and knew it. While I always loved English, French, art, the piano, and anything to do with performing, at everything else I was utterly useless and had no intention of making an effort. I was always bottom in most subjects, except those I enjoyed, and my main concern was to make the class laugh. This I did by indulging in outrageous cheekiness to some of the teachers for whom I had no respect (a foible often mentioned in my reports) and a kind of impolite sarcasm that I liked to think was wit. There was a moment that it occurred to me I should pay more attention to history to please my father. But, as I have mentioned earlier, our teacher's methods put me off history for life. I have from time to time tried to repair this disgraceful state of affairs, but have always been frustrated by such understatements as 'they went into battle'. How? How did they prepare? What weapons did they employ? It's difficult to get answers to such questions. Perhaps it's not important. But to me, like everything else, history should conjure pictures in the mind.

Two years before I left, everything changed, due to the arrival of Miss Dillon-Weston to teach English.

While we were lucky at Lawnside to have several teachers who conveyed a love of their subject extremely well, Rosemarie Dillon-Weston was in a category of her own. She it was who inspired generations of pupils, many of whom had never been interested in literature or writing essays. Whenever the subject of an inspiring teacher is broached, Miss Dillon-Weston is my example, and for many years I've been trying to work out exactly why. Yes, she was brilliant: she got a first at Lady Margaret Hall, Oxford, and had intended to go on and be a don. But she gave up that idea in order to look after a fragile sister. They lived together for many years in a cottage on the Ludlow side of the hills. After a spell at various other schools she came to Lawnside and, like the others in the old guard, stayed for many years. What was it about her?

DW, as we called her, was, physically, a singular figure. She wore, mostly, a brown suit of scratchy-looking tweed, brown lace-up shoes and yellow ankle socks. I have no memory of her ever in stockings. Curiously, she, like Brag, might have appealed to Rossetti to paint, with her curved brows, dark brown eyes, good bones. Her smile was spoilt by teeth darkened from her constant smoking; her soft voice, compelling you to listen, never rose. She was possessor of that elusive thing, *presence*. We would be larking about in the form room after some uninspiring lesson, DW would waft in with her pile of corrected exercise books, and there was instant, awed silence. The forty or so moments of the lesson would pass in a flash as she sparklingly led us through the bloody path of Macbeth, or Milton's sonnets, or the Romantic poets. When it came to writing essays, her means of explaining to those who were not naturally imaginative how to conjure a story were brilliant. She set exercises that succeeded in making many girls realise they could do things that previously they had thought impossible. Forty years later, as a visiting teacher in many kinds of schools, I have set the same exercises and had the thrill of seeing them work. Her praise – not easily given – was a reward like no other. I remember the rapid beating of my heart while waiting for her to give back an essay, over which I had tried with all my might, and which I had loved writing. Ticks in the margin meant she approved of an idea or a phrase which, often, had taken no second thought. Snippets of overworked, purple prose were less likely to earn her praise.

Apart from bringing literature scintillatingly to life, she managed to sow in us a general love of learning – she was scathing to those who lacked curiosity. She it was who made me suddenly realise that subjects that had previously been closed books must now be opened. I found myself making great efforts with the everlasting dairy farming in Denmark, and the Tudors, because DW would have been shocked if I hadn't. This led to rising from the bottom of the form to the top – a very unusual position for me, but which naturally encouraged me to try even harder.

There were several girls who were particularly drawn to DW – myself included: these feelings were not 'pashes', which most of us went through for senior girls from time to time; it was more that we craved her undivided attention, just wanted to listen to her and her wise, sharp comments, for far longer than the official time. At some point she mentioned in passing the then fashionable Christopher Fry. I bought all his books, began reading them. This seemed to please her. She invited me to her small room on several occasions to discuss Fry's plays. I made notes of all she said. Decades later, I met Fry at a birthday party for him and Sir John Gielgud at the Garrick Club, and showed him the books he had signed (and sent back to me) when I was at school. This news delighted the old, and by now very frail, DW immeasurably.

It was she, of course, who prepared us before each play at Stratford. So suddenly, instead of being confused and sometimes bored by Shakespeare, it all became brilliantly clear as things she had explained happened. Not content with just seeing the plays, she began a Shakespeare Club: once a week, a keen group of us would take parts and we read through a good many plays. On another evening of the week we went to her Poetry Reading, where a poet was discussed, his poems read by some of us. These were wonderful, unforgettable evenings in the hall: low lights, quiet voices, discoveries. They ended late. I imagined DW called a taxi to take her on the longish journey home. Only much later did I find out that she insisted on catching the last bus to the Wych Cutting where she lived on the other side of the hills. Weighed down with exercise books, she would walk the last half-mile in darkness.

On the occasion that I made the speech at Prize Giving, twenty-two years after I had left the school, I was able to pay tribute to her, and the entire gathering of parents and children spontaneously stood up and cheered. She was very cross with me. But it was good, though unsurprising, to see how many others owed her the same debt as I did.

We kept up a correspondence for forty years, and I visited her in her cottage, where a stream of pure Malvern water ran through the garden, every few years. Everything I wrote I sent first to her, and it was her opinion that meant more to me than any other. She was thrilled when my novels began to appear, and always wrote pertinent observations when she heard me on the radio. After her sister had died, she took little care of herself, and spent most of her time writing to old pupils. When my daughter Candida was doing *Lear* for her GCSE, DW sent six pages of 'reflections' of rare brilliance, which I am keeping for future generations.

She didn't like retirement and suddenly became very frail. Concerned, I asked the man who ran her local post office to ring me if ever he was worried about her. In 1993 I got a call saying the paper boy had noticed papers and milk bottles were gathering outside her door. She was found unconscious on the floor of her bedroom, and rushed to Worcester Hospital. She died before I could get there. At her funeral there was a large gathering of pupils who would never forget her. For me, she was an inspiration, and an influence only matched by my father: a rare and extraordinary woman.

Friends, of course, were the most important part of school life, and I made a great many. Just as in grown-up life, some best friends were instantly detected, and beyond them an outer circle of others not so entirely in tune with one's own idiosyncrasies. Somewhere in the outer regions there were a few enemies, easy to avoid. In my second term I was in the same bedroom as one Rohais from Scotland, renowned for her sophistication. She had minute feet, pre-Raphaelite curls and, for thirteen – and the first among us to wear a bra – an astonishing cleavage. Rohais would rub Nivea cream into her arms every night after lights (a practice that went undiscovered so was never punished) and, when she had had enough of that, she would dance a solo reel between the beds, commanding that one of us should follow her progress with the beam of a torch. Rohais and I would stay with each other in the holidays, but followed different paths after school parted us.

There were others I found on exactly my wavelength, but Felicity was Best, the one who survived the constancy of a lifetime of friendship. She had coarse, sticking-out straight hair and an original way with her ankle socks that hung over her Idler shoes (somehow, she got away with not wearing uniform straps) and a smile of particular sweetness. We had a love of the arts in common, and her quiet sense of humour was a constant delight. As my parents never came to take me out, I was always included when hers drove down to give us lunch at Ross-on-Wye. Our mothers, who lived near each other in SW1, became friends, and found they had the same kind of interests. They had many a lunch together, gossiping about news from Jaeger and Peter Jones, and their hopes for their daughters' marital life.

As the end of school life approached, DW summoned me to talk about future plans. I was fifteen. I was set to take school certificate in shamefully few subjects. DW assumed I would stay on in the sixth form and then try for Oxford to read English. I could not think of a more exciting plan, and put this to my mother.

'Certainly not,' she scoffed. '*We don't want a bluestocking in the family*, thank you. You can go to Paris for a year, learn more French.' There was no changing her mind.

Many decades later, I went to an Old Girls' Reunion lunch at the Basil Street Hotel, a quiet and timeless place, for lunch. As on all such occasions, there was much clichéd astonishment about the changes that had taken place in our physical being. Some were almost unrecognisable. Some had become very fat, some very skinny. Many of them seemed to be wearing exactly the clothes that we had considered fashionable when we changed into mufti in the Fifties – Gor-Ray pleated skirts, elastic belts. But, fascinatingly, none of their hands or feet or legs had changed. I could have recognised every girl had I only seen these parts. Their mannerisms had not changed, either. A girl who often gave out notices from the front of the hall always stood with legs apart, one arm folded behind her back and held by the other. After the lunch, perhaps to show her normal role still existed, she stood up to make an announcement, and her stance was exactly as it had been fifty years ago. A very strange, long-ago, déjà vu.

Lawnsidians' memories of the school are mixed. Some, like my sister, who left after a year, hated it. Others regret the lack of learning in hard subjects. Those who shared my wonder at DW's inspiring talent, and the encouragement of all things concerned with the arts, look back on our time with affection and appreciation, though we agree our overall education was certainly lacking. Very few went on to university, though many went into distinguished jobs. Unsurprisingly, writers emerged in various fields – Mary Keen, Elizabeth Luard, Phyllida Hart-Davis. Lindy Guinness became a famous painter. The school magazine produced news of many a 'good' marriage, as Brag would have called it.

I left in July 1954 aged fifteen and eleven months. My parents, with Felicity's, came to the last Prize Giving where, as usual, my name was not called. On the way back to London we stopped for dinner at a pub at Minster Lovell, near Oxford. In a clear night sky there was a single star. Felicity and I competed to be first to observe that it was Rupert Brooke's 'slippered Hesper'. We faced our future spell abroad with some foreboding.

In 1994 the school closed down. In the Old Girls' News we were assured that the famous grand piano, its silver plaque telling of the historic moment when Shaw and Elgar played a duet upon it, was safely housed in another Malvern school; safe for ever.

6

Paris and Florence

After leaving Lawnside there were a couple of months before the dreaded departure for Paris. Felicity and I had a small taste of two different sorts of excitement. There was the impact of Men, and the bliss of Exmoor.

At Docking, in Norfolk, where Felicity's parents rented a cottage, she had come across two handsome, entertaining brothers. Their father had been a housemaster at Eton. Mickey, the oldest brother, was an unconventional product of that school, although in many ways both brothers were deeply conventional – golf players, sailors, a love of playing bridge. They were some ten years older than us, well established in their careers, though Mickey's was never very specific – something to do with paper and America.

Felicity, having met them first, zoomed ahead of me. She went out with Antony – 'went out', in those days, meaning for lunch or dinner. Their first date was dinner at The Berkeley. Antony wore a black tie. Felicity had been advised by her mother always to order the cheapest thing on the menu. She chose grapefruit, Antony went for the smoked salmon. And he put his feet up on the neighbouring chair, which rather impressed her. He took her home in a taxi and she was lightly kissed. Every detail she reported back to me, and we discussed High Hopes. What the hopes were for was not entirely clear.

Felicity skilfully arranged an evening out *à quatre*. We went to the Café de Paris. I was dressed in peacock organza. Vertical frills trailed down its skirt. Marlene Dietrich, more restrained in top hat and smoking jacket, was the cabaret. 'Falling in Love Again' reached across the gilded room, with its two branches of curving stairs, in a voice that quavered like smoke and lighted our amorphous yearnings. Mickey and I danced: 'Cheek to Cheek', 'You Do Something To Me' – all the old evocative tunes. His dancing, I had to admit to myself, was a disappointment: he was of the school of the rhythm-less shuffle, one arm pumping up and down like a piston. So I was denied the chance to show off my Lawnside ballroom expertise. Still, our noses touched. His searingly blue eyes dazzled into mine. In a trice I was in love.

I confessed this to Felicity next day, on the train to Exmoor. She felt the same about Antony, she said, though she did not sound entirely convincing. Still, it was a good thought: best friends in love with brothers.

We were to stay with a widow who lived in a remote farmhouse opposite Dunkery Beacon. It was a farm that had turned into a charming shambles because one woman could not possibly keep much kind of order. In the chaotic kitchen, sheets and clotted woollen socks hung from a ceiling rack, warmed by the stews that constantly rippled on the stove. Outside, the farmyard was equally disorderly. Sheep, cows, horses and hens gathered democratically, unhindered by any regulations. The tottering stables, cluttered with cobwebs, smelt of old saddles marinated in decades of sweat, while steam rose from the dung heaps.

It was high on a hill, Cloutsham Farm, protected by trees through which there were glimpses of the moorland. Felicity and I walked for miles over the moors, climbed Dunkery Beacon, and talked about love, love, love. We were suffering from that post-exam Wordsworthian ecstasy that afflicts some teenagers, when every small fist of new bracken was of inexplicable significance. We kept rushing to our exercise books to unleash our souls in a gush of purple nature notes. Looking back at some of our unusual adjectives for clouds and sunsets, I laugh. What tosh! But to scoff is to be unfaithful to the past. It wasn't tosh then. It was simply the beginning of a new understanding that being in what seemed to be love changes the common order and perception of everyday. Simply because of the existence of another person, every mundane place and thing is a-quiver – no matter that the love is unrequited, and the love objects are innocent of its existence. We could not resist sending postcards (of stags) to the Butterwick brothers: it was a wonder we managed to exercise some restraint in the messages.

Several times, in my later teens, I returned to stay with Mrs Young on my own in order to hunt with the Devon and Somerset staghounds. Terrifying days out, those: galloping down steep wooded hills, I wondered whether my horse was going to charge through the wide stream at the bottom of the valley, or whether there was a chance of pulling up. There was one unforgettable day: I was cantering at the back of the field – an undulating heathery stretch. A very large horse ahead of me had a red ribbon on its tail. We came to a five-barred gate: I followed the horse over. Once on the other side, its rider fell off. While I tried to grab its reins, the rider was writhing on the ground. I secured the rein: the horse whirled round. It was then that I saw, still attached to the saddle, a leg in a hunting boot. The man on the ground, struggling up, had only one leg.

We were miles from anywhere. Other riders were long gone over the horizon. The horse was seventeen hands high. The only possible aid to mounting was the gate we had just jumped over. The agitated man managed to hobble onto a low rung. His horse shied away, snatching the reins from my hand. Many frustrating attempts were made, and I succeeded in hoisting him into the saddle after a wearying hour. But trying to heave a large, one-legged man onto an enormous horse, at the same time keeping my own skittering mount under control, was a hunting experience not likely to be forgotten.

After our post-school visit to Exmoor, we had just one more night out in London with the brothers. A subdued nightclub was chosen. The sparkle of the Café de Paris was missing. We were all rather quiet. Our departure loomed.

I have no idea how my mother came across the lodgings she found for me in the Rue Spontini, just off the Avenue Victor Hugo. She had many friends in Paris, so perhaps it was through one of them. I know she went and looked at the flat, in the *seizième* arrondissement, and met the owners. She declared them to be charming. Monsieur Guiard was an *ancien diplomat*. That would have appealed to her.

Their flat was on the far side of one of those Parisian courtyards surrounded by such grimly soaring buildings that the sky stands no chance of shedding any light. My mother chose not to come with me for my introduction to the Guiards' apartment. The ancient lift groaned up to a space of darkness. After much fumbling I found the door, and a deep-throated bell clanged. The door was opened into more darkness. 'Bonjour, Madame,' I said brightly to a shadowy figure. But it was the maid, Katrine, who lived in some far-off attic.

Monsieur and Madame Guiard were hovering about in the sable-coloured air of the *salon*, with its high-backed painted chairs and hideous sofas. Monsieur Guiard kissed my hand. He was a small man with tufts of white hair, a blue suit that, worn for half a century, shone as if floodlit. A speck of the scarlet *Légion d'honneur* adorned his lapel. His wife's scant hair was scraped so viciously on top of her head that the bones of her temples were overexposed. She had the eyes of a marmoset monkey, and wore patches of scarlet rouge each side of them, instead of on her cheeks. My presence seemed to unnerve her. Her head constantly nodded like a tired puppet. She was trembling as we felt our way through the dark passage to my room – a narrow slit of a room whose window looked on to the prison-like courtyard. There was just space for a bed, basin, table, and one small table lamp. The basin was a bonus, because the bathroom down the passage, as far as I could see in a different texture of darkness, was not fit for human use. A thick layer of moss lay on the bottom of the bath.

'*Qu'est-ce que c'est, cette mousse?*' I asked quietly – I hoped it sounded more of a horticultural query than a complaint.

'*Ah, Mademoiselle …*' Madame Guiard gave a squeak like a

demented bat and led me on to inspect the unspeakable lavatory. Later that day the other lodger, a tall blonde German, Christa, arrived. She was to have the bigger guest room. During her tour of the bathroom and loo I could hear Germanic exclamations of horror, and for the rest of the year I heard her sobbing herself to sleep every night.

The Guiards, like many retired couples, plainly needed extra income. Like many of their contemporaries in Paris at that time, they were able to take advantage of English teenagers who came to be 'finished'. They charged a high rent, but gave little in return. As I soon learnt, not only were they mean, but they had some nasty, sadistic ways. Madame Guiard, for instance, was allergic to the telephone – or at least to the very idea of my using it. So if a friend rang she would answer curtly, but desist to come and fetch me. '*Quelqu'un vous a téléphoné*,' she would report, hours later, but she had not bothered to ask for a name. So communication with friends was very difficult. I had to lurk about waiting for the rare moments when both Guiards were out to make a few hurried calls.

Economy of lighting was another of her preoccupations. There was one small, dim light in my room, and the rule was I could not put it on before it was pitch dark. This meant that in winter, in order to read, I had to sit with my head out of the window hoping for a moon. But her even fiercer economy was food. What was cooked was fine, but the exiguous amounts meant Christa and I were always hungry. So, it seemed, was Monsieur Guiard. Sometimes, when I came back a little early, I would find him at his desk, wrapped in a rug (there was no heating), eating a crust of bread. He would guiltily brush away the crumbs, and his look begged me not to report him to his wife. I had £2 a week pocket money – enough for bus fares and postage, but not enough for supplementary food, apart from a rare baguette or brioche. The hunger was uncomfortable, making concentration on work a struggle.

Monsieur Guiard's sadism was of a more subtle kind. It concerned my post. In the gloom of the dark life with the Guiards, the one thing there was to look forward to were letters from home. Nanny continued her Canterbury tales, Trish wrote from time to time, and there were wonderful letters from Miss Dillon-Weston. The concierge would deliver the post at 8.30 every morning. I could hear the lift clank up to the *deuxième étage*, and Katrine fumble with the thunderous bolts of the door. I would slip out of my room, but Katrine, in cahoots perhaps with her boss, hurried into the *salon* before I had a chance to ask for my letters, and handed the whole bundle to Monsieur Guiard. He would snatch them up with extraordinary fierceness for so diminutive a man, and lay them on the seat of one of the high-backed chairs. Then he would kneel on them, clasp his hands and start to pray. I knew his daily prayers took anything up to an hour, so was not able to wait for him to finish. As I made my way past the glass doors of the *salon*, he would flick me a pitying look and carry on praying – for forgiveness, I hoped.

It was the kind of household where you were forced to wonder if there had ever been happiness, or light, or fun. The two crabbed old codgers seemed to live mostly in silence, though Monsieur Guiard conveyed a glimmer of good manners at the pathetic suppers, when he made some attempt at conversation. He sometimes treated us to eloquent soliloquies on

Racine, but hunger usually deterred his concentration as his head bent lower and lower over his meagre bowl of soup. Christa sat opposite me, silent tears pouring down her cheeks. Madame Guiard sniffed. Oh, they were merry evenings.

I did, from time to time, describe life in Rue Spontini to my parents, but my mother was adamant. There was no question of my moving somewhere more congenial. In her view, I was very lucky to be with an *ancien diplomat* in the *seizième*.

As a result of her forbidding me to stay on at Lawnside to take my Higher School Certificate, I decided I would do it anyhow, in English, while I was in Paris. I had saved up my pocket money and signed up to a correspondence course in Cambridge – cost, £5. But as the syllabus had to be completed in three terms, rather than the two years it took in schools, this meant writing four essays a week – difficult, in my circumstances, because of being at art school all day, and impeded by the lighting restrictions in the evenings. I once bought a candle which caused Madame Guiard a near heart attack, so in the end struggled with a torch. By starting very early in the morning, and carrying on late every night, I did somehow manage the weekly essays. Waiting for their return was an excitement, though clouded by Monsieur Guiard's cruel ways with the post. I was lucky enough to have an extremely good and encouraging tutor who sent encouraging notes on my essays. Miss Dillon-Weston, too, was a help, providing copious thoughts on *Emma* or 'Lycidas' or anything I needed. Just as my imaginary world had protected me from the emptiness of East Burnham House, so hiding myself in the English literature syllabus was my saving in the gloom of the time in Paris.

Although I constantly yearned for England, rather than home, and hated the Guiards' apartment, in my cloak of disengagement I was not actually unhappy like the sobbing Christa. And the days were good.

I was lucky enough to have been accepted into the École des Beaux-Arts, and was assigned to one of its *ateliers* in Avenue Victor Hugo rather than its main building. The studio was not large: there were only some twenty pupils. It was warmed by a wood-burning stove – not quite warm enough for the nude models, but fine for the rest of us. Everyone smoked Gauloises, whose smell for me came to symbolise hard work, and wore long scarves. The great joy, the privilege, as I now see it, was our tutor, Monsieur Souverbie. Once again I had been lucky enough to chance upon a remarkable teacher. On one occasion, when he praised some minor still-life I had done, I again began to think of becoming a painter. But that thought soon vanished. I knew in my heart I was not a painter.

Monsieur Souverbie, with his unruly hair, filthy old corduroy jacket and black fingernails (a caricature old French artist), had been a pupil of Matisse. Each one of us felt a sense of awe and trepidation as he approached our easels to look over our pathetic attempts to convey the blue-skinned model, in paint, pencil or charcoal. He never said much, but you could tell what he thought by the scrunching of his eyes. Sometimes it would simply be: '*Plus comme ça, Mademoiselle.*' Then he would take the pencil from his pocket and draw a few lines beside my effort, and at once I could see exactly how I had gone wrong. One of his favourite exercises was to slap down a thick line of oil paint on a canvas – say, yellow. '*Regardez ça,*' he would say. '*Regardez, regardez.*' Then he would paint a strip of another colour beside the yellow – red, perhaps. '*Et, maintenant – qu'est-ce que vous voyez?*' What had the red done to the yellow? The yellow had changed the red's *nature*. It didn't change its colour, but it did do something to it that it's visible to the keen eye: a subtle shift that either enhances or diminishes it. As I'd always believed there was something magical about colour, I was enchanted by this revelation, which has been of great help whether painting, decorating or choosing clothes. And, since Monsieur Souverbie's observations, I've found myself over-critical of fabrics, carpets, wallpapers and clothes designed by people who have not learnt to appreciate the art of choosing neighbouring colours.

Those were good days, at the art school. I was the youngest pupil, at sixteen, by some four years. My peers were an appealing group, in their scruffy, glamorous way, and kind to me. I was glad of my French, for none of them spoke a word of English. In the lunch break we gathered round the stove. They were generous to the *pauvre petite anglaise* who came with nothing but an apple or a sliver of cheese – shared their *saucisson* or *baguettes au jambon*. But despite the camaraderie at the Beaux-Arts, I was never invited to their get-togethers at the end of the day. I suppose they thought I was too young.

Indeed, social life scarcely existed. Luckily Felicity was lodging just an avenue away. Her landlady, a stern but good-hearted old *marquise*, was also careful about the food, but of a different order from the Guiards. As neither of us was welcome in the other one's flat, we spent some free moments sitting on walls by the Seine, or half-heartedly exploring the Louvre. There was no money to go to the cinema or the theatre. The best we could do was to spend an hour in a café, an electric fire on the table, eating two dry *flutes*.

There were some respites. Bois, the headmistress at my mother's finishing school, had retired to Versailles by the time I went to Paris. She was my godmother, and dutiful. We had an open invitation to go there for weekends. The fare had to be saved for, so visits were not that frequent, but longed for. I remember we would arrive on a Friday night and have six helpings of soup, several helpings of cassoulet and a great many éclairs for pudding. Bois was shocked by our hunger. She, too, wrote to my mother, but to no avail.

They were not lively weekends. Apart from stuffing ourselves against the hunger of the following week, and having baths morning and night to make up for the lack of Parisian bathing facilities, there was little to do. Bois, a kindly old soul, lived with another retired spinster teacher, Mademoiselle Monet, with her pince-nez and lugubrious parrot face. Intelligent conversation flicked between the two old Balzacian figures, and they were interested and appalled that our experience of Paris had possibly put us off the city for life.

The small, elegant house was within walking distance of the palace. We often went there – I remember it best in deep snow, the complicated pattern of box hedges piled with white on white. And inside we came across much of the sort of furniture my grandmother would have leapt upon to be copied. At least, chez Bois, there was peace – and light – to read our books: Felicity, too, was taking her Higher English by correspondence course.

Perhaps because of the lack of central heating at the Guiards', I caught pneumonia. I was in bed for over a week, tossing about in sweaty sheets which were not changed because the six-week sheet-changing day was not due. Madame Guiard put

122

her head round the door only once, and frowned to see that my bedside light was on at five in the afternoon. Katrine brought me thin soup once a day. I felt too weak to write letters or indeed to telephone any friends, even if I had been allowed to do so. Sometimes I put on my portable wind-up gramophone and played nostalgic 1950s records and thought of dancing cheek-to-cheek with Mickey. Never had time gone so slowly.

Some sort of high life, which I had imagined might come about in Paris, did not materialise. Once my godfather took me to dinner at the Eiffel Tower, and once friends of my mother invited me to a dinner at SHAPE, Supreme Headquarters Allied Powers Europe, where very senior army folk made interminable speeches. And once Felicity's father took us to dinner at the Jockey Club. But we were not leading the life of Parisian teenagers. There were no entries into the world of French youth. In the whole year there was only one real treat.

My father had, at that time, formed a production company with Douglas Fairbanks. They were in the process of making thirty short films for American television. The films were being made in Rome. My father was both directing and writing several of the scripts. I knew he had made some effort to persuade my mother to change my Paris lodgings, with no success, but his letters were deeply sympathetic. He suggested that one Easter, instead of returning to London, I went to stay with him in Rome.

That was the most exciting Easter of my life to date. We stayed in the Grand Hotel: there was a car to take us wherever we wanted to go. By day, while my father and Douglas were working, I was left with Mary Lee Fairbanks, blonde tufts of hair among the dark, and her eldest daughter, Daphne.

Shopping was very much on their minds, and indeed mind-boggling; these were shops of a different order from anything in London or even Paris. As for the food, three days into the visit I was at last no longer hungry. My father managed to get away for an hour or so to take me to the English Cemetery, where I found Keats' and Shelley's graves, and took photographs for DW with my Box Brownie. There was not much sightseeing – the female Fairbankses preferred shopping. But I did manage to sit on the Spanish Steps outside Keats' house, listening to the sizzle of passing Vespas, and watching the afternoon skies deepen into the ambers that must have been familiar to the poet as he lay dying. In Rome, there were moments of pure happiness. I quickly loved the city as much as I hated Paris. I asked my father to put to my mother the idea of spending some time in Italy after Paris. He said he would do his best.

Every evening we joined him, Douglas and a few others (disappointingly, none were young) for dinner in some wondrous restaurant. Douglas exuded his famous charm. He was funny, kind, encouraging. He listened, he told amazing stories of his life in films, and he had huge admiration for my father. They were a good team.

It was Douglas who arranged for Daphne and me to visit to the studios where Sophia Loren was filming. We met her on the set. When she tossed back her stripey hair and laughed, I saw that her teeth were very thick: they had an unnatural kind of backing. I suppose they had been capped – not, in those days, a frequent occurrence. She suggested we might like to meet her make-up man. Stumped, perhaps, about how to entertain two sixteen-year-old girls, he first sat me down on a sort of dentist's chair next to a table crowded with lotions, powders and brushes. He began to work on what he called the 'canvas' of my face, explaining each flick of rouge or lipstick and, most useful of all, how to make the most of my eyes. To this day I ignore all fashionable theories about this, and stick to what he told me in 1954.

There were dozens of English girls in Paris who spent their days at a finishing school where they learnt no French, and met at the English church on Sundays, all wearing their uniform feather hats that curved over their flat hair like an Alice band. I did join them, occasionally, but far preferred being with the students at the art school. There were, of course, some rare good moments in the city, when the sun glittered on the Seine, or Notre-Dame was almost empty, but the frustration of having no money meant it was impossible to do many things we would have liked to have done. The grimness of life chez Guiard coloured the whole experience, and often it would feel as if the entire French nation was alien. I would walk down the Avenue Victor Hugo early in the morning to the art school, and a sour-faced old woman would come out of her pâtisserie and throw a bucket of water over my feet. This happened so many times it could not have been an accident, and a dislike of the French population began to gather in my sixteen-year-old breast. However, I was able to escape all the things I so abhorred about Paris by reading my set books and writing my essays, when I wasn't at the art school. And never will I regret going to the Beaux-Arts: a whole year in which to *look* – echo of Miss Derby at my prep school – and to learn about anatomy and colour and tone, all to the evocative smell of two dozen Gauloises, was some compensation for not going to university, and certainly not time wasted.

But the year in Paris was depressingly long. Decades later I was interviewed by the *Independent* for a series of articles about the worst time in various people's lives. Paris was not, in fact, the worst; it would have been unwise to describe *that*. I heard myself telling the journalist about the numerous dispiriting elements of my French sojourn with some glee. But the grimness of that time made an indelible impact. I did not return to Paris for twenty-five years.

I put it to my mother that to be able to speak Italian as well as French could be an advantage in my future life – I mean, I might marry a diplomat, I cunningly added. This idea lent weight to my point. She agreed. So I was allowed to go to Florence for six months before what she regarded as the serious part of my life, the Coming Out, in the old-fashioned sense, i.e., being a debutante. She was worried to find the finishing school cost £80 a month, which included trips all over Italy, as my father's film business was going through a lean time. But she gamely stuck to the plan.

I went with my tall, pretty, funny friend Sally Hambro, who had also had a less than joyous time in Paris. The contrast of our lodgings there and in Florence was overwhelming.

The school – some dozen pupils – was in a large house not far from the Piazza Santissima Annuziata. Sally and I had adjoining rooms on the top floor from which we could see the *duomo* brooding above interleaved roofs. On a lower floor there was a communal sitting room, and a dining room where we were waited on by a maid in white gloves. The food was sensational.

This extraordinary establishment was run by the Musatti sisters, two handsome, grey-haired Italian women of fierce cheekbones and warm smiles. They did not speak much English, despite many years of entertaining English and American girls. As soon as we had picked up a smattering of Italian, we were encouraged to speak at meals.

Our lessons were with a very old, brilliant *contessa* who lived in a castle by the Arno. Sally and I had tutorials together. On the first occasion we met our teacher, she gave us a piercing look and asked if we would consider 'getting through the grammar in six weeks, so we could then hurry on to Dante and Boccaccio'. We agreed. She also taught us history of art – lessons in Italian, notes to be written in Italian. So it was hard work, but enthralling. But there were other ways, we soon found, to become quickly fluent.

The Musatti sisters had a friend, Piero, who was a heart specialist. The son of one of their friends, some years older than their pupils, he was one of those thin, dark-haired Italians; huge eyes, slightly underhung jaw. He wore badly fitting flabby suits. His shoulder blades jutted through the material of his jacket. Despite the dozens of pupils he had practised upon, his command of English was poor. 'You are the world's most experienced girl,' was his most accomplished sentence, inspired by a Pan American Airways advertisement, and his well-worn introduction to a flirtation. He came to lunch at Casa Musatti every day. Our parents had been absolutely assured that none of us would ever have any communication with men, but somehow the Musatti sisters seemed to think Piero did not count. And he, daily surrounded by nubile British youth, had acquired a charm and an ease that none of us could ignore.

It was well known that out of the previous year's intake, he had lighted upon the beautiful Mary Nicholson (later married to George Christie), fallen in love with her, and followed her to England. This had not been a success, most especially with Mary's parents. When we arrived, he did not look as if he was still pining, but perhaps he was simply a good concealer of a broken heart. I think he concentrated on me because I knew Mary, and we could talk about her. Just a few days after sitting next to him at lunch (and the Musattis did make some attempt to shuffle the seating, in the belief this might be a deterrent to any possible flaring of interest), he asked me out. 'Not unless Sally comes too,' I said. 'Very well,' he agreed. 'I have friend who can be for her. He's a heart specialist, too.'

Going out with Italian men, although absolutely forbidden, was not impossible – indeed, illicit meetings were wonderfully easy. We were trusted, and the Musattis did not employ any spies.

Piero, in his silver Fiat, with his friend Jorio, would come and collect us from our lessons and drive us to a café for a drink before taking us back to Casa Musatti for lunch. It felt slightly wicked, but it was innocent. And in no time, with all this extra means of learning the language, we were jabbering away in Italian. After a while invitations changed key: would we like to go to Fiesole and look down on Florence as the sun set? We would. Three or four sunsets later included the first kiss. We had to smooth ourselves and brush our hair in order to look innocent at supper. Sometimes Piero would appear there, too. He would come jaunting in, 'straight from the hospital', he claimed, and cast a quick, sly look at me. 'Ah! Most experienced world's girl! What have you been doing today?' The nefariousness of it all was thrilling.

Piero and Jorio introduced us to their friends Massimo and Franco: two smallish, enthusiastic young men who had a flat. We were asked there to a 'party' one Sunday afternoon. This was so exciting we abandoned our Italian verbs for a few days to concentrate on sartorial matters. I had a pair of bronze stiletto shoes made by a cobbler, and decided on a purple tweed dress of my own design (yes, I had brief thoughts of becoming a dress designer) with a rose silk lining.

Guests at the party were Sally and me, and our two friends in their second year, Davina Darcy de Knayth and Susan Baring. In Massimo/Franco's tiny sitting room we were given a glass of wine. The lights were switched out before we could drink it or put down the glass. A record was put on.

Che bella pansé che tieni,
Che bella pansé che hai,

Words which could be taken in two ways. The smooching began. It was innocent smooching, but lively. Partners changed from time to time, though neither Massimo nor Franco approached Sally because they would only have come to her navel. Sally was obliged to stick with Jorio, although kissing him was 'like kissing a jellyfish', she said. Low lights were sometimes put on, mouths wiped, laughter. Many Sunday afternoons were spent at these parties.

But then Piero was sent to work in Rome, and Jorio mysteriously evaporated. The impatience of Italian men, we were learning, was considerable. Perhaps Jorio realised he had gone as far as he would ever be allowed, and was off after some Italian girl of easier persuasion. But we did not mourn our heart specialists. They were quickly replaced by Piero's dentist friend, Willy, for me, and Willy's friend Maurizio for Sally. Willy had the rather goofy good looks common to some Italian men: huge sleepy brown eyes, a slow smile. He constantly wore an enormous sloppy tweed overcoat, which was his idea of an English coat. Maurizio, just tall enough for Sally, good looking from some angles, was a manufacturer of bras, though I don't remember there was much discussion about his business. Although not quite so hot blooded as our original escorts, life with Willy and Maurizio continued in much the same way as it had with the doctors. There were variations. Maurizio took Sally one day to see where Willy worked. Willy and I went to meet them. We found Sally lying back in the dentist's chair while Maurizio pumped her up and down. His foot on the pedal, the whole chair was rising and falling.

We never declared we were in love with these Florentine men: love was far from our minds and, I think, theirs. Instead, they were fun, generous in their offers to show us Florence and to entertain us. Of course seduction was their chief objective, but I think they were wary of young English virgins and the trouble that could be caused by going too far. But the enjoyment of a sunset in an Italian car with a good-looking Italian man did, of course, further enliven our days which, anyhow, were overflowing with an almost tangible daily happiness and excitement. And all that in a setting of such acute beauty that we felt, as Elizabeth Bowen said in one of her letters, as if we were living in 'that world which is the background of an Italian picture'.

My days were particularly full because, besides the daily Italian lessons, I was also continuing art at Pietro Annigoni's school. This, after the Beaux-Arts, was a terrible disappointment. Instead of live models, we had to do prissy little sketches of small statues with a soft pencil, rubbing in the shadows with a finger. Colour was frowned on, Monsier Souverbie's feeling for brightness totally abhorred. My box of oil paints was forbidden. Annigoni himself was sometimes at the studio: a dour, silent man. He would come and look at our dreary little sketches and sigh. At the time he was working on a portrait of the Duke of Edinburgh. The place was littered with rough sketches. A marvellous draughtsman, these sketches had a liveliness which seemed to be lost in his finished paintings. I learnt little there, and often skipped classes to meet one of the suitors.

Italy, in 1955, was still relatively tourist-free. We were taken on jaunts to dozens of towns and cities to see churches, paintings, galleries, museums; and wherever we went was empty of other people. There was an unforgettable night we spent in a convent in Assisi. We had silent supper at long tables with the nuns, and slept in modest but clean rooms. In the night we were woken by a wild storm. Out of the window we could see the plain below us, lighted by grape-green flashes that, for seconds at a time, paled the dark cypresses. Huge clumps of the sky parted, then clashed together like fighting monsters. Freezing at our window, we watched the storm's slow decline. By dawn there was silence, and it had begun to snow. Donkeys were provided for us to ride up through the white-quiet streets to the church of San Francesco. We joined the nuns for Mass. They, too, had also travelled on donkeys, the hems of their black habits skimming over the snow. The only sound was the tolling of a single, melancholy bell. The smell of early baked bread, coming from open windows, was the only warmth.

Just eleven years later, in Assisi with my husband Quentin Crewe, the silence had gone, the crowds and buses had come, the sellers of plastic relics had set up their stalls. I realised how lucky my generation of students had been just a decade earlier, when uncluttered silence was the norm. Awe was undisturbed.

We were taken by a marvellous guide to see everything there was to see in Florence itself, and would return many times on our own. We walked everywhere, overwhelmed by the beauty, the light, the smells. In a tiny street we found a house where, for a few lire, *bombolini* (doughnuts) would be sent down a pipe, too hot to eat immediately. Sugar-fingered, doughnuts cooling in paper handkerchiefs, we would walk to the straw market or the Ponte Vecchio to the squealing music of the vaporetti, whose drivers shouted hilarious compliments.

It was during that time in Florence that I came to understand the passion of Keats, Shelley and Byron for Italy. I felt it myself, a tangible thing that has never left me. Day after day we were faced with the kind of beauty only poets and artists can adequately convey. We wanted to stay for ever.

But our six months hurried towards their inevitable, dreaded end. My mother, previously a rotten correspondent, suddenly sent a flurry of letters. Well, she had something important on her mind: the Season, and all that it entailed. There was much to plan, and she was an efficient planner. Her most pressing concern were the clothes I should wear to be presented at Court. She kept sending me small scraps of salmon-coloured taffeta for my approval. I didn't approve at all, but could not be bothered to disagree. It was irritating to be interrupted from the glorious daily life in Florence. I didn't want to think of another world.

So sapphire-blue scraps of velvet followed the pink taffeta, and ideas for two different hats – one for a rainy day, the other for sun. At the time this suggestion came, I had found a sonnet by Michelangelo translated into English by Wordsworth, and I was enjoying trying to translate it back again into Italian. How far from the original would my attempt be? The last thing I wanted to attend to was the choosing of hats. Mean of me, I suppose. My mother, who was often disappointed that our interests did not coincide, was trying. But the two years running of organising debutante life for Trish and me was more for her own pleasure than ours.

Felicity, during the Florentine episode, wrote regularly. We both enjoyed nature notes, so regaled each other with pages of descriptions rich in adjectives – hers of India and London, mine of Italy. She also mentioned, ever more frequently, Mickey. I had said to him, before leaving for Florence, 'Look after her.' He had said he would. Seemed he was looking after her very well.

Then came the letter explaining that they were to be married. Felicity was eighteen. Her parents were apprehensive – hence the 'break' in India, and she was still to do the Season. Possibly, they reckoned, she might be deflected by some other, slightly younger man.

I felt the kind of jealousy that doesn't mean one wants whatever has gone for oneself; I was left, for a short time, with the silt of nostalgia for what might have been. I had never thought of marrying Mickey. But he was my first love, a friend for life. I knew that I would never marry anyone who was not his equal in fun, intellect, sympathy. He was a supreme life-enhancer. What he provided for me was a standard by which all future men, I thought, would be measured. Very useful.

So, for Felicity and me, there was no breach in our friendship.

Sally and I left Florence in the spring of 1956 to face the dotty business of becoming debutantes.

7

Debutante Interlude

For many years into my working life I kept very quiet about ever having been a debutante. It was something to be embarrassed about, almost shameful. Certainly, if you were after a serious job, this blot on your past went against you: you were automatically put into the category of flibbertigibbet, not serious, probably brainless. On the other hand, those who scorned the Season were also fascinated. When they questioned me about it (and I felt I had to answer truthfully), they laughed, they scoffed, but they wanted to know more. Some years later, working for a Sunday newspaper, the editor tried many devious ways to make me write about those ex-debutante friends whom he snobbishly felt were interesting. I never obliged.

It's now sixty years since I came out and I have mellowed a little. By now I look upon the whole business as being as quaint and peculiar as many other antique practices. When discussed, with a light laugh, it's a perfectly acceptable area of reminiscence, though not of spectacular interest. Many ex-debutantes have written books and articles about their own experiences: there is probably little left to say. I am merely going to look back with a quizzical glance at what it was like for me. The big change I feel is that I am neither ashamed nor embarrassed by my long-past participation in that peculiar rite of passage. After all, I was a student until it happened, I began a salaried job the moment it was over, and have worked ever since. The parties themselves lasted for precisely *fourteen weeks* of my life – surely not a long enough period to be the cause of serious remorse.

On the way home from Florence (once our suitors had got off the train at the French border), Sally and I had reflected a little on what was to be expected. Those of us embarking on the dizzy life, with all its weird habits, had heard a good many stories about the horrors that could tip the balance of the fun. Would the day come when we would have to hide in the Ladies for lack of partners? Find our own taxis home? Watch the man on whom we'd pinned our hopes clasped night after night to someone else? In order, I suppose, to guard myself against such agonies, I devised a plan. I would not fall in love with anyone, and thus avoid heartbreak. This would not be difficult, as I doubted any of them would come up to the standard of Mickey. I would cultivate men *friends,* primarily those who danced well. Above all, I would believe myself to be invisible. That would be excellent armour, I thought. At a cocktail party, less than entranced by the man I was talking to, I would just walk away with no excuse, and he would not notice. I could flit about a crowded room or dance floor, appearing to be intent on finding a particular person. The thing to avoid was the panicky expression of one lost, embarrassed and drifting. Of all my peculiar theories, this was one that worked very well indeed. I have made it a practice ever since – it's as useful in middle age and old age as it was in youth. The belief in invisibility brings many rewards.

Home, heart still in Italy, I found my mother in a state of acute excitement. Plans, lists and dozens of invitations swirled through her mind. Energy at full throttle, she was in her element. We were off.

First thing to be done was to concentrate on clothes. With a budget far smaller than some, there had to be caution. Just one dress from Belinda Bellville, the rest from an inspired dressmaker. This suited me well, for it meant I could get back to my dress designing. After a morning spent in Allans of Duke Street (we bought so many yards of material that they gave us a huge discount), we came home with bales of taffeta, silk, organza and chiffon in glorious Matisse colours. I drew dozens of pictures and dresses were quickly and expertly made. My 'signature' was skirts that were shorter in front than the back, so that contrasting frills on the inside of the hem would flash as I danced. Next came the white satin Dolcis shoes (27s. 6d. a pair), dyed to match each dress. None of that was onerous: it was rather fun, suddenly having ten new dresses. In their prime, it was impossible to imagine they would be in shreds three months later, but they were.

Far less entertaining were the lunch parties that had to be attended and, even more bizarrely, the tea parties. Huge quantities of the fashionable coronation chicken was eaten in private houses, or private rooms in a hotel. Many of the girls I already knew from school, Paris or Italy, and I lighted on some sympathetic new ones among the strangers. But at these gatherings it was impossible to have a proper conversation; you were obliged to take down addresses and telephone numbers and keep saying '… and you must come to my dance, too'. While I was at the youthful lunches, my mother was enormously enjoying herself at 'Mums' lunches', gathering sheaves of information about available dates for a dance, and 'available young men', whose eligibility was no doubt being weighed up.

The lunches, teas and cocktail parties were over at last by the end of April, quantities of information and some new friends gathered. The presentations kicked off the start of the more enjoyable part of the Season. My mother had relentlessly invested in the salmon-pink taffeta, sapphire velvet coat and the cautionary two hats: as it was a greyish day, the velvet one was chosen. There were queues, glimpses of silken walls and glorious pictures in Buckingham Palace, a lot of nervous shaking. Many of us had been rigorously coached in how perfectly to bend a knee – it was all so quick that I came away feeling it hadn't happened. There was a band playing jolly traditional tunes, and excellent chocolate cake. That was it. Being presented at Court in earlier years was a glamorous occasion: long dresses, tiaras, ostrich-feather fans. By 1956 there was a feeling of curtsey fatigue … No wonder the event only lasted another two years. It must have been an ordeal for the Queen, who was bound to acknowledge each tottering debutante dip with a glimmer of a smile, and the back-up members of the royal family, who had to spend several hours sitting bolt upright, hands neatly placed as their eyes glazed over at the tedious parade.

That evening, at a cocktail party at the Hyde Park Hotel (there were many, many occasions in the hotel's sombre ballroom), I met one Tim Renton. He turned out to be one of the friends I had hoped for, and so well did we get on that my invisibility did not have to come into play. Good looking, extremely intelligent and funny, his added charm was his excellence at dancing. Apart from meeting at parties, we kept up a correspondence: very long letters with our views on authors and books and life in general. He remained a friend not just through the Season, but for life.

The weird summer began: a rigorous pattern that did not change. On weekdays the dances were mostly in London. The venues became familiar: 6 Belgrave Square, 63 Pavilion Road and the popular Hyde Park Hotel, where you could escape the dance floor for a breath of night air on the balcony, and study the moon silvering the dark trees in the park. Sometimes there were dances held courtesy of one of the great livery companies of the City of London – the Fishmongers, the Grocers, and so on. These were very grand dos, with much gold and silver plate on show, and a certain sombreness scarcely enlivened by a weary band. Sometimes vast marquees were put up in garden squares, which made a nice, though often chilly change. In the much used *endroits*, hosts made an effort to do something a mite different in the way of decoration and flowers, but by the end of the summer many of us had had enough of the uninspired rooms of the Hyde Park Hotel and 6 Belgrave Square.

Claridge's, though, was different. Those who hired Claridge's seemed only to want to make it extraordinary, memorable. Once its ballroom was converted into the *plage* at Nice: the

139

walls had become sky with clouds, there were distant vistas, walls, palm trees. We could believe ourselves to be in the South of France for the evening. On another occasion the ballroom was turned into a lifelike jungle, with a density of trees, bamboo and greenery, from which stuffed lions, tigers and exotic birds peered in amazement. Goodness knows what such transformations cost, but money was mentioned only in the gossip columns.

Musically, hosts were less adventurous. There were no young pop musicians to call upon – only Tommy Kinsman in his dinner jacket and neat, sloomy players, or Bobby Harvey, a touch wilder, with his untidy hair and enormous consumption of the free drink which kept him singing as well as playing. So no matter whether it was among stuffed tigers, or in hotel ballrooms unadorned except for stiff, triangular arrangements of gladioli on pedestals, we jogged about to 'Tea for Two' or 'Dancing on the Ceiling' and a few numbers from American musicals. The bandsmen had registered that young Elvis Presley was causing a stir, and did sometimes launch into 'Rock Around the Clock' towards the end of the evening. Then we took off. Crinolines (there were quite a few about: I had three) would flip, hard-set hair would fling as wildly as it was able, the men would go so far as to loosen their black or white ties. Many of us had boned bodices to our dresses, the better to show off our waists. (Mine, in 1956, was 18 inches.) These did not marry happily with rocking around the clock. There were occasions when, twisting incautiously about, real bosoms would escape from their boned cages, and for a moment the careless dancer seemed to have four breasts.

* * *

Before the dances were the dinner parties. These came about in a way peculiar to the whole ritual of the Season. Either mothers would arrange them between themselves, or you would get a polite letter from a mother asking if you would 'care to dine' for so and so's party. It was essential to go to a dance with others: to have arrived alone could be unnerving. So you accepted, and on the appointed evening bundled your tulle/taffeta/organza skirts into a taxi and set off to often unknown hosts in Chelsea, Belgravia or St John's Wood. Notting Hill, in those days, had years to go before it became fashionable.

The dinner parties were hit-and-miss affairs. Sometimes the hosts had hired someone to cook and wait; sometimes they had plainly spent the day doing it all themselves. Effort always seemed to have been made: extravagant flowers, rich food – chocolate mousse was at the height of its popularity – and good wine. The fathers, exhausted after their day in the City, exuded something between tolerance and reluctance, in their white ties and tails, as they made polite conversation to the couple of unknown girls chosen to twitter at their sides throughout dinner. The mothers were sometimes close to hysteria – so much to organise and worry about. Their main worry was transport. How were the bevvy of young to get to the party? Few of them had cars, and the 'young men' who did own an MG or a Sunbeam Talbot were not drivers to be relied on. So it was up to the hostess to designate groups to share taxis, while she and her husband would give a lift to a couple. Once she got her group safely to the dance, the giver of the dinner could relax. The real problem came with dances outside London. Driving after a good dinner – and the young men took full advantage of the wine – was obviously a hazard. On one occasion the charming, wild, reckless Richard Strachan, later to become my brother-in-law, came to dinner with us. He had a fast but rackety car, but nobly volunteered to drive three of the girls who had been at dinner. Richard's reputation as a driver was famous. But my mother disguised her apprehension and agreed. The rest of the party set off in various cars and made their way to somewhere in Kent.

At 2 a.m., Richard and his three passengers still had not turned up. There was nothing to be done but to wait and hope. They arrived at 3 a.m. The girls, all in white dresses, were soaking wet. Green weed clung to their sodden skirts. Mud was smeared over bundles of dead tulle. Water squelched from satin shoes. But they did not seem to be hurt. Richard braved my mother.

He explained that he had come upon a pond, in a village, into which the road seemed directly to lead. And, well, he had followed it right into the middle of the pond. The car was still there, half submerged. But he'd managed to get the girls to the party in the end, hadn't he? It was the last time he was chosen to drive anyone.

Usually there were a few friends at those pre-dance dinners, and occasionally there would be an appealing stranger who became a friend. But there was always the danger of being put next to some gormless young caricature of a man – brainless, arrogant, altogether incapable of amusing or entertaining. I always thought it was worth trying, however dull my companions on either side, but often I completely failed to ignite a glimmer of life. After one dinner I was told a small guardsman, with whom I'd had no conversation, was to take me to the party. He had a low, roaring sort of car, of which he was very proud. We drove past Buckingham Palace, and round the Victoria and Albert Memorial. Then round again, and again, and again. Eventually I asked why we were doing this so often.

'Just want to make sure the muckers on guard see me,' he said, glancing at the rigid sentries standing in front of their boxes. If they did see him, they chose to remain impervious. Not a raised eyebrow in acknowledgement.

My mother was a keen hostess. She revelled in giving dinner parties and went about the whole business with huge energy and spirit. Welfare, our old butler, managed to last the Season, laying the table beautifully with silver polished to a dazzling brilliance. But Mum did all the cooking herself – it would take a whole day. Her culinary repertoire was limited, but anything she did cook she did very well, with an extravagance of butter and cream. Despite three courses, she spent a long time making small rounds of fried bread on which she put various concoctions of egg, curry, smoked salmon – *amuse-gueules* designed to go with drinks before dinner 'to break the ice'. She never grumbled about the amount of preparation because she enjoyed it. She liked to invent things: her pink fish, for instance. Small soles rolled up in a secret pink sauce of her own devising. She was famous for her pink fish, I often heard her telling people. She liked to be famous for her cooking. She wanted these dinner parties to be done really well, and took enormous trouble with the smallest detail – and indeed years later people would remind me of the many merry occasions in our flat in Eaton Square.

Over the summer I think we gave some dozen dinner parties, each time for ten guests. And my parents were good hosts. Many of the young found my mother an amusing companion as she told stories of when she was a deb herself: certainly she was witty, high spirited, often funny, extremely politically incorrect. But I always sat through the pink fish with one eye on her glass, willing her not to drink enough to fire those smeary glances that came after a normal martini evening. But, to be fair, some inner rein took a hold. When entertaining the young she restrained herself. Perhaps the one thing she didn't want to be famous for was drinking, and made sure that didn't happen.

Oh, those evenings. Anticipation (though I could never be sure what it was I was hoping might happen) fizzed throughout the routine. The long bath. The going to the huge cupboards, where my collection of billowing dresses was huddled under dustsheets. The working out who I had seen when I last wore the yellow taffeta, in which I had always had a good time, or the lilac chiffon permanent pleats over a crinoline petticoat … The choosing. The careful make-up, according to Sophia Loren's make-up expert. Then, to the drawing room, with its elaborate furniture with its hints of Versailles, and its thick, clammy scent of lilies on the piano, bunged into a cut-glass vase. (My mother could never be famous for her flower arranging.) My father would come quietly in, wretchedly tired, for he was up at six every morning in order to be at the studio by eight. His furrowed, handsome face would crumple into the smile with which he would always greet me. He would pour himself a whisky and soda, stand stooping a little in front of the fireplace, fiddle with his white tie, quietly wonder how soon he could get away from the Hyde Park Hotel, or wherever it was we were to go. He never complained, though he must have been desperately worried about what all this was costing, and there was Trish to be accommodated the following year. But he knew better than to suggest to my mother any sort of cutting back. It was her fun, this Season. She'd been waiting for it for years.

Then Welfare would open the door, and in would come the first of the young men. My father braced himself to smile again, shake hands, offer a drink.

'Good evening, sir.'

'Dear boy.' And then they were off, easily. For somehow my father's acute natural interest in everybody he met guided him to the very thing that the blank-faced visitor could eagerly talk about. My mother would still be in the kitchen, apron over her Hartnell dress, putting finishing touches to her *chef d'oeuvre*. I always dreaded her joining us, for her way of coming into a room full of people was always noisy. She had a big, stomping walk, swaying from side to side. You could not miss her entrance – which was strange, for she often said she was very shy. Hers was not the gait of one who was shy, but perhaps it was intended to disguise her shyness. I sometimes wondered if I should recommend my invisibility theory, but that would not have been a conversation I would ever have considered having with her.

When she appeared among the white ties and bulbous dresses, the drawing room instantly became smaller, as it had on the evening my grandmother's red velvet train had consumed most of the floor. I have to admit her self-deprecating jokes made everyone laugh. I always longed for her to quieten down, but plainly my feelings were not shared. Many of the guests told me what 'good fun' she was. Certainly she was much easier than many of the more rigid mothers. I recognised that. Perhaps my father, Trish and I were the only ones so often embarrassed by her.

Within a few weeks of the Season, I had chosen my 'regular dancers' and my plan seemed to materialise extraordinarily well. Perhaps this was because they were all men eager to avoid the difficulties of a high romance for the few months that the parties lasted but, like me, wanted uncomplicated friendships. And indeed, on the many occasions when I looked round a ballroom and saw couples jammed together, hardly moving, knowing the girl was desperate not to lose her man to some predator nearby, I was hugely relieved to be whirling around with someone I liked very much, knowing there was no chance of either heart being broken.

I don't know where my dancers learnt their art. Only one of them – Tim Renton – some fifty years later, confessed that when he was at Oxford he used to sneak off for secret ballroom-dancing lessons at classes in a room above Boswells, the department store in The Broad. None of the others mentioned tuition, but they were all masterly, including Johnny Wright, who talked a lot about God and danced like Fred Astaire. (He was once seen, in his late sixties, dancing all alone in Athens Airport while waiting for a plane.) Antony Snow, with his infectious laugh when we missed a tricky step, would sometimes walk me home from Belgrave Square; we would put on the radiogram and carry on dancing in the drawing room till we heard my father leaving for work. Tim Elwes was particularly skilled. Occasionally we would leave a dance to go to the Allegro nightclub, where Hutch (Leslie Hutchinson, cabaret star from Grenada, who was rumoured to have had an affair with Edwina Mountbatten) sang and played. We would start to dance, and suddenly everyone else left the floor. Appalling showing off, we knew, but irresistible, a whole floor and throbbing music all to ourselves. We were rewarded for our 'entertainment' with free drinks.

To love dancing, I learnt, was both an advantage and a disadvantage. To go to a party and have to lumber around the room with a man who can only pump his arm, and lurch about with no sense of time, is depressing. Then suddenly to be partnered with someone who can skim across a room, as light as a zephyr, makes the spirits soar. Never since 1956 have I experienced again the luxury of proper dancers night after night: they are definitely in the minority and are too old to learn. Nowadays, at an (infrequent) dance, I simply hope to run into Rupert Lycett Green or Nick Paravicini, both stars to whom jiving, the Charleston and Viennese waltzing are second nature.

Often the best dances were in the country, in some castle or huge house. The fun of whole out-of-London expeditions was never knowing quite what to expect. We came to understand that there are innumerable English country houses of grey stone covered in wisteria, porches cluttered with gumboots, dogs of all sizes lumbering about – and hosts who made an extraordinary effort to ensure the enjoyment of the strange young things they had been asked to accommodate for a night. At Paddington Station you would join up with girls in skirts still influenced by the 1947 New Look, and giggle your way to the West Country, or Sussex or Hampshire. An agreeable old host, his gardening interrupted, would meet us at the station and drive us to the usually enchanting house. His wife would pounce on us with tea and sponge cake, and show us to cavernous bedrooms with four-poster beds and the bathrooms leading from them – never referred to as *en suite* – with baths from the last century and mahogany loo seats with wicker lids.

We changed, we bathed, the mundane acts all heightened by anticipation, despite the fact that the men in the house party did not hold much promise. Then, at drinks in the drawing room – wounded sofas dipping beneath their aged Fowler chintz – a glance out of the vast windows showed distances of unspoilt English fields and hills that rose beyond a ravishing garden. Pre-dinner communication was always a little stilted, as so well captured by William Douglas-Home in *The Reluctant Debutante*. People really did talk about the way they had come, road numbers, the advantage of the train, how they planned to get back to London … But by dinner everyone had discovered how many people they knew in common, which made for greater ease. At these dinners, again, I used to marvel at how much trouble our hosts had gone to, often for a gathering which did not include a son or daughter of their own.

Dances in the country were considerably more of an undertaking to arrange than those in London. Except in houses like Firle Place, in Sussex, marquees not only had to be erected, but also their basic canvas disguised. At one dance in Hampshire, the tent extended over flights of steps up to a beautiful Georgian façade which became one wall of the tent: the tent itself was thickly studded with gardenias perched in greenery. We learnt somehow that the flowers alone cost £1,500 … and the thickness of their scent, that extraordinary evening, wings back to me every time I smell a single gardenia decades later. There is powerful nostalgia in scent.

Another memorable dance was at Eridge Castle, in Sussex, to which the Queen and several members of the royal family were invited. There, in the magnificent ballroom, I was waltzing with Richard Strachan of the village pond incident – he was as reckless a dancer as he was a driver. We were twirling ever faster, perilously close to the Queen. I urged him to stop, which goaded him to further speed. And suddenly we were splayed on the floor, my crinoline tipped up to expose undignified suspenders, Richard bellowing drunken laughter. The Queen chose to observe none of the wretched scene, and swooped away as we struggled up. Later, to show I had forgiven him, we walked round the garden between the long avenues of yew hedges. He confessed he'd thrown his previous partner into one of these hedges, for no particular reason. But she, too, had forgiven him, and scrambled out unharmed.

The unforgettable part of the country dances was the return to the house at which we were staying to find the brilliance of the previous evening veiled in early mist, melancholy wisteria drooping more heavily, mourning doves cooing – all so uniquely English that tears almost came to tired eyes. Knowing such dawn experiences would soon be coming to an end added to their poignancy. Many a country-house host must have received very over-the-top thank-you letters from me: they were a chance to air my nature notes.

I never ceased to rage about not being allowed to go to Oxford or Cambridge (and that particular regret is as alive now as it was then), so in the heady summer of 1956 I accepted as many invitations as possible to both places. In those days the long-lashed undergraduates, who by night restrained themselves at least for the first half of a party, in their own habitats of colleges saw no reason to curb their wild spirits. They wore a kind of uniform of corduroy turn-up trousers, often of shocking cream, and good tweed jackets. The laughed a lot, drank a lot, jumped out of windows, gave crowded parties in their rooms with no food and bad wine. For the Commem Balls at Oxford, rich colleges funded extravagant bands, inventive decorations and, often, cabarets. Johnny Wright, one of my platonic dancer friends, took me to the Balliol Ball where we behaved like Fred Astaire and Ginger Rogers for some six hours, scarcely stopping for a sip of Coca-Cola. We never mentioned feeling tired. Indeed I rarely ever felt tired, despite night after night of going to bed at dawn and sleeping only for three or four hours. I tried to remember this when I remonstrated with my own daughters over their penchant for endless late nights, but the feeling would not return.

In Cambridge I had two particular friends, one of whose family house was where Tennyson wrote 'Come Into the Garden, Maud'. I was excited by the idea, but Peter plainly was not. We never spoke of poetry, but he often took me to the Pitt Club to dance in pitch darkness. Then there was Michael Macleod, of the longest, thinnest legs I have ever seen, and a lugubrious but appealing face. He was in the Coldstream Guards: very poor but ridiculously generous, he would never let a girl pay for anything. I sometimes ran into him in the street in London, when he would swish off his hat, bow, seem ecstatic to see me, and suggest another Cambridge outing; he was an undergraduate at Pembroke College. On one occasion he gave a party for me in a large room in his college. There were fifty-three men, and me.

It was unusual for anyone to enjoy their own dance as much as they did other people's, and I was no exception. Mine began with sartorial preparations: more fittings at Worth, because my grandmother insisted on giving me the dress. It was a horror – salmon organza over a crinoline with a hand-beaded bodice leading to the nineteenth-century waist. Pure Gracie Fields at the Palladium, which caused me as much embarrassment as it did discomfort – and guilt. I was told many times it cost £150, but still could not like it, and rarely wore it.

The dance was held at Shoppenhangers Manor, near Maidenhead, which belonged to friends of my parents. It was a seventeenth-century house of aged darkness, but boasted an impressive garden where flights of steps clambered down terraces. It looked enchanting, but a few years later it was wiped out by the M4 motorway.

As hostess, you danced with every polite man doing his duty – not much fun for one as critical as me. I remember a particularly dreary turn with the man soon to become Lord Lucan. My own party was not the one that I remembered with any particular enjoyment, but I was glad that my parents, who had tried hard, were much congratulated.

Those three summer months (I remember no rain) passed in a kind of multicoloured skein of sounds, sensations, colours, candlelight, and the intoxication of gardenias, roses, clouds of sweet peas. As a non-drinker myself (in reaction to my mother, I daresay), I had no trouble in finding myself in the high spirits that some of my contemporaries needed to spark with many a glass of champagne. The parties did not seem to pall; obligatory daytime events were less enjoyable. The Berkeley Deb Dress Show (for me, the first and last time on a catwalk), the opening of the Royal Academy Summer Exhibition, where my mother and I were photographed in quilted coats, looking like a couple of beds. I did enjoy Ascot, waving my Edwardian lace parasol and concentrating on the horses. I even enjoyed the Henley Regatta, where I was photographed wearing a lilac cardigan. 'Dullest Henley of them all' said the headline in the *Evening Standard*.

The spinning, glittering ball of time came to an end in mid-July. There were only the Northern Balls left – a very different and rather alarming matter. Felicity and I went to stay with her uncle in Inverness-shire: he was a stickler for strict routines, and adamant that we should not put a foot wrong in a night of reels. To this end we were urged to practise on the gravel drive after tea: it was cold, and confusing. But the old Lawnside training clicked in, and the steps came back to us. We dreaded the procedure of being given dance cards, tiny pencils attached. How were they to be filled? As soon as we got to the first ball, our host and a couple of other old men who had been at dinner kindly signed us up for a reel or a waltz, as did the two young men also in our party. But that left many dances unaccounted for, and I daresay we shamefully sat out a few. But the balls, for all their regimentation, were enjoyable. By day, we were urged to go for walks. One of the men staying in the house, a rum cove by the name of Lumsdaine Sans Lumsdaine, came with us on one occasion. His way of entertaining us was to climb very high up an unexpected pylon, then jump to the ground – 'Just to prove,' he said, 'I wear nothing under my kilt.'

(above left) The Huth family on the steps of East Burnham House.

(above right) My father, whose joy in hard work never faded.

(left) My mother in the garden of Pullens End.

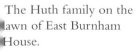

The Huth family on the lawn of East Burnham House.

Rosemary Dillon Weston, English teacher extraordinaire.

(above) My father leading me up the aisle in 1961.

(left) Quentin's last walk – out of the church.

My grandmother at my first wedding, guarding her famous pearls.

Wootton House, Bedfordshire – some thought it haunted.

Quentin and Candida, August 1964.

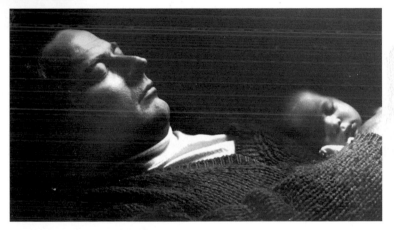

First sight of irresistible Ladybird Cottage.

Tap dancing with Cleo Laine on *How It Is*.

Second wedding, June 1978.

Candida with the bride, June 1978.

The judges of the Booker Prize 1978 (Freddie Ayer, Angela, P.H. Newby).

With Eugenie in the early 1980s.

Eugenie and the Admiral in France.

Quentin and Candida in the garden of Pullens End.

My sister Trish in the garden of Pullens End.

Filming *Landgirls* in Devon, 1997.

With Eugenie at a tap-dancing show in the Cowley Workers Club, May 2004.

Temple House, found after a two-year search.

Sally Ashburton, childhood friend and former sister-in-law.

Eugenie reading to her sons, 2017.

Candida in her Oxford study, 2017.

Together with my grandsons, Norfolk 2017.

I think most of the debutantes had been copiously kissed — in taxis, parked cars, moonlit gardens, darkened dance floors. But we doubted that more than two or three had 'gone all the way'. 'You can always tell which ones have,' people said, with a sagacity based on nothing but surmise and vague scrutiny.

Among our lot there were some who were definitely daring in their approach: they widened their eyes, flung their hair, suggested they 'went for a breath of air' in the orchard when the waltz was over. They were the ones, we thought. The rest of us were too nervous. Birth control was expensive and complicated, and some of us clung to the old idea that keeping oneself for a distant husband was a good idea. So 1956 produced a majority of virgins prepared, now, for real life. For Felicity it would be marriage. For me, work. And Charlie.

In those few months of myriad parties, I had not given much thought to the matter of love, and certainly not to marriage. That was a far-off hazy thing that would descend one day, but it was too big and serious a matter to be confused with dancing. Many of my girlfriends declared themselves to be 'wildly in love', though I never asked them what that felt like. Then, at parties, I saw them having a horrible time as their love objects cast their eyes over the many variations of pretty girls they were faced with every evening. I think only two girls from that summer of '56 went so far as to marry in the autumn, and both were divorced after a very few years.

I had read enough writers who were able to describe precisely how love could be, and I waited patiently for that time to come. I knew that love changes the shape, the smell, the colour of things, and that everything becomes significant simply because of the existence of another person. But that strange state of being had not yet hit me, though the almost non-existent relationship with Mickey, when I was sixteen, had certainly instilled a thrilling urgency about every day. And I had known then that this would return, eventually, with more besides.

At nineteen, working hard and with plenty of friends to go out with (that is, to dinner, the cinema and theatre), it was easy not to think about loving anyone. But once the dancing stopped, Charlie kept on asking me on dates. I began to cogitate again. Was this love?

I had only a vague picture in mind of a husband. He would have to be in the world of arts: a writer, painter, actor, musician. He did not have to be rich, but he did have to be clever so that I could constantly learn from him. Ideally he would speak fluent French and one other language. He could ride, he could dance. He would want children, and want to live in the country. If he was anti-hunting he could not be considered, though such an idea scarcely existed in those days. Odd requirements, perhaps. But, in my early twenties, my ideal.

What I could never contemplate was a businessman, no matter how rich, nor a Member of Parliament. A city dweller, a drinker who often drank too much, a man who neither knew nor cared for books, theatre, paintings – none of those would do. Nor would a man whose idea of fun was to spend hours watching cricket, football, motor racing and billiards. None of those would do either.

No: he should be a man whose presence was exhilarating, who had a good sense of humour and of language. Kind, thoughtful, generous. Looks were also on the list of things that would be my ideal: to wake up every morning to see an unattractive face would not be easy. I had always gone for good-looking men. To find one also blessed with brains, humour, imagination, a lover of both the arts and the country, I knew was a tall order. But I kept hoping.

8

Advertising and America

Merriments over, there was no great sadness. The crowd of parties was unreal, not designed to last long. By the end of the summer we were all feeling burnt out and eager to start earning a living. I had no money apart from my grandmother's allowance of £60 a year, which did not go far, even in 1956. Work was imperative. What was it to be?

For as long as I could remember I knew that all I wanted was to write, and to try to earn a living that way. But, at eighteen, there was small chance that I could produce a novel that would instantly solve the financial problem. And I had no intention of admitting that was what I wanted to do. Ever since the time my mother had shown my snippet of purple prose to her friends, I had kept silent about my intentions. If one day I did manage to get published, she would be surprised.

She goaded me to do something in the field of art. 'You've had all that time at art schools,' she said, not unreasonably. But she could not understand I was not an artist. Being a faintly competent watercolourist, and able to draw figures with a fairly accurate line, does not mean you are an artist. I was not one of those people to whom art is life, and for whom not a day goes by without being driven to paint. If I had never picked up a pencil again, it would not have saddened me. She could not understand any of that. In the end she agreed I should try to get a job on a magazine.

Equipped with nothing more compelling than a piece of blank verse about lamplighters who worked in a mews off Trafalgar Square, I slogged round magazine offices trying to persuade editors I could be of some use to them. They were not impressed. Day after day I had to return home and admit I was still jobless. My mother was good about curbing her impatience, but it was a frustrating and anxious time.

Eventually, a charming old man took pity on me. He was the managing director of the magazine *Harper's Bazaar*, and declared he liked the badly typed sample of my writing. He said he was sure there was 'something' I could do in the fashion department. I could start at once: £5 a week.

My elegant friend Philippa Wallop, a girl of brilliant taste and fashion sense, had arrived at *Harper's* a few weeks before me. There were no other jobs in the fashion department and, no, I could not *write* anything for the magazine, said the whiney little features editor: that job required *experience*. I wondered why no one was keen to give beginners a chance, thus furnishing them with the elusive experience. But I was grateful for the job as a fashion assistant: a foot on the ladder, at least.

I soon discovered it was a position too hopeless to keep. There was no way of progressing from taking hats to photo-shoots, and constantly making tea for the entire editorial department, to becoming a journalist – which I had never wanted to be, but thought might be a good beginning. It occurred to me that, before giving in my notice, I could gain promotion by suggesting ideas. In hope, I sent lists of possible features to the editor who was so set on experience. She used every one of them, but commissioned others to write them. Her excuse was her old refrain: my youth and inexperience.

I gave in my notice after three months. The glamour of sometimes cowering in a studio, yards from a famous model being photographed by a well-known photographer, was not enough. I needed a stimulating job in which I could be of some use, and earn a decent wage. Five pounds barely covered bus fares, and sandwiches for lunch.

'Right,' said my mother, in a voice that proclaimed she knew she had been right all the time, 'art.' One of her assets was to produce great energy when she thought she could be of help. She rang the chairman of J. Walter Thompson, despite my protests about not wanting to go into advertising, and my embarrassment at pulling such strings. I went for an interview, carrying my folder of Beaux-Arts work. The chairman said I needed another year at art school. He suggested the Byam Shaw. Then, he would be delighted to employ me 'in some capacity'.

A year at the Byam Shaw was excruciatingly boring. We were only allowed to draw small statues with soft pencils. Never a live model. No paint or colour allowed. No progress made, just further conviction that I did not want to carry on with art.

But the chairman of JWT seemed to approve of my lifeless sketches. I was given a job not in the art department – 'no experience' – but in the art-buying department. This was a receptionist's job of a lowly kind. You took storyboards from one person, delivered them to another. You merely had to be efficient, for £6 a week. The 'excitement', I was told by others in the office, came from meeting all the famous photographers who passed by. Norman Parkinson was a constant visitor; as I was by then beginning to think about photography, I engaged him in eager conversation. He was friendly and helpful. From time to time I was allowed to sit in on planning meetings, when a lot of smartly dressed men would spend long hours discussing the next promotion for a client's new product. I used to look from one to another of them, trying to imagine their lives. They were well paid, of course, and came to the office in chauffeur-driven cars. But what in their day was there to look forward to? Hours of tedious talk about cereal and washing powder. There were few jokes, or even light-hearted moments. It was all numbingly earnest, and dull. I had so little to do that I took the opportunity to write my first novel, a clichéd autobiographical first book about an art student. Finished, I put it away and never looked at it again.

One of the senior copywriters, Robin Douglas-Home, was a friend. Ever hopeful that something more interesting than my particular job might come up, I asked his advice. He suggested I try for the standard test that all would-be copy-writers are given. It was one of those tests in which you have to fit circles into squares and solve all kinds of meaningless puzzles from which, apparently, your character and ability are judged. There was no writing required.

I failed. A haughty woman in charge of the Horlicks account told me I would have to wait for several years to be a copywriter.

'How can someone of your age possibly know what goes on in the mind of a fifty-year-old woman who finds Horlicks comforting?' she demanded.

'Imagination?' I suggested.

She sniffed, bored. Then, predictably: 'You could try again when you've got some experience. Until then, you'll have to wait.'

'Keats didn't have to wait for experience,' I snapped, too angry to be ashamed of my rudeness. The name Keats did not seem to register in her Horlicks-coloured face. I dashed from the office.

There was one minor compensation for my brief time in advertising. A skinny employee with an underhung jaw who came regularly to the art department, always keen to talk, told me he was a professional ballroom dancer. At the office party at Grosvenor House he was my constant partner. How glorious it was to swish round the ballroom, doing all that dipping and swaying and reverse-turning, with someone who knew how to do it to perfection. He smelt a little too strongly of hair grease, Old Spice, chewing gum and sweat, but his sure-footed, utter command of the floor drained such trivial matters of almost any importance. The next day he proposed: would I be his professional partner? It would be a wonderful life, he assured me, travelling round the country, winning silver cups. I said I was honoured to be asked, and thanked him, but turned down the invitation. He took it well.

But I sat down and wrote a thousand-word send-up of the office party which, anonymously, I sent to the editor of the house magazine. It was published in full. There was much guessing in the copywriting department, Robin said, as to who had written such a funny, scurrilous piece. No one ever discovered it was by a junior in art-buying.

At the end of a year I asked for a rise. After much cogitation among those in charge of salaries, they said I would be pleased to hear they could give me another pound a week. The thought of £7 for another tedious year was not appealing. I thanked them, and said I was off. Before leaving, I enjoyed writing a note to the smugly experienced Horlicks lady, saying what a pleasure it had been to be published at length in the house magazine, by an editor who had plainly not been concerned by the writer's lack of experience.

During the frustrations and boredom of this working time, there were the evenings to look forward to. Trish was now doing the Season, and I was invited to various dances. Some of the men, who took advantage of being constantly in demand, carried on for several Seasons, and were old friends. And then there were copious invitations to dinner with Charlie.

He had been among my top dancing partners – not brilliant, but much better than average. He worked in insurance: I never discovered the exact nature of his job. But it meant that, at pre-dance dinners, he felt it prudent to slide up to talk to the host when the girls had left for coffee in the drawing room. This, he explained, was often an opening to 'a bit of business'.

He was a man of sweet and generous nature, a proper countryman with a love of horses and racing – his father had once won the Grand National. In London, we went out to dinner several times a week. He earned a great deal more than me, but could not be said to be well off. But he would have found any suggestion of my sharing the bill offensive. Those were the days of car doors being opened, men leaping to their feet at the entrance of women, and always paying, even if they could ill afford it. We went mostly to a small restaurant off Belgrave Square. It had a tiny dance floor and we spent much of the evening on it. Charlie took a polite interest in my literary aspirations: I took no interest in his world of insurance. I'm not sure what we talked about, but it was nothing very profound.

I frequently went to stay at his parents' house in Hampshire. Sometimes we went racing at Sandown – not my natural idea of enjoyment, but I was determined to try to fit in. My instinct was constantly to observe other ways of life; to remain a spectator rather than to join in. But Charlie was kind and enthusiastic. To try to look like a natural race-goer was the least I could do.

I bought a suede jacket – a clumpy thing in a hideous shade of orange-brown. This I wore to several race meetings and many a point-to-point, happy that I looked the part of a horse-loving woman, unhappy with the rasping of the jacket. It seemed to have independent sleeves that forced my arms to move before I had given the command. But nobody seemed to notice. The picnics at point-to-points were merry enough occasions, but it occurred to me many times that years and years of that sort of Hampshire life would not be for me.

One afternoon, walking over the fields of the family estate, we came upon a small, pretty house of mellow brick. This was the place of Charlie's plans.

'How do you like it?' he asked.

I said it was lovely, which was true. I liked its proportions, its remoteness, its views. But it was not where I ever wanted to live. I should have made this clear at the time. As it was, Charlie was led to believe that there was some hope of a future for us. I think he recognised that we were inspired by different things, and our aspirations were worlds apart, but perhaps he thought that did not matter. I knew in my heart it would never work. So, having left JWT, I decided the best thing to do would be to get right away. With extraordinary speed, and the encouragement of my parents, I arranged to go to America for six months. Absence, I imagined, would ease the parting.

My idea was to work in New York, earn enough money to travel round the States, and somehow get something published. Then I could return to England equipped with a fragment of *experience*.

To begin with I shared an apartment in New York with a girl who had also left JWT. Later, I moved into a lovely flat on 57th Street with a childhood friend, Henrietta Tiarks – her mother and my father had once been engaged. I found a job in Mary Chess, the (then) famous house of many scents. I did try for higher things – *Vogue*, the *New York Times* – but was always turned down for the usual reason. So I had no choice but to spend three months in the stifling, airless shop in an arcade in the Waldorf Towers Hotel, and felt much like a battery hen. It was one of those plate-glass shops where your every movement could be seen by passers-by, and there was no glimpse of sky. I wondered at all the people who work, and often live, in skyless places. But, oddly, many of them seem not to notice this lack. The air in the shop was thick with jostling scents that clung to my clothes for weeks – heavy, sickly, that produced a kind of claustrophobia that followed me everywhere.

But I was lucky to have a job at all, and much needed the $50 a week wage – my $150 capital was fast running out. And by the time I left, at Christmas, I had acquired a vital art, highly prized in the States: I had become masterly in the art of gift-wrapping.

Every box and bottle that left the shop had to be wrapped in gold-embossed paper, and tied with ribbon pulled into bobbing ringlets. There was a day when a woman in a swirl of floor-length mink ordered ninety different things.

'All gift-wrapped, honey, please, by six thirty.'

They took me all day. I was quite proud of my pyramid of beautifully decorated presents, and she was delighted. But at 9 a.m. next morning a forlorn-looking man appeared with a trolley piled with the gold parcels.

'Apologies,' he said, 'but my wife has a weird disease. She goes round shops ordering dozens of things we don't want or need, and has them gift-wrapped. I have to take them all back. I'm so sorry.'

While the days were long, claustrophobic and dull, the evenings were lively, late, and fun. My old friend Tim Elwes was also working in New York. At least three nights a week we would carry on with our 1956 dancing, or go to listen to George Shearing and other great jazz players. Tim's weekends were well provided for. He was a friend of the J. P. Morgan family and invited me frequently to their estate on Long Island. There was a magnificent main house, and satellite smaller houses meted out to relations. The old matriarch, whose electric chair looked like a perambulator and needed to be pumped up every night, chuntered about visiting members of her family. On Sundays they were all invited to lunch in the big house. On some occasions I was included. It was a spectacular contrast to my weekday lunches of hot dogs in Chock full o'Nuts.

For decorum's sake, I imagine, on my visits to the Morgans I did not stay in the same house as Tim – despite the fact we were merely platonic friends – but in the main house. My first arrival there was memorable. I was greeted by the English butler.

'For madam's breakfast,' he said, 'would it be coffee or tea?'

'Coffee, please.'

'And would that be Brazilian, Kenyan, Continental ...?'

'Continental, please.'

'And milk, madam? Jersey, full fat, skimmed?'

'No milk, thank you.'

'Oxford marmalade, I presume.'

'Lovely, thank you.'

'As to the toast: would madam like white toast, or prefer brown?'

'Brown, please.'

'Wholemeal, or plain?'

'Wholemeal.' I could hear my answers becoming fainter.

'And how would madam like the toast toasted?'

'Oh, God, I don't know.'

'That is, well done, or lightly?'

'I don't mind, thank you. Really ...'

'I'll leave it to the chef, then.'

The next morning, a tray arrived in my room, heavy with the precise orders. Through the open window I could hear the sound of sweeping. It was the man whose sole job was to clear the front drive of autumn leaves.

* * *

Sometimes, in New York for a weekend, Henrietta Tiarks and I would have a glamorous time, too. Henrietta, renowned for her looks in England, was now the toast of New York. She would invite me to go with her to Sunday lunch with her friend, Aly Khan. I remember only two things: the view of the UN building out of the vast window, and dancing with Aly mid-afternoon. Like Henrietta, I had to remove my high heels, for Aly was not a tall man – but he was good company, a good host.

My last night in New York was New Year's Eve 1959. Tony Armstrong-Jones, who had become a friend in 1956, was working with Penelope Gilliatt on an article for *Vogue*. We discovered we had both been asked to the same rather grand parties. Tony suggested it would be much more fun to go down to the Bowery. There, we went to various clubs to see cabarets performed by myriad comedians, dancers, transvestites and many characters of diverse oddity. Tony took hundreds of photographs. It was the kind of thing he most liked recording. I shadowed him, saying not a word. By the time the night was over, I had decided to try to become good enough at photography to illustrate any articles I wrote. I was not to know that day was still a very long way off.

In the 1950s, to travel round America on a Greyhound bus appealed to many English young in search of adventure. Very tame, in comparison with all those gap-year students today who scour the world, often choosing journeys fraught with various kinds of danger. But the Greyhound bus was fast, efficient, cheap and safe. In the 1950s, $100 would take you round the entire States on any route you chose. Today, it has all changed. Travelling alone, particularly as a woman, is not advised. The bus stations themselves are crowded with drug addicts, alcoholics and robbers. Even my intrepid daughter Eugenie, who regards almost nowhere as off limits, having travelled much of the world, spurned the Greyhound when she was in America. I was lucky to catch the golden age of bus travel.

I quickly realised the much-anticipated journey was going to be another dip in my life that always seemed to be jagged with contrasts. It was a particularly bleak winter. The boring stretches all across the Midwest seemed to go on for ever, clouding my vision with its sameness. Luckily my friend from J. Walter Thompson had decided to come with me part of the way, so at least there was someone to talk to. And talk was mostly about how to manage on our scant dollars. Money had suddenly become a huge worry. By the time we got to Denver, I had less than $100 left to last for three months and fifteen thousand miles. (As a matter of pride, we did not even consider telegramming our parents for financial help.) To economise, some days I ate only the free saltines and drank the free water at the bus stations. We couldn't afford to stay in a motel, so spent many nights uncomfortably on the bus. Fatigue impeded the recovery of our low spirits.

But then suddenly we were in California – sun filling the sky, tangible warmth. We were to stay with friends of my sister's godmother in Pasadena, home of the magnificent Huth Library, started by one of my ancestors. We had proper beds, the best of American food, and a spell of fun. There was racing at Santa Anita, where some kind old millionaire put $50 on a horse for me: it won. That took care of money worries for quite a while. We were taken to lunch at MGM with the actor, director and producer Mel Ferrer. There, we met George Hamilton who, amazingly, took me out to dinner. I couldn't stop gazing in wonder at his perfect tan, brilliantly shining black hair and a vast stretch of Hollywood-white teeth that taxed the narrowness of his face when he smiled. His was a face that, today, is very familiar. Then, it was definitely before its time. He encouraged me to eat a great deal against future weeks of saltines and water, and was quite (only quite) interesting about the problems of being a famous, ambitious film star. But there was no igniting on either side. It did occur to me he might have found me of more interest had I not been wearing a demure, boat-necked tweed dress that my mother had assured me I would need in Hollywood. But I was not bothered by our lack of mutual spark. Just having dinner with a film star was a bonus for my diary.

There was a final treat before we left the West Coast. Through one of those recommendations that are so prevalent in America, we had an invitation to visit the Sedgwicks' ranch near Santa Barbara, built on high ground overlooking the Pacific Ocean. We had taken a cab from the bus station. The driver, in some awe, was approaching very slowly along the rutted drive. The house was still a distant shape when the view of it was suddenly obliterated by a cloud of dust and we heard a shout of welcome. It was our host, the magnificent-looking, grey-haired Duke Sedgwick, riding a horse and leading two others.

'Thought you might like to help round up the cattle,' was his greeting.

The prancing horses looked eager to be off. Somehow we

managed quickly to climb into the Western saddles. In all my years of riding as a child, I had never tried a cowboy saddle. There was no time to think. We followed Duke at a flat-out gallop up into the hills. We watched, rather than helped, when it came to rounding up the enormous herd of cows, fearful of falling off if the horse did one of its quick turns. The skill of the cowboys was extraordinary. It was all routine, daily stuff to them, but a performance of intense excitement to us. By the time the herd was rounded up, a sophisticated sunset of chiselled clouds had burnished the Pacific so brightly that it hurt my eyes to marvel.

We galloped to the house for an evening of guitar playing and singing, and briefly met the Sedgwicks' daughter Edie, famous for her life in Andy Warhol's world. A dinner of wondrous French food was served by, yes, an English butler. Well, this was no ordinary ranch. And at breakfast next morning there was more Cooper's Oxford marmalade ...

When we left California, some of the people we had met kindly pressed dollar bills into our hands. Our precarious finances left us with no choice: we had gratefully to accept them.

The journey back to the East Coast was very different from the outward journey, and due to our tips we were able to spend the odd night in a bed. Everywhere we stopped I spent an age taking photographs, still determined to be an occasional photographer.

Our first piece of good luck was arriving in New Orleans the day before Mardi Gras, and tracking down some hospitable friend of an acquaintance who had us to stay. The second piece of good fortune was much more extraordinary.

By this time I was travelling on my own on Trailways buses, altogether a more congenial bus company. Their routes went through small towns and roads: great relief after all the miles of highways. Somewhere near Charleston, a middle-aged woman got on the bus. There were many empty seats but she chose to sit next to me, guessed at once I was not a local and began to talk in that friendly way that is second nature to Americans. Her name was Lavender. When she had established that not only had I come from England, but also that I used to live near Windsor, excitement overcame her.

'You see, my late husband knew someone who went to school at Eton,' she said, in her enchanting Southern accent. 'So I think that's a very good reason for you to come and stay for a few days, see what the South is like.'

She lived alone in a huge white plantation, of a type familiar from *Gone With the Wind*. Her widowhood was not lonely: dozens of friends dropped in most days, all old enough to be my grandmother, and exhaustingly interested not only in my English life but in every mile I had travelled in the States. There was a clam bake given in my honour, and a Sunday lunch which turned out to be horribly memorable.

Lavender employed a single black servant, Ella, in the house, who apparently did everything, and seemed to be more of a friend to my hostess than a servant. On the Sunday of the lunch she wore a hat made of imitation mimosa, and was elated by the whole idea of cooking for twenty or so people. We were seated at two long tables. Ella and two of her friends went round serving huge amounts of Southern food from wooden platters. When the main course was finished and the plates cleared away, there was a very long pause. I looked at

Lavender. She looked at Ella who, with her two friends, had sat down at the end of a table where there were some spare places. They talked merrily among themselves, impervious to the furious looks that were coming from the grand elderly guests. Lavender had turned pale. She whispered to those sitting next to her. Someone told me the dessert would be on its way, then all would be well. But the pudding did not arrive, and Ella and her friends did not move.

Then suddenly, with one accord, the twenty guests rose, left the tables and hurried out of the room. I could not understand what was happening. I looked at Ella, who was grinning.

'They don' like to sit down with no black person,' she said, and her friends giggled. Embarrassed, I did not know what to do. Should I offend her, or Lavender?

'You go on up, then,' said Ella. 'I don't want you in no trouble too.'

Upstairs in the drawing room, there was chaos. Lavender was crying, apologising. She was shaking her way round the room, touching each of her friends on the arm or the shoulder. She seemed to be in shock.

'Never in my life has such a thing happened,' she moaned. 'What came over Ella? What was she thinking? What was she doing?' Many of her guests were in sympathetic tears. She plainly thought Ella's act of defiance – if that was what it was – had caused some irreparable damage to her reputation as a hostess, and was distraught.

The guests, in some haste, disappeared, leaving me to try to comfort Lavender. It was of course the time, the late 1950s, of strict segregation: special public lavatories and buses and diners for Negroes, as they were called then. Passing through small towns on the bus I had seen notices saying 'No Blacks', but I suppose I did not register just how important this was to Whites. So Ella's unusual behaviour must have been deeply shocking to Lavender and her friends: incomprehensible for a servant – a black servant – to take such a liberty.

After that, the spirit seemed to go out of my hostess. Her enthusiasm to show me more of the South dwindled. She could not believe the ghastly occasion had not put me off Americans in general. I did not like to say that the only thing I had found shocking was the behaviour of her guests. I tried to convince her that it had not been that traumatic – people sometimes behaved out of character. Maybe Ella had been trying to send a message to me, a foreigner, I thought, though I did not mention this.

'But Ella's been here for twenty-five years,' Lavender wailed. 'She knows the boundaries. What came over her? What was in her mind? What do I do now?'

I did not discover what she did, for I left the next day for Savannah, the town in America I would most like to live, and then travelled on up through Virginia. From New York I boarded a Dutch boat for an uncomfortable, but not uneventful, journey home. There was a small, stocky, ersatz cowboy among the passengers who was out to cause trouble. He was threatening. People avoided him. On the second day at sea he held up dozens of passengers in the bar, waving his gun straight at us. Luckily a couple of Dutch waiters managed to throw him to the ground, relieve him of his gun and escort him in handcuffs to the ship's prison.

When we docked at Southampton, I checked the state of my finances: 55 cents. Still, I had just made it without calling upon parental help. It had been a wonderful six months and I had grown to love America. In my suitcase were three short articles I had managed to get published in small-town news-papers (a visit from an English girl, in those days, was a rare event of great interest, so editors were eager for a foreign correspondent, no matter how juvenile, to write for them). I was now a published writer, I could claim to editors who would soon be hearing from me, and I could boast that, at last, I had snared a measure of that elusive thing – *experience*.

9

Work

I soon discovered there were very few employers who are prepared to give an eager but unqualified jobseeker a chance. Well, the risk is high. Not many bosses were prepared to take it. But a few did exist – possibly some still do. I was lucky enough to find just two men happy to take me on. The first was Jocelyn Stevens, and to him I remain eternally grateful.

It was 1959. Jocelyn had just bought *The Queen* magazine and was in the process of overhauling it in a radical way, changing its name simply to *Queen* in the process. There had been much publicity, and many renowned writers, photographers and fashion people were queuing up to be part of an exciting new publishing venture. Just the place I'd love to be, I thought. But how to go about it?

I wrote Jocelyn one of my enthusiastic letters, declaring my overwhelming desire to write, but also to do *anything* so long as I could join the staff. No reply. Several weeks of despair. Then I discovered we were both going to be at some party. I armed myself with yet another *billet d'enthousiasme*, adding that I had been published in America. I slipped it into his dinner-jacket pocket. As he whirled round the dance floor – he wasn't much of a whirler – I heard him say the magic words: 'Ring me.'

A meeting was arranged. In the cramped offices in Covent Garden, Jocelyn roared about, exuding his famous charm. He was the kind of blond handsome that is observable from fifty yards: he was noisy, energetic, full of ideas, and determined to make *Queen* the most sought-after magazine of a completely new kind. With palpable enthusiasm he explained many of his ideas. I was amazed how long he kept me, considering I was but a young aspirer who had trapped him at a party.

'Published in America?' he said, eventually. 'The *New York Times*?'

'Not quite. But published, I promise.'

'How old are you?'

'Twenty-one.'

'You can have a job as a secretary.'

'Thank you,' I said. 'But I don't want to be a secretary. Once a secretary it's hard to be switched to something else. I want to write.'

He contemplated this bold ambition. Then gave a gust of friendly laughter.

'All right, then. You can do some of the rewriting. A lot of our contributors know about their subject but they aren't writers. Start on Monday – ten pounds a week. OK?'

Beatrix Miller, the editor, headed a team of diverse and lively talent. There was Mark Boxer, art editor, Francis Wyndham, literary editor, Annie Trehearne, fashion editor, and Quentin Crewe – title-less, but hired to be a General

Inspiration and Purveyor of Ideas, and to write major articles such as a definition of The Establishment, which caused a huge reaction. My immediate boss was the attractive and sparky Drusilla Beyfus.

And my first job was indeed rewriting. Many an evening I stayed late trying to put some life into Stirling Moss's car reports, the beauty editor's deadly articles and the cookery writer's turgid prose. In turn, Beatrix made great efforts to teach me how to be a journalist. Not a comma nor a semi-colon went unjudged, discussed, deleted or improved. When it came to the time that I was allowed to write some minor story myself, my own first draft, nervously wavered on to her desk, was covered with crossings-out, and snappy comments cluttered the margin. The first reporting story I was given was to interview David Attenborough about his goldfish. Even then he was famous, but the trepidation I felt was due to my lack of knowledge about goldfish. I nervously asked him a few feeble questions, worried about writing every word in my notebook – having spurned the idea of secretarial work, I had not learnt shorthand.

'Would it be helpful,' he asked ten minutes into the interview, 'if I asked the questions myself?'

The result was two hundred and fifty words of pure, wonderful Attenborough, on which I was congratulated by Beatrix, and somehow it was too late to confess how the excellent interview had come about. I became, of course, a lifelong fan of Sir David.

Then I was asked to go and report a wedding in Scotland – not a happy prospect. I had no wish to be a journalist at a wedding. It turned out it was the wedding of Tim Renton, my old dancing partner, and his constant love Alice Fergusson, to which I had been invited anyhow. The fact that so many friends would be there made it both better and, in some respects, worse. It was a strange feeling, officially observing, taking in every detail, trying to think of illuminating phrases. I told no one of my job, and enjoyed the day.

Back at the office I wrote the two hundred and fifty required words – the piece was to be mostly photographs – and took it to Beatrix. She was busy. 'Ask Q to take a look at it,' she said.

Q was Quentin Crewe: both loved, and somewhat feared, for his sharp tongue. He was diagnosed with muscular dystrophy at the age of six, but always chose to dismiss it. The doctor he was taken to as a child told Q in a cheery voice that he would be walking normally by the time he was sixteen. This was contrary to the advice he gave to his mother. 'Your son will be dead at sixteen,' he assured her. Q succumbed to a walking stick both at Eton and Cambridge, but still would insist on dancing (barefoot and precariously) at parties, and only took occasionally to a wheelchair in 1956, when he lived in Japan for a year with his first wife. By the time I met him at *Queen*, he was in a wheelchair all the time, though he did manage to walk a few steps, occasionally, and was used to falling down.

He was a handsome man, though not in the conventional sense: heavy-lidded eyes, a sharp nose and the most captivating, winning smile. He had a beautiful voice, exquisite handwriting, an acerbic sense both of humour and of language, and gave absolutely no sense of being a 'cripple', as he called himself. He hated all euphemisms for disablement, and would never use them. When I went to his office with my report on the Renton wedding that day, I was both nervous and intrigued. I very much wanted him to think that what I had written was fine, because as a brilliant writer himself his opinion would mean much to me. He gave me a quick, friendly glance, took the copy. His pen began to hover over it. A single smile followed.

'I think there's probably some hope of your being a writer,' he said, handing back my copy a few moments later. It was lacerated with red underlinings, crossings-outs, changes, and notes in the margin. Dispirited, I took it away, studied it. I saw at once just why it was now so much better than my original, and how in future it was the kind of reporting I should aim for. So my immediate feeling about Q was gratitude for such a precise, helpful lesson.

There was a high sense of fun, working for *Queen*: constant laughter, a good many rows and disagreements, the feeling that everyone was bursting with ideas. And if even a junior, such as myself, came up with a good idea, they were allowed to give it a try. I wanted very much to do long interviews with half a dozen people whose jobs were very boring – get them to describe what went through their minds as the slow hours of each day chugged by, and photograph them. (By now I was allowed to take pictures for the stories I had suggested, which saved Jocelyn money.) But my boss Drusilla Beyfus was doubtful about my idea. Would a lot of factory workers describing their eventless days fit in with the high-powered, smart, glossy, fashionable content of the new magazine? It was Jocelyn who was adamant.

'Fantastic!' he roared. 'Go and *do it.*'

I spent two weeks in grim northern factories talking to stalwart, stoical women who spent eight hours a day watching torrents of chocolates rolling past them, alert to the slightest imperfection and, even more dizzy-making, other women who were paid a pittance to watch thousands of cigarettes streaming by. I returned to London full of self-reproach: why should I be so lucky as to have a privileged background, a comfortable life, an exciting job, while so many would never be able to acquire these things? I returned in a subdued mood and took a long time to write the article. It was spread, with my photographs, over some six pages. That was both surprising and cheering. It also encouraged me to keep on photographing. Apart from the enjoyment of it, it brought in a much-needed addition to my earnings.

Just as I was never a real painter, I was technically never a good photographer, though my art training was a help in composition. But I was good enough to get an agent and my photographs were published. I never quite managed to understand about settings and speeds, and this failing caused some embarrassing moments. There was the incident involving Churchill's first great-grandson: every newspaper wanted a picture of the baby, and as I knew his mother Edwina, she asked me to take it. I went round to the nursing home where she had given birth, accompanied only by my small Rolleiflex camera. I snapped away, aware it was rather dark, and gave the film to a messenger waiting downstairs on a motorbike.

Home, there was an instant call.

'None of them has come out,' said the kindly man who ran the agency, and who treated me as a rather unusual sort of client, 'and there's a deadline. Could you hurry back to Edwina and I'll send someone round with lights ...'

Which he did, and I took several more rolls of film, knowing the lighting was perfect and they would come out. Next morning, they were all over the papers.

Although I often photographed friends and their children, what I most liked to capture was life far from my own: the very poor parts of Naples, washing strung across the streets, ragged children, skeletal old men. I would go to Bermondsey, where Richard Carr-Gomm, a friend, had begun the Abbeyfield Society, housing the impoverished poor. There, sad old men in bleak rooms played away the days on their mouth organs, or smoked, while telling me of their better youth. These were my best photographs, but difficult to sell. What was wanted, just as it is now, were pictures of celebrities. One summer, Peter Sellers invited Q and me on holiday in Ischia. His wife, Britt Ekland, had a part in a film that was being made there: I think Peter wanted the company of non-film friends while she was on the set. I photographed nonstop for a week: Peter and Britt were not averse to publicity. And my agent did a wonderful selling job. Ten years later I was still receiving cheques from all over the place – a great boost to the precarious finances.

I had not been at *Queen* for long when Jocelyn summoned me to his office, where he did his usual roaring and pacing, to tell me about the promotion he proposed.

'Thought you could be travel editor,' he said, stomping to the window, out of which he had once flung a typewriter in a rage. I knew this was meant to be a piece of good news, but as one who was never a keen traveller, I was not entirely enthralled. I asked what it meant I had to do.

'It means you can go anywhere in the world you like,' he said, 'so long as I don't have to pay for it. Ring up the airlines.'

I began with Middle East Airlines, said I wanted to go to Beirut. In fact, I had never thought about any such thing. I was not a natural traveller who dreamt of visiting far-off places. Beirut was just the first name that came to mind. No problem, said the man at MEA – a phrase which meant more then than it does today. They would arrange a first-class flight for me, and put me up at the best hotel for as many days as I wanted. I was impressed, but nervous. What on earth was I to do alone in Beirut, knowing no one? Luckily, Q had a friend, Geoffrey Keating, who was the head PR man for BP. He knew what he called 'everyone', everywhere – indeed everyone seemed to know him, not always the case in such a boast. But contacts were both his work and his lifeblood. He would have benefited from today's methods of storing information. For him, it was boxes and boxes of small cards with vital names, addresses and numbers. He was a kindly and a genial man; he so often became a proper friend to some of his 'contacts', and always seemed willing to help, even though he asked for no payment unless it was a business arrangement.

Geoffrey had a talent for thinking up amusements for visiting VIPs whom BP wanted to impress. When the King of Jordan came to London for a three-day visit, Geoffrey discovered there was nothing in his schedule but official meetings. He immediately started to telephone friends to ask if they would mind giving a party one night *this week* for the king. None of them did mind. None of them said it was impossible at such short notice. It was extraordinary how many famous people were free to attend amazing parties three nights running: one given by Chips Channon in his house in Belgrave Square, one by Lord Bessborough, and one by another illustrious host whose name I have forgotten, at The Dorchester. The king was delighted. Geoffrey was delighted, BP was delighted.

Sometimes it occurred to Geoffrey that so-and-so would like to meet so-and-so, no particular reason. One day, he rang me to say he had arranged a small lunch for Paul Getty and thought he and I might 'get on', despite some fifty years and many millions between us. Intrigued, I accepted this rather weird invitation, and agreed to pick Getty up at Claridge's and drive him to the restaurant.

I had been given a lilac and white Triumph Herald for my twenty-first birthday: not a large or solid car, but – to my mind – glamorous. I was not an experienced driver, and wondered vaguely, should there be an accident, if my insurance would cover damages for the richest man in the world.

Paul Getty was waiting on the pavement, one hand on the doorman's arm. His lugubrious face went from rigid to frozen when he realised he was to be transported in my frivolous car. There was some difficulty about him getting into the small lilac front seat, but he remained politely silent. Such was my concentration, and his natural taciturnity, we spoke not a word all the way to the restaurant, where another doorman had been primed to heave him out of the car. I sat next to him at lunch – again, scarcely a word passed between us, and as soon as the coffee was ordered, he slipped away with never a mention of contributing to the bill. Geoffrey's face fell. He was a great tryer, Geoffrey, but never seemed to realise that sometimes his introductions were inappropriate. (Years later, I found myself seated next to Getty again. Up against the usual silence and lack of response, I eventually turned on him. 'Are you always so boring?' I asked. He perked up. 'Not always,' he said, and became, by his standards, quite lively.)

Occasionally, Geoffrey misjudged the benefits of bringing people together. Once he rang at 9.30 p.m. to say an American millionaire had just flown in, was having dinner at Claridge's, and would be glad of company. The wretched man was exhausted, longed to go to bed. Politeness forced him to have a long supper with two or three English people he did not know, did not want to know, and would never see again. But Geoffrey, always keen to organise unlikely mingling, was never aware of others' fatigue, or simple reluctance.

He was the perfect person to approach about 'contacts' in Beirut, and as always he was helpful. Immediately he rang some millionaire businessman (he knew few people, anywhere, who weren't millionaires), who was apparently 'delighted' to put his Mercedes and chauffeur at my disposal. (What had Geoffrey said, I wondered?) A visit to Madame Sursok, famous for her money and her horses, was arranged in her palace, and there was a racehorse owner evidently keen to show me his horses.

It was an extraordinary week. I had breakfast with rose-petal jam every morning in my very grand suite, which seemed to be made of beaten gold. I pondered on the turn of events: so recently on a Greyhound bus, penniless, jobless; now, in a job in which I could go anywhere I liked in the world … in return for nothing more than a friendly article.

The owner of the Mercedes, a hefty, smiling man of no great attraction, decided he would take a few days off (from what job, I never discovered) and accompany me around Beirut. He was courteous, polite. It never occurred to me he had anything further in mind than to be helpful to his old acquaintance Geoffrey's young friend. At the Sursok Palace, where I was able to interview the legendary octogenarian who owned it, guests lay on their sides by pools cut into the marble floors, and threw rose petals into the water. Somehow the scene brought to mind Frankie Howerd in all those toga television sketches, but I kept a straight face. There was a certain amount of sightseeing, whizzed from place to place in the Mercedes. My host seemed to know interesting things about passing camels, but very little about buildings. So there was not much exploring of ancient sites.

On my last day, the plan was to visit the racing stables that belonged to a friend of Mr Mercedes. There was a vast, white-sanded stable yard, palm trees, glossily painted stables. Dazzling horses pranced under their hand-sewn rugs, rearing up against the sun that chequered their brilliant coats. My host was under the impression I was keen to photograph his horses – which I was. One or two. Each one was brought out, made by its tiny groom to stand just so, as if to please a judge, while I clicked my Rolleiflex. Once I had captured seven horses, I explained that was fine. I had got all I wanted. But I failed to make myself understood.

'That is absolutely no bother,' smiled Mr Mercedes. 'You must photograph all the horses.' There was nothing I could do but carry on. By the end of the afternoon I had recorded 156 ...

I had rather hoped that this, the last night, I could be alone in my suite. But no: the invitation was to dinner in Mr Mercedes' flat.

It was huge, grand, intimidating. Footmen in white gloves glided about, balancing trays of skinny glasses of different champagnes. We ate in a dining room overlooking the city. Again, I thought it all so very odd: a junior travel writer being entertained in this extravagant manner.

Delicious food; Turkish coffee. Once that had been poured, Mr Mercedes indicated to the three footmen that their work was over. They slipped away.

'Now,' said Mr M, in a soft, new voice. 'I have a little surprise for you.'

He pressed a button. The huge, mahogany doors slid open. Then, *the entire wall* disappeared – I did not see where to. There, before us, was an elaborate, gilded bedroom, its bed large enough for a football team to romp upon.

I leapt up, shakily.

'I don't think you understand,' I said.

'Oh, I do,' he sneered, moving round the table towards me. 'I give you a good time. You English girls …'

I fled. Ignored the Mercedes waiting downstairs, took a taxi back to the hotel and taxi to the airport the next day. I was keen to tell my side of the story to Geoffrey first – a story which I had not expected, and did not feature in my article.

Once I was working on *Queen*, my life seemed even more removed from Charlie's. He knew none of the writers and photographers I now spent time with, and he was not particularly interested in the magazine world. One evening I braced myself to tell him that he and I had to come to an end. He took it in a dignified manner, and gave me a beautiful gold bracelet, which had cost him, I guessed, at least a month's wages.

Then, just two weeks later, I behaved outrageously.

My lilac and white car was parked in Jermyn Street. On my way to fetch it, I saw Charlie dart out of a restaurant where he often ate. He told me he had seen a parking meter attendant approach, so had dashed out and put more money in the meter. Overwhelmed with gratitude, I agreed to join him for coffee. He suggested we did not entirely stop doing things together and, prompted by another surge of deliquescent gratitude out of all proportion to Charlie's kind act, I agreed. This period of seeing each other again did not last long: there was too much against it, though Charlie remained as charming as ever. There had to be another ending. Again, he behaved beautifully, and I have never quite shaken off the shame of my bad behaviour.

Queen magazine, now thriving, moved offices from Covent Garden to Fetter Lane. They were bigger, but still not big enough. The managing director apologetically explained that as there was no room for me on the editorial floor, I would have to have a desk in Quentin's large office.

Q, apart from writing major articles for *Queen*, was also putting together a history of the magazine. He had two extraordinary helpers: Auberon Waugh, and the beautiful, brilliant Judy Innes who, at Cambridge, had inspired Andrew Sinclair's novel *The Breaking of Bumbo*. The banter and the jokes between the three of them enlivened every day. I would listen, join the laughter and, as a travel editor still not keen on travel, carry on ringing airlines whose planes flew not too far from home. I apologised to Q for being thrust upon him, as it were, but he did not seem to mind. Most days he insisted on sending out for smoked salmon sandwiches for lunch, and telling me about the divorce from his wife Martha.

He invited me to go with him one weekend to stay with his brother Colin, who was married to Sally Churchill, previously one of the naughtiest girls in the school at Lawnside. It was a glorious weekend. The two brothers sparked each other to great heights of wit and humour.

Very shortly after that, both at our desks in the office one afternoon, he asked me to marry him.

'Give me a few moments to think about it,' I said, in something of a dither. By now I was without doubt devoted to Q, but had not thought of marriage. I remembered my decision, in 1958, never to contemplate marrying anyone unless they were in possession of all the qualities I loved in Mickey Butterwick when I was sixteen. Q was certainly that man. I loved his company, his humour, his courage, his sharp and questing mind, his dotty generosity. I loved him completely, though had never had that conversation with myself. As for his being lame – it did not occur to me that this was the slightest impediment to a happy life if you loved someone enough.

I went out into the corridor. Mark Boxer was running down the stairs.

'What are you doing?' he asked, for I suppose I looked serious.

'Trying to decide whether or not to marry Q,' I said. He gave an uproarious laugh and said he guessed what the answer would be.

I gave myself just time to reflect that all the things I had been so moved by in Mickey Butterwick were to be found in Q, plus many more. I hurried back into the office and accepted.

In a trice we were off to Collingwood's to find an aquamarine ring, and to make plans.

First hurdle: my parents. Quentin was thirteen years older than me, divorced and with two young children. He would never recover from muscular dystrophy, only get worse. How would I manage with a man in a wheelchair? And what were his *prospects?* my mother would be bound to ask, meaning financial.

It turned out not to be a hurdle at all – Q effortlessly enchanted both parents. There was no hesitation, no apparent doubts. But my mother insisted he had a 'talk' to my father – not to ask for my hand, as we were already engaged, but just, well ...

Q and my father sat at the dining-room table one night, easing themselves into the odd encounter with a certain amount of whisky.

'I'm not sure what I'm meant to be asking,' my father apparently said, confused by his role of future father-in-law.

'I expect it's about money,' said Q, helping him out. 'Have to say I haven't got much, and probably never will have.'

'Same here,' said my father, and that was the end of the official conversation. My mother was disappointed there was not more to report, but satisfied the exchange had taken place.

Travel editor was not a demanding job, and I did not work at it with any great enthusiasm. Luckily, I was also allowed to do other articles of a more rewarding kind. For instance, I was sent to interview four 'up-and-coming young men', who were about to put on a show called *Beyond the Fringe*. For some mysterious reason, the photographer decided the interview should take place on a traffic island in Piccadilly. It was almost impossible to hear either questions or answers against the roar of the traffic, but it was plain the four young men were some of the funniest and most original ever. I kept in touch with Peter and Dud and, years later, when they were in New York for a run of *Beyond the Fringe*, I saw them regularly.

At about this time, the regular *Queen* restaurant critic fell ill and was unable to visit some restaurant: the copy date was only hours away. Could you do it? Jocelyn asked Q, who knew little about food but could write about anything. He came back with the most hilarious article ever written about a restaurant and was immediately made into the regular critic. He changed the nature of the job for ever. Others were quick to copy, but no one ever matched his original humour and piercing observation. His criticism was often lacerating, but restaurant owners loved it and did everything they could to persuade him to come and be rude about their establishments. He was constantly offered free food, but never accepted.

It was plain that now we were engaged Q and I could not go on working for the same magazine, let alone in the same office. It was also plain Q should be the one to stay: he had the major job, I had the minor one.

Q had a journalist friend, Derek Monsey, who one day was looking at some of my photographs. Without asking my permission, he took them away but left no message as to where they had gone.

I then had a call from Charles Wintour, editor of the *Evening Standard*. 'I've been talking to Derek Monsey,' he said. 'Would you consider choosing five good-looking men, writing a few hundred words about each one and photographing them?'

Payment: £100. Flabbergasted, flattered, I accepted at once, not imagining that would be difficult.

But, surprisingly, it was. All the obvious men I approached turned down the idea, horrified they should be considered good looking. I ended up with one old politician, a couple of minor actors and a man who wrote saying he had heard about the forthcoming article and would 'like to offer himself up'. The series was advertised on the top of all the *Evening Standard* vans. I felt briefly rich. Perhaps, I thought, encouraged, I should try to get a job in tougher journalism than that offered by *Queen*. And, not a week after the Good-Looking Men appeared, I was summoned to an interview with John Junor, notorious editor of the *Sunday Express*.

It seemed the writer of the Woman's Page had taken a year off, and a replacement was needed. Would I be interested? All I had to do was to fill a page a week with women's stuff – not my idea of exhilarating, but obviously I could not turn down a job that paid £25 a week. It also solved the problem of Q and I not working for the same proprietor.

It was a strange year that I spent in Fleet Street – not enjoyable, although there were some friendly people on the paper. The kindest, to a young novice like me, was Susan Barnes, a particularly good writer, who later married the Labour Party politician, Tony Crosland. I would arrive every morning, pass through the main room where the clatter of dozens of typewriters was a kind of constant music, and go into my own, large office. I had a secretary, several telephones and a huge desk. I would sit down and wonder what to do, how to fill a page by Friday. I was allowed to include several paragraphs about non-fashion stuff, interviews and so on, and that I enjoyed. What I hated was scouting about for fashionable clothes, and all the palaver of getting them photographed. But I soon found a way round this. John Junor – he confided to me with the utmost delicacy – had some favourite models. As long as I arranged to have a weekly photograph of one of them, preferably in a nightdress, that would fill up a large part of the page.

Every Friday afternoon I was summoned to his office to go through my copy. What made him cross was that I absolutely refused to write about my friends, those who he snobbishly considered would 'be of interest'. Often he lost his temper, shouting insults while sweat poured down his scarlet face. But I remembered advice from Anne Scott-James, who had had a page on the paper before my time.

'No matter how angry he gets,' she said, 'never cry. He despises women who cry.'

So I never cried, and in fact was not tempted to do so. And most Saturday mornings I received a large bunch of flowers, chosen by his secretary, with an apologetic note. One Friday, just three weeks after I had started working there, I found John in an unusually benign mood. 'I'm going to give you a rise,' he said. 'Thirty-five pounds a week.' I was suddenly a millionaire, at twenty-two. No matter how much I disliked the job, I realised I would have to stick it out for a while.

I learnt some odd lessons: most crucially, about expenses. One week I put in a receipt for the 17*s* 6*d* I had spent on a taxi. I was summoned by a features editor, apoplectic with rage.

'Don't you realise you're making fools of us all?' he yelled. 'Never, ever put in for such a paltry amount again, even if it was what you actually spent. The unspoken rule here is that we all add to our actual spending what we have to pay in tax … I don't want to speak about this ever again.' For a moment I contemplated suggesting this method was horribly dishonest, but another outraged glance from him and I abandoned the plan. Much of my time at the *Sunday Express* was spent trying to make up expenses. Later, I found myself having to do the same thing at the BBC.

My job at the *Sunday Express* became less and less appealing. When the real writer of the page returned, John Junor offered to keep me on. But no: it was my chance to escape. And by now I was beginning to think that television would be a good alternative.

It was the time when new television companies were starting up, and hundreds of young hopefuls, mostly with no experience at all in front of the cameras, were trying to get jobs. But it was very difficult to be fairly judged, due to the nature of the auditions. I must have gone to dozens of these: the pattern was always the same. Long train journey, a crowd of us ushered into a studio. One by one we would be asked to stand in front of a camera, and an electrician would ask two questions: What's your name, and where do you live? Hard to make your mark answering them.

But by now I had an agent, Diana Crawford – a friend from 1956 – who had two major first clients: David Frost and Bamber Gascoigne (later host of *University Challenge*). She was widely known as the best agent ever, brilliant at coaxing large sums of money from tough employers like the Grade Brothers. Also, unlike these days, when agencies are divided into different departments for television, books, plays and film, Diana managed the lot. It was an act of extreme friendship to take me on, as I had nothing to offer: I had merely ground out a page on a Sunday newspaper for a year after leaving *Queen*.

Diana did not succeed in getting me a job making documentaries, my goal, but managed to get me on to some popular light entertainment programmes. My first appearance on *Juke Box Jury* was a disaster. The Everly Brothers were being discussed, and somehow I had never heard of them. David Jacobs, the chairman, was so infuriated by this ignorance that he shut me in a hospitality room when the recording was over, and subjected me to his extreme contempt. Diana also got me on to *Call My Bluff.* Colour television had just got into its stride, but precautions were still being taken. We had to put Max Factor foundation between our fingers lest, if we gestured with a hand, the whiteness of the inner finger be shown. It was an entertaining programme to be on, with writers and raconteurs Frank Muir and Denis Norden being very witty, and I was allowed to replace the definitions of words that researchers provided with my own.

But still no offer of a job in television came. Desperately needing to earn some money, I did some freelance articles for various national papers, but with reluctance. By now it had occurred to me that I might be more successful *writing* for television. I wrote fifteen half-hour plays, always bearing in mind that expense was an issue, and to have only two or three characters and one set was an asset. Diana did her best. She sent scripts all over the place. Response, in those days, was quicker than it is now, but not exactly fast. There had been several encouraging notes when the scripts were returned, but they were always 'not quite the thing we are looking for'. Just as I'd more or less given up, and was trying to think of something else to do, I was called upon by a man at The Stables at Granada Television.

'I'm not interested in doing any of the plays you've written so far,' he said, 'but I'd like to commission another one.'

So my sixteenth play, *Special Co-respondent,* went into production. The thrill of seeing your own words given life by actors was as extraordinary as I had always thought it might be. The play was about a man who, unable to find a co-respondent in his divorce (a necessity then in cases of adultery), persuaded his wife to play the part. Maureen Lipman was the star: it was her first television play, too.

Somehow the timing of the play went a little awry when it was being recorded. It was several minutes too short. I was not asked to add another page or two. Instead, the decision was made to play it at a slow pace. I remember trying not to giggle when the obliging actor playing the husband, opening a bottle of wine, pulled out the cork more slowly than any cork has ever been extracted from a bottle. Luckily the play was put out too late for any but insomniacs to watch it, and I never met a single person outside my loyal family who did in fact see it.

But it was a shard of ice broken and, as I was to learn, as soon as something has been produced somewhere, however bad, it is easier to get commissioned to do something else.

Quentin and I were married in August 1961. I wore a white satin dress I designed myself, and had made by a dressmaker called Gina Fratini, who later became a famous designer. There was a small ceremony in a register office, and what was meant to be a blessing at St Bride's, Fleet Street, the following day. But the delightful old vicar became a little confused. He had fortified himself with several glasses of sherry, and seen that I had entered the church in a white dress. Wedding, he thought, and gave us the whole floribunda of matrimony according to the prayer book, thereby delighting everyone.

Quentin, in 1961, rarely left his wheelchair. He said many times he was determined to walk down the aisle, but I doubted he could manage that. I was expecting to find him in his chair.

Instead, at the end of a very long aisle, he was standing, very upright and tilted slightly backwards, at the altar. He had one hand on the shoulder of his best man, who was used to helping him – Jim Douglas-Henry, the TV reporter who was married to the novelist Elizabeth Jane Howard. Q stood, unflinching, throughout the service, then loped down the beautiful aisle, hand always on Jim's shoulder. Next challenge: out along the path to Fleet Street, and into the car to go to the reception. It was a nerve-racking journey, and nobody thought he would ever make it. But he never faltered. It was the last time he ever walked for more than a few yards.

10

Synaesthesia

In the early 1960s, soon after we married, on holiday in Italy we ran into a journalist friend of Q's, Julian Holland. Talk turned to Vladimir Nabokov. Julian was intrigued by the writer's weird ability to see abstract things in colour.

'But I've always done that,' I said. 'It isn't at all weird.'

'Nonsense,' scoffed Julian. 'It's a very rare condition. It's called synaesthesia. The only person I know of who had it is Nabokov. And he was a genius,' he added with a sharp look. I agreed I wasn't in Nabokov's class, but insisted I was telling the truth. 'I'll test you,' he said.

He wrote down all the colours I have always seen for days of the week, months of the year and some numbers. To be precise, Monday is a cloudy pink, Tuesday a deeper pink, Wednesday mulberry red, Thursday dark blue, Friday yellow, Saturday May green, Sunday stainless steel. February, incidentally, is the same as Sunday, September the same as Tuesday, while the figure eight and August are of the same blue as Thursday. A year later he produced his notes, questioned me again and was astonished I got 100 per cent right. Of course I did. The colours had been with me for as long as I could remember. Reluctantly, Julian admitted I must be a synaesthete and wrote an article declaring there were now two people 'suffering from this incomprehensible condition'. I recall no interest or response to this major discovery, and I thought no more about it for fifty years when, having been asked to give a series of lectures on the *Queen Mary 2* ocean liner, it occurred to me that synaesthesia – by then being researched in various universities – might be an intriguing subject. I talked about the idea to my former sister-in-law, Sally Ashburton, and happened to mention the red of my Wednesday.

'Red?' she shrieked. 'Wednesday is *blue*! Always has been.'

This was the first time Sally and I, who had talked our way through so many years, discovered we were both synaesthetes of the same kind. Why had neither of us mentioned it before? 'I thought everybody saw abstract things in colour,' she said. 'Too obvious to mention.' I had thought the same.

It's no wonder that synaesthesia has been called The Strangest Thing, for it's a psychological and neurological state concerning the visual and auditory areas of the brain. The vast majority of people have five senses: sight, touch, hearing, taste, smell. For synaesthetes there is a mingling, an overlapping of some senses – two or more combined. *Aesthesis* comes from the Greek word meaning sensation, and *syn* means together, or union. For synaesthetes this union means that either one of the senses, at the sight or the hearing of a letter or a number, produces a colour in their minds. For some people it's abstract things that conjure these colours, for instance my days of the week. Those of us with this particular form of synaesthesia are considered more rare than those who only see coloured numbers and letters. More rare still are those for whom taste, smell and music produce colours.

Interest in this condition, as it is called, began in the 1880s. The phenomenon never made it into neuroscience, but research continued up till the 1920s. There were complicated theories about what in the brain caused synaesthesia, way beyond my understanding. But there was one thing on which several researchers did agree, and I found amusing: the test cases all turned out to be 'persons who are unsparingly critical'. That caused a jolt, for I know that one of my great failings is to be unsparingly critical. A couple more interesting things came up in those early researches: synaesthetes were nearly always women and nearly always concerned with some sort of creativity – artists, musicians, writers, whatever. In fact, it's been discovered that it is seven times more common among *them* than in non-creative people. I have not found this backed up by authors of books I've read on synaesthesia, in which only examples of unknown women synaesthetes are given. The famous synaesthetes they listed were all men, including the poet Rimbaud, composer and pianist Alexander Scriabin, artist Wassily Kandinsky, Nabokov, and the composer Olivier Messiaen, who once described the piano part in one of his compositions as 'the gentle cascade of blue-orange chords'. Baudelaire was another synaesthete, and he described the state in a verse in one of his poems. It's better in French than in English, but it still conveys the sensation:

Synaesthesia

Like long echoes, which from a distance mingle
Into a shadowy and deep unity as vast as night and light –
Perfumes, colours and sounds reply to one another.

I doubt any scientific explanation could improve on that.

In those early days of research it was generally believed that only one in 250,000 people were synaesthetes, but for some reason, after the 1920s, research withered away and pretty well died for fifty years. In the 1980s, inexplicably, interest in the arcane subject was reborn among neuropsychologists and other scientists. Research started up again and was conducted in a much more sophisticated way. Learned books were written, research projects were – and still are – being carried out in universities. A new figure of 'sufferers' was suggested: one in 25,000. By the 1990s the whole nebulous subject had become almost fashionable – and you can understand why. Making TV programmes about people who talk about seeing blue when they hear Beethoven, or seeing green when they smell frying sausages, produce good viewing figures. Room for humour there, not to mention awe, wonder, and of course an element of disbelief. And by now the reckoned number of synaesthetes had changed again: one in 2,000.

Most of the books on synaesthesia are too complicated for the layman: the exception, I found, is by John Harrison, senior neurologist and research fellow at Cambridge. The thing that most intrigued me about his fascinating insights was his confession that, having studied the subject for so long, he can *imagine* it, but can't *know* what it's like. This is understandable because – no matter how articulate and vivid a synaesthete may be – it's near impossible to describe. The reason for this is perhaps because the colours are – to me – obfuscated by what I can only call *cloud*. I have tried to be precise, dozens of times. I've tried to describe my colours by explaining they are a bit like a tongue-and-groove fence that stretches across my mind, and each plank of wood is a different colour. But the colours are not like samples from a Dulux catalogue. They're not clear, but misted, as the skin of a dark grape is sometimes misted. The colours could never be reproduced in real life – though I do find some of the Dutch grape-painters get pretty close to my Thursday.

And, for me, how do the colours work? Could we meet on Monday? someone asks. The very thought of Monday instantly triggers the dusky pink panel in my mind. What I have never understood is if you don't have synaesthesia, how *do* you think of Monday? I often ask people. 'I imagine a page in my diary' is a common answer. But most say they don't think of anything. That is something I cannot imagine: not visualising anything when you imagine something abstract. Surely you would feel ungrounded, lost. What a peculiar state seeing nothing must be: to me, it seems mystifying, inexplicable.

Among contemporary researchers is an idea that synaesthesia is inherited, genetic. (Both Nabokov's parents were synaesthetes.) Not so in my case – though I can't be sure because it was a subject I never thought of discussing, assuming as I did that it was as much a part of everyone as an arm or a leg. My father was a man of vivid imagination; my mother had none at all – apart from her ability to imagine parties she was planning to give. They are both dead, now, and I wish I had asked them. My guess is that my mother would have thought I was off my head, while my father would have understood and would have been intrigued.

The fact that synaesthesia has become a more common subject of conversation means insights about people one thought one knew often surprise. And it often produces funny, surreal dialogue, such as the argument between Sally Ashburton and me as we disputed the reds and blues of Wednesday and Thursday (my blue).

Professor Vilayanur Ramachandran, the distinguished Director of the Center for Brain and Cognition, and Professor of Biology and Neuroscience at the University of California, who gave one of his Reith Lectures on synaesthesia a few years ago, admitted that when research recommenced again a few years later, one of the possibilities seriously considered was that all synaesthetes were crazy. Or were on drugs. I disagree totally with these theories, as does Professor Ramachandran. No, we're not crazy. But like any minority whose condition is hard to understand, doubts arise about whether it exists at all.

Contemporary researchers have rather naturally come up with the idea that maybe synaesthetes have merely got particularly good memories, and giving colours to the alphabet and so on is just some kind of party trick. To prove the sceptics' point, tests were carried out: the synaesthetes' colours for numbers and letters were given to a group of non-synaesthetes who were invited to remember them. They did quite well – got 37 per cent right. The synaesthetes themselves, of course, got 100 per cent.

It was only quite recently that I began to reflect on what effect synaesthesia has had on my own life and work. This was prompted by a reviewer of my novel *Land Girls* who said, 'She writes like someone who has synaesthesia.' What did that mean, I wondered? Was it a compliment or a criticism? I still haven't decided.

The nature and effects of colour have always been part of my being. From a very early age I had my distinct preferences and dislikes. I remember that my mother's choice of ubiquitous eau-de-nil walls instilled in me a strange gloom. They had a dispiriting effect that I failed to understand. In contrast, the yellow nursery exuded warmth and safety. This lifelong sensitivity to colour has its advantages, but also its drawbacks: there are many colours, mixed chemically with no reference to nature, that literally hurt my eyes. I recall having a conversation about marigolds with my father. I said their brightness hurt my eyes and made me feel rather sick. I was not more than five. Even now the variations on yellow and orange flowers glaring in municipal roundabouts induce in me the same queasiness. Barclays Bank used to employ a particularly harsh turquoise. I could not look at it. And for decades I've raged round Marks & Spencer and other shops whose colours – especially at bathing-suit time – seem to be designed to offend their customers. These colours never appear to change over the years: blistering lime green, pinks that are ghastly, hopeless imitations of Schiaparelli, reds that are simply variations on tomato ketchup. But I admit that when I make such observations, most people don't seem to understand what I'm talking about. Perhaps the majority of the population doesn't perceive colours as vividly and in such nuances as we did at the Beux-Artes, during Monieur Souverbie's classes, and is simply not affected by colour: it gives neither profound pleasure nor acute pain.

When it comes to writing, I'm certainly not conscious of 'writing like a synaesthete', though one of my firm beliefs about writing is that the author should constantly be painting pictures – vivid pictures – in the reader's mind. There should not be a page without a picture that you can see completely clearly. To achieve this is no easy matter. It calls for acute observation, accuracy, precision, and it's particularly important – to me, anyway – when it comes to colour.

I find myself frustrated when authors are careless in this respect – all those who mention blue sky, for instance. What kind of blue do they want us to imagine? Postcard blue? Estate agents' brochure blue? That weird thing called baby blue? There are a thousand different blues: I want to know exactly which one the writer has in mind. A green dress – what kind of green does the author want us to see? I want the exact picture again. 'Lovely' green won't do, because the writer's lovely green might not be mine, and it's his I'm after. Admittedly, to describe a colour so that it instantly leaps into a reader's mind is not easy – almost as difficult as describing music in an attempt to convey the sound. But it can be done if you choose a description which can be recognised very clearly. I never use apple green because there are hundreds of different green apples. I've used chive green, because chives are a regular, unchanging green. Everyone can picture them. As for blue: bluebell is a safe bet because most people are familiar with that very particular blue.

Despite its difficulties, finding ways to describe things precisely is one of the many challenges that I love. In one of my novels I was describing a wood in winter, trying to think how I could best convey the almost non-colours of winter bark, with its streaks and ridges. I have no idea if I succeeded. What is visible to me may be invisible to readers. In a new novel, water, with its myriad colours, is a problem. There are few writers who are brilliant at describing water – sea, rivers, sluggish ponds. (Adam Nicolson, I think, is a rare exception and, very recently, John Lewis-Stempel, whose two books set in his few acres of Shropshire land are as compelling as any thriller.) My hero spends a lot of time on cruise ships, leaning over the rails studying the sea. I contemplate leaving the reader to imagine how he sees it, rather than disappoint by falling into lustreless cliché. In this same book the heroine works in a huge building of dusky glass. Problem: would the dark glass change the colour of the passing white clouds? That's the sort of question that frequently confronts me.

I have often written about fire, flames – another challenge, and harder than you might think, considering that oranges and yellows merge with blue and purple. The man who loves cruises is by trade a man who designs fireworks. Reluctant researcher though I am, I spent a day at a firework factory, but learnt more about computer technicalities than how to describe all those colours torrenting through the sky. Sometimes solutions to such problems are solved out of nowhere: words just come to mind. But of course I have no idea whether they paint the picture I am trying to produce in my readers' heads.

Looking back over my novels and stories, I've been trying to find those parts that made a reviewer declare me to be a synaesthete. My husband reminded me of a story I wrote long ago called 'Mind of Her Own'. The story is about a put-upon woman called Alice who is always persuaded by her loutish husband and sons to spend their annual holiday on a dreadful old boat on the Norfolk Broads. There, it rains every day, and she spends her time peeling potatoes. When one year she shows small signs of rebellion, and refuses to go, her family declare she is insane. They eventually persuade her of this, and get her admitted to a psychiatric home. Alice is not as put out by this as might be expected, simply because she is, and always has been, blessed with what she thinks of as 'the yellow of co-operation'.

Co-operation was pale yellow in Alice Lee's mind. A primrose yellow, to be precise, sometimes almost metallic: a colour that started in her head, flowed down through her body filling it with warmth and making her limbs waxy, deliquescent, so that her movements, to onlookers, would sometimes appear clumsy. Most days Alice experienced these yellow sensations in some measure. The fact that she was used to them in no way diminished their rewards. They represented inexplicable happiness that was her only secret, her only area of absolute privacy.

When there was no more she could do for any member of her family, Alice felt flat. They were the moments she most dreaded. The yellow of co-operation thinned in her blood, leaving her physically lighter, feeling she might take off in a west wind. Tasks were her anchor ... getting the breakfast, she felt just as usual: the same subdued pleasure, a lovely saffron colour at this time of day, soon to flower later into the inevitable chrome ...

That was a story I read on the radio, and received several letters from women who said their own feelings of co-operation were a colour in their mind, though none were yellow.

In another story I used colour not to convey a sensation, but to do something positive. The story, 'Monday Lunch in Fairyland', is, as the title suggests, the tale of two people having the most romantic of affairs, but who know there is no hope of any permanency. They are just very lighted-up ships passing in the night. Here's a fragment of what is going on in the mind of the girl, Anna, as she thinks back to their meetings in Cornwall.

Oh my love that wet and shining winter beach sandpipers pecking at the frills of sea you said they were sandpipers I didn't know and you said quietly now if we go quietly we won't disturb them and we came so close before they flew away a small bush of wings in the grey sky urged higher by their own cries of alarm and me with my arm through your absurdly bulbous anorak of dreadful tangerine so out of place I said on this empty shore shouting against the wind so you could hear and laugh and feeling you shorten your step to coincide with mine …

I think what I've done here is to use the horrible tangerine anorak to pull the whole thing down to earth a little, to counteract any soppiness in the girl's reflections – to make one small point of ugly colour in a bleached, watercolour sort of landscape. But I can't be sure that was my intention. I'm hopeless at analysing my own work. I just copy down a sort of dictation in my head. It's only if I'm required to look back on past work, or do so out of curiosity, that I can start attributing motives that certainly were not there when I was actually writing. So it could be that my whole thesis about the tangerine anorak is invalid.

I cannot be precise about how young I was when I became conscious of my colours, but think it was at a very young age. Of all the known synaesthetes, Nabokov is probably the most lucid: his explanations go a long way to making us understand. For him, it all began in his seventh year.

'I was using a heap of old alphabet blocks to build a tower,' he wrote in his autobiography. 'I casually remarked to my mother that their colours were all wrong. We discovered that some of her letters were the same as mine and that, besides, she was optically affected by musical notes', which Nabokov never was, no matter how much he was exposed to operas and concerts. He went on to say his mother did everything to encourage his general sensitivity to visual stimulation and, again from an early age, was quite clear how his 'fine case of coloured hearing', as she called it, worked – though he added that 'perhaps hearing is not quite accurate since the colour sensation seems to be produced by the very act of my orally forming a given letter while I imagine its outline. A long A of the English alphabet has for me the tint of weathered wood, but a French A evokes polished ebony. The black group also includes R – a sooty rag being ripped. N is oatmeal, and the ivory-backed hand-mirror of O takes care of the whites.' His list of such detailed colour associations include the steely X and the thundercloud Z, while S is a curious mixture of azure and mother-of-pearl.

It's not hard to understand, reading a list like that, why non-synaesthetes assume us colour-touched folk are a bit peculiar. When his letters gathered to make words, Nabokov must have been dazzled. I'm relieved my own form is only triggered by days, weeks, months, and a few numbers.

'The confessions of a synaesthete must sound tedious and pretentious to those who are protected by more solid walls than mine are,' Nabokov finally admitted. I agree with him entirely. Though for the 'afflicted' it has so many uses, not least as a conversation starter. 'What colour is your Monday?' is an unfailingly good opener. But is synaesthesia merely a strange and useless condition, or is it a gift? I can't be sure of the answer. I only know that its constancy is reassuring and, without it, I'd be at a loss. There would be no structure to the pictures in my mind. I'd be bereft. As it is, I'm eternally grateful to my internal rainbow.

11

Television

Quentin owned a perfectly agreeable if rather dull house in Flood Street, Chelsea. Economically, it would have been wise to stay there. But as a naïve young bride I was loath to live in the previous wife's house. Q conceded to this selfish whim and agreed to move.

We found a wonderful flat in Wilton Crescent, ground floor and basement. There were good rooms and a terrace garden downstairs, a large dining room and a magnificent drawing room on the ground floor. Just the place for giving parties, and the 1960s were beginning to unfold. Q was still working at *Queen*; I was doing a little freelance journalism. It was an era for us that teetered between huge fun and financial panic.

Then, out of the blue, came a strange job in television. The American company NBC were to make a documentary about the English privileged classes – a subject that has always appealed to filmmakers. They needed a couple of researchers. I was chosen to be one of them. The other was an unknown young man called David Frost.

David had just come down from Cambridge. He was thin, faintly spotty, eager, energetic, funny – scintillating company. We had great fun at the expense of the producer, a great Canadian bear of a man, as he floundered about, totally confused by the class system, deeply in awe of any title. The job was hard work and did not pay well, so David and I had many a scant lunch of fish and chips. Years later, when we met in New York, things for him had changed, but however famous and rich he became, he remained loyal to old friends, and generous. In the days of our frugal lunches, he talked of a programme he was trying to set up called *That Was The Week That Was*, which was soon to change his life.

One of the major contributors to the programme, when it came on, was Bernard Levin, an old and close friend of Quentin's who was a frequent visitor to Wilton Crescent. At the time he was theatre critic for the *Daily Mail*, and often asked Q to the theatre. But Q didn't fancy all the palaver of getting in and out of theatres – his driver would have to give him a fireman's lift – so he rarely accepted. Bernard's invitations were then directed to me: as I loved the theatre, I always accepted.

But, in those days of early acquaintance, I felt some unease about going with him. He could be unnerving. The pattern of our evenings out was always the same. He would arrive at Wilton Crescent in a black tie, and a smart coachman's coat that reached to the floor. He never failed to bring a transparent box holding a very expensive orchid from Moyses Stevens, which I was urged to pin to my bosom. This I dreaded. What if I were to run into a friend wearing an extravagant great bloom? Sometimes I put it on my coat, so that at least when we got to the restaurant I could get rid of it. Bernard would have several glasses of wine, the taxi's meter ticking up outside all the while. This always shocked me, for often at least £5 was on the clock by the time we set off.

During his time as an interviewer on *That Was The Week*, Bernard was constantly attacked in the press – goodness knows why, because his slot on the programme, though abrasive, was compelling. Often, as we slipped unobtrusively into the theatre, he would be booed at, sometimes even spat at. Bernard ignored it all. He would make small grunting noises as we made our way to our seats. It seemed that he found comfort in these soft sounds, as some people do when they hum. Walking down a street, travelling in a taxi, going up in a lift – if there was no talk, the quiet between us was filled with his rhythmic grunts.

The play over, we would hurry to his office in a taxi, where he would write his review. Rarely did it take him more than twenty minutes. Then another taxi to dinner. This was always in some very grand and expensive restaurant – The Connaught, The Savoy, The Ritz. Not for Bernard one of the popular small *trattorie* that were springing up all over London. Pasta wasn't his thing. He was a major gourmet with a huge knowledge of – and love of – food.

Sometimes, sitting in front of a dazzle of white napery, I would suppress a sigh as Bernard went very slowly through the menu. There would be at least two hours of eating ahead, and conversation was never easy. We would discuss the play we had just seen, and move on to his reports of a music festival or concert he had recently attended. (He tried for years – but failed – to persuade me to a love of opera.) One evening, as I felt the approach of a new wave of silence, I thought: this is ridiculous. We can't go on like this. We must talk properly. 'Do you have a girlfriend?' I dared myself to ask. 'Are you in love?'

'Well, well, well,' he muttered. 'Funny you should ask that.'

And the floodgates were opened. He began a long spiel about whoever was the girlfriend (or potential girlfriend) of the moment. He put to me the highs, the lows, the difficulties, the hopes. He seemed to want my opinion, my advice, and this continued for many years. He would take me out to lunch in order to ask whether he should send a car to the airport for Arianna Stassinopoulos – his girlfriend of the time – and whether or not he should send her red roses as well. On one occasion, over lunch at Fortnum and Mason, he invited me to a weekend in a hotel where all sorts of odd things were to take place in order to ease the participants' way to finding themselves. This was because he and Arianna had become disciples of the Indian guru Bhagwan Shree Rajneesh, whose message combined traditional spiritual teaching and pop psychology. When later the guru was involved in some scandal, Arianna's support evaporated, and Bernard's with it – for his part, with some relief. He himself was not fundamentally in favour of all the gobbledegook, but valiantly tried to support it out of loyalty to Arianna. He wanted me to come on one of the weekends where amazing things would happen to enhance my life.

'You'd find it very interesting,' he said.

'I couldn't possibly afford it,' I said, honestly.

'I'd take care of that,' he said, ever generous.

But I had heard of odd goings-on at these expensive

gatherings. In the process of one of the weekends, a fellow novelist, wearing a pink tutu, had been seen lying on the floor kicking her legs in the air and making odd noises.

I thanked him, and said it wasn't my sort of thing. He pressed me no further. But I did agree to go to just one of the followers' meetings, where Arianna spoke passionately on the guru's behalf. I studied Bernard's face, and felt for him.

Bernard lived for many years in a stately flat in Devonshire Place. Occasionally girlfriends lodged for a while, but for much of the time he was alone in this hotel-like flat. Usually, before a play, we would meet for a glass of champagne somewhere near the theatre. Only once he asked me round to the flat. I was not sure what to expect.

The sitting room was large, with a very high and wide window. No view, because a curtain was drawn against the daylight. The curtain was made of silvery stuff whose folds glinted disturbingly: it was easy to imagine it had been bought from a provincial theatre, and in its heyday it had been the sparkling background to one of those organs that rises up from the floor and booms out 'I do like to be beside the seaside ...' I sat down, pondering all this, and Bernard disappeared through a slightly open door.

He was away for a very long time, almost half an hour. I wondered what he was up to: opening champagne couldn't take that long.

Eventually he came in, carrying a small tray. On it were neatly laid delicate china plates, a rack of triangular toasts, a bowl of foie gras and two glasses. But what had to be seen to be believed were the napkins. They were made of that stiff, dense white damask, and moulded into the most perfect water lilies I have ever seen achieved in a napkin. I realised that there was nowhere from where Bernard could have acquired ready-made damask water lilies, and could only conclude he had spent the afternoon in his kitchen making them himself ... I was filled with a whole new light of wonder and appreciation.

Bernard assured me his greatest wish was to get married and have children. But this never quite came about. He had dozens of girlfriends – clever, famous, aristocratic: a disparate but impressive bunch, to whom he was devoted and immensely generous. He assured me he was going to marry Arianna Stassinopoulos 'once we have found a house', which Arianna insisted upon. They looked at dozens, but somehow never found the perfect thing. (I had a feeling Arianna's heart was not entirely in the search.) So their affair came to an end, but not their friendship. Arianna went to America and married her millionaire politician. Bernard, naturally, was invited to the wedding in Washington, and went. When I asked how it was, he assured me it was a 'splendid' occasion.

'I helped lay the tables,' he said.

Q and I made him godfather to our daughter Candida, to whom he gave stupendous presents, and organised various 'treats', which she dreaded. He would arrive at the door bearing a plate on which lay a circle of small flowers, such as a child bridesmaid might wear, covered with a napkin. On many occasions she was urged to put this floral halo on her head and set off with her godfather, in a pink dinner jacket, to see a play at the National. Once, at Oxford Station, they were confronted by a crowd of yobs who were obscenely rude. Candida wanted to die; Bernard seemed not to notice them. On another occasion he described a new Greek restaurant he had found in

Stratford where after dinner you could *both smash plates and dance*. Would she like him to take her? Luckily, there was some valid excuse for her not to go.

Bernard found a remarkable woman with whom he spent his last years before having to move to a care home. He remained loyal to his friends, above all Quentin. When they were both ill, Bernard would still make the train journey to Moreton-in-Marsh, hire a taxi, collect Q and take him out to lunch. They were both in a state of some confusion and frailty by then, but clear enough to know they wanted to go on meeting. They would still exchange charged opinions about current politics, swap humorous stories of their present lives. Until the time came that neither of them could journey to the other, they still enormously enjoyed each other's company.

In 1962 I was pregnant, and delighted. Although feeling horribly sick all the time, I carried on working with David Frost for the Canadian film company.

One weekend Q and I were invited for the weekend to stay in Hampshire with my friend Philippa Wallop. Q's driver at the time was an amiable young Australian called Grant. When he saw the park in which a herd of deer was grazing, he decided to get his air rifle and take a few shots. It was with considerable difficulty we halted him from doing this. He failed to understand why a park, and deer within it, should be private property, but obligingly held his fire. Often Grant was confused by the fact that British life was so different from life in Australia, but he was one of the best of many drivers employed over the years and was devoted to Q, whose various employees were a constant source of both frustration and amusement.

There was a weedy one called Smith who, when he came for an interview, explained that if he lifted up one leg he was bound to fall over. With that, he lifted one leg, and fell at Q's feet. All the same, he was hired. Then there was the mad-looking but very strong man whose chauffeur's cap rode precariously on his wild gypsy hair. At some point Q mildly chided him for being late yet again. In revenge, when carrying Q to a meeting in a hotel, the outraged driver threatened to drop him down a lift shaft. Disaster was averted by a passing waiter, but it was a very frightening moment for Q, who naturally made light of it. But the man was plainly a psychopath: he was sacked. A few days later, glancing out of the window at his car – a beautiful second-hand Rolls; goodness knows how he had mustered the money for that – Q saw that acid had been flung over it, ruining the paintwork.

On the Friday evening we arrived in Philippa's house. By now, seven months pregnant, I was faintly alarmed by the constant pain nagging my back, and rang the local doctor. He said I should put a couple of bricks under the legs of the bed.

It was a sleepless night, and by morning the pains were stronger. My gynaecologist suggested I should return to London as soon as possible. I said I would, after lunch. Lunch happened to be with Xandra and Robin Douglas-Home. Xandra, too, was pregnant. We were warned before we arrived at their house not to talk about pregnant matters as it was not a subject Robin enjoyed. All through lunch, under a hot sun in the garden, I squirmed about, trying to disguise the by now very regular and strong pains. Back at Philippa's house we rang the doctor again. It was a weekend, he said, and he was reluctant to turn out. When eventually he arrived he announced that, if we didn't make Winchester Hospital in time, it would be no trouble to deliver the baby in a ditch.

It was a long and excruciating labour and Caspar was born at dawn. He looked very like Q, and weighed just one pound. His lungs were underdeveloped. He was put into a primitive-looking incubator. We were not warned his chance of survival was small, so were surprised when there was a sudden flurry of people suggesting the vicar should be summoned for a quick christening.

Caspar died aged two days old and was buried in a small Hampshire churchyard. Q, in his autobiography, wrote 'and not a day goes by when I don't think of him'. Over fifty years ago since his birth, now, I frequently do the same, though time has dulled the frequency of remembering and tempered, a little, the sadness. But the sense of loss remains: a small, persistent echo.

Our flat in Wilton Crescent seemed to be a place where friends frequently dropped by. Quentin was regarded as a kind of sage. People liked to sit at his feet and listen to him. He was marvellous at giving both advice and encouragement. Among the disparate listeners was Sandie Shaw, the singer, and Magnus Linklater, just down from Cambridge, who wanted to be a writer. Q managed to find him his first two jobs as a journalist. Years later, as editor of the *Sunday Times*, Magnus commissioned Q to do various articles. And in 1997, at Q's memorial service in St George's, Hanover Square, he gave an eloquent and touching tribute to the man who had always been his hero.

We began to give parties; nothing very elaborate, but the guests – mostly writers, artists, painters – were an entertaining lot. I have memories of Edna O'Brien in entranced conversation with Shirley MacLaine, Elaine Dundy sulking under the grand piano, Keith Richards arguing with Anthony Blond, Kathy and Ken Tynan swooping in, the ultimate glamorous couple ... We would have some ten people to dinner, then invite twenty or thirty more to come in afterwards. For them, it was just drink. But on frequent occasions these gatherings went on till 2 or 3 in the morning.

Jocelyn and Jane Stevens asked us to one of their dinner parties, to which Tony Armstrong-Jones and Princess Margaret had been invited. It was not long after they were married. And being invited to meet a member of the Royal Family, in those days, meant a certain standard of dress was called for: black ties for the men, long dresses for the women. I went so far as to pay a visit to Collingwood's, the jewellers, to borrow a diamond brooch, a story which decades later my daughters greeted with laughing scorn.

The dinner was a great success, actually enjoyable. We knew Tony well anyhow, and Princess Margaret was in sparkling form – beautiful, lively, always questing to learn about disparate things. In those days she and Tony sparked each other off – stories, mimicry – brilliantly. There was much laughter. It was hard to believe it had all been so unscaring and easy. A few days later, Princess Margaret rang to ask us to lunch at Kensington Palace, into which they had just moved.

Kensington Palace was like a large, comfortable, cosy country house in the middle of London. We were shown all round it, Tony explaining what had had to be done to each room. He was particularly proud of the colour he had chosen for the kitchen – 'copied from a brown egg'.

There were about twenty people at that first lunch, including Noël Coward, John Betjeman, Anne Scott-James and Osbert Lancaster. I remember being amazed by seeing Osbert's hand shaking so much that his gin and tonic swayed about in his glass. There was a slight feeling of nervous tension, guests wondering how to behave. But the princess and Tony were good and lively hosts, making people laugh and putting everyone at ease.

After that occasion, Q and I then decided that perhaps we should ask them to one of our parties – nothing at all grand, I explained, but usually an interesting gathering of people. The princess accepted at once. She was naturally drawn to writers, artists, dancers, actors – the arts world – so was delighted to find a lot of people to whom she could talk about the things that most interested her. And she danced and danced. We judged that first invitation to have been a success, because they did not leave till 7 a.m. After that, we became close friends until she died some forty years later. The invitations, to and from, were numerous over the years, both before and after PM and Tony were divorced. They are all recorded in the diary I have kept since I left school, and that is where they will remain.

But I would not be giving anything away by insisting that the standard portraits of the princess in the press bear little resemblance to the reality as we knew it. Yes, there were the occasional untoward moments, and she was sometimes impatient with people who were not entertaining. But my chief memory of her is the constancy and the firmness of her friendship: she was kind, imaginative, wise and had a marvellous sense of humour. She was always wanting to learn, and when she came to stay with us (James, my husband since 1978) in

Oxford, she taxed dons on various subjects, wrote down all they said, and remembered it. She was a friend I shall always miss.

I became pregnant again in 1963. This time I was commanded to stay in bed for five months, which meant difficulties, as Q was unable to assist me and we had no help. Trying to find a live-in cook was almost as difficult as finding the perfect driver. But eventually a vicar's daughter appeared, apparently eager to work for us. The first morning she arrived I took out a book in which to write suggested food. She wrote *apple crumble*, I wrote *kippers*. After that, we were stuck. I have never been much interested in food, and hate having to think of what to buy. To this day I abhor cooking and balk at being at the stove when I could be reading or writing. But I have tried to learn a few things, English puddings being my *pièces de résistance*.

Dawn, the vicar's daughter, struggled for about three months before she left, taking with her most of my jewellery. I read countless books and watched television. I wasn't exactly bored, but longed to get up and go out. The only news that stirred the bedroom was when Q arrived home one afternoon to say that President Kennedy had been shot.

Princess Margaret was pregnant with Sarah at the same time I was having Candida, and was sympathetic about my incarceration. She suggested she and Tony came round one Saturday evening for supper, bringing a film which Tony would set up in the bedroom. I had to confess I couldn't provide supper: the vicar's daughter still had not been replaced.

'Don't worry,' Princess Margaret said, 'we'll send it round.'

For the next month or so, every Saturday evening, a van from Kensington Palace would arrive with a delicious cold supper, plus silver, china and wine. We would eat in the dining room (I took the risk of climbing one flight of stairs), then go back to the bedroom to watch whatever the film. I was allowed up, finally, a month before Candida was born. By then Princess Margaret was in bed, waiting for the birth of Sarah. It was our turn to be invited for picnic suppers in her bedroom.

Candida was born in June 1964 – a much happier occasion than Caspar's arrival, due to the relatively new aid of an epidural, which meant I could see and enjoy her birth rather than screaming in agony. A Portuguese housekeeper was found, and an obliging young nanny – necessary because I was to go back to work. Everything became easier, though the flat often seemed overcrowded. There was a libel case going on with our friend Jeremy Fry, and some other libel case concerning Randolph Churchill. They and their advisers all constantly met in our drawing room, wanting Q's opinion. We longed for a bit of peace.

While we were living in Wilton Crescent, my parents moved nearby to Lowndes Street. By now my father was ailing, with hardening of the arteries. His last major film had been *The Trials of Oscar Wilde*, starring Peter Finch and Yvonne Mitchell. Ken Hughes and my father wrote the script, Nic Roeg (to whom my father had given his first break as cameraman on a film called *Jazz Boat*) was the cameraman. As with all Dad's films, I spent a lot of time in the studio, photographing the actors in the hope that one day the pictures might come in useful. The excitement lay in trying to get this film out before the one being made by another company, also about Oscar Wilde. *The Trials of Oscar Wilde* did, just, open first, and the film was highly praised.

But it was my father's last major work. He had become slightly confused, and very upset that his working days seemed to be coming to an end. He spent most of the day at home reading thrillers. Then Cubby Broccoli, with whom he had been working a few years previously on the Bond films, kindly gave him some 'work': it was to read most of Dickens's novels with the idea of adapting the whole lot for television. My father knew most of them almost by heart, but settled down to read them again, making copious notes and suggestions. Cubby paid him well for this enjoyable 'work', and my father regained a sense of being useful.

He was delighted Q and I were living so near, because it meant he could amble round most days and spend the afternoons with me and his granddaughter. He would have a sleep in my study, then talk about whatever work I was doing, giving advice, and wanting to know every detail. His great wish was for me to write a novel. I promised I would, although I told him I might wait a few more years so as to avoid a juvenile autobiography.

It became too difficult for my mother to look after him. A home, run by monks, was found for him at Park Royal. I think his move there was more searing for us than it was for him, because by then he was in a state of great confusion. For the journey to the home he wore his dinner jacket, thinking he was going to a party. He then confused the grim building with The Dorchester, which had been round the corner from his office and where he had gone every day for a drink. He was shown to a long ward, every bed filled. His eyes dragged over the many sad, sleeping old men.

'Who are these actors?' he asked.

The home was only fifteen minutes from the BBC, where by now I was working. So I was able to visit him every day at lunchtime. Every half-hour visit was sad in a slightly different way: sometimes because he was in a melancholy mood, sometimes because looking at his handsome, crumpled face, the signs that he would not live long were horribly apparent. I knew he had been counting the minutes to my visit since he woke in the morning, and would be counting the hours till my return next day. He always made an effort to entertain me, and retold many of the stories about his Devon childhood that he used to tell Trish and me when we were children. Often he thought he was back in a film studio, and grumbled because one of the old bedridden men had not learnt his lines.

After a couple of busy, happy years in Wilton Crescent, Q began to feel the call of Abroad. He went to South Africa and wrote such an outraged piece about shantytowns that he was forbidden to enter the country ever again. He crossed the Empty Quarter accompanied only by his wheelchair: no English speaker went with him. One of his companions had his jugular vein slashed in a fight. Q, who admitted to being squeamish, somehow managed to sew it up and saved the man's life. His courage and determination were astonishing, until well into his old age. Until he broke his back after a year in India, he continued to challenge himself with expeditions to uncomfortable parts of the world. He turned these adventures into compelling travel books. Sometimes, keener on the travel than the actual writing, advances had to be returned, but this never seemed to faze him. Early on in our married life he had the idea of writing about the *piazze* of Europe: he was commissioned to do a book. Compared with his later travels, whirling round Europe in his huge, bouncy American car, this was no hardship – a kind of extended holiday. I was reluctant to go with him: there was work, and I did not fancy twelve weeks on the road. But I did join him for a while in Italy, keen to be reunited with all the places I loved. We ended up in Venice.

There, we were to stay with Q's old friend Anna Maria Cicogna, a fearsome old *contessa* who had built a huge marble house just off the Grand Canal. She sent one of her two gondolas to fetch us. We sat on red velvet seats as the *gondoliere* skimmed us through the murky waters, singing Neapolitan love songs. It was such a perfect cliché we could only laugh. Then the gondola calmed down, edged slowly down a narrow side canal to an elaborate landing stage. An elegant woman appeared from the house, dressed in cream silk, plainly Chanel. A bevy of gold charm bracelets rattled round her elegant wrists. When she realised that getting Q out of the gondola and into the house would be complicated, and require several helpers, disapproval twisted her face. I knew at once I was not going to like Anna Maria.

She was not our hostess, it turned out, but the housekeeper. She led us up a narrow staircase (more grumbles) to a small but charming bedroom, from which the Santa Maria della Salute could be glimpsed. Our embarrassingly shabby bags were dumped on the floor.

'What,' the snooty woman asked, 'shall I take to iron for you tonight?'

I was stumped. I knew she would disapprove of us even further when I explained about the roughness of our journey. Her English was poor so, to try to win her sympathy, I launched into vivid descriptions, in Italian, about the different hotels every night, nowhere to get clothes washed or ironed … She sniffed, not interested, pulled a rubble of crumpled things from my bag, held them up with disdainful fingers. After several moments of horrible suspense – would we be cast out as we had not got the right clothes? – she eventually chose a dress that had been turned into a rag by the imperfect packing conditions. She held it up, waved it in my face, the better to force my agreement of its dreadful condition.

'I suppose,' she said at last, 'this could do *for tonight*. But not for tomorrow night, when we have a big party. Tonight there are just a few guests: Sir John Gielgud, Isaiah Berlin and his wife, Nancy Mitford …' She stomped off without even looking at Q's bag, probably imagining the state of his shirts.

'Stupid cow,' he said. 'Anna Maria won't give a toss what we wear.'

He was right. Our hostess never glanced at our clothes but gave a smiling welcome. She had been devoted to Q for many years and seemed keen to extend her friendship to his twenty-three-year-old wife, apologising for the age of the other guests. We had a glorious dinner on the terrace with a chocolate soufflé that almost flew out of its dish, such was its lightness. I sat between John Gielgud and Isaiah Berlin, who seemed almost to be competing to make a young wife feel at ease:

a dinner, at the beginning of two very spoiling weeks, that I will never forget.

When Q's trip was over, and we were back in Wilton Crescent re-establishing normal life, it soon became plain that his initial enthusiasm for writing the book about piazzas had seriously dwindled. The trouble was, the advance had been spent and funds were very low. We should have had a serious discussion about jobs, and earnings. Q was always good, though, at putting such worries to one side. There were a happy few months when he enjoyed recounting stories of his European travels to the old band of droppers-in, and playing with Candida. But it was imperative that one of us started to earn regular money.

My old idea of working in television re-emerged, and somehow I was granted an interview with Desmond Wilcox, who had become well known for launching a documentary series on the BBC called *Man Alive*. I had merely written to him saying I had almost no qualifications, but I was a fan of his new documentary programmes, and would love to be a reporter. I got a quick reply, possibly due to the fact that Desmond liked the idea of our address. He would be delighted to see me.

Desmond, previously a newspaper reporter, went on to make his name in television with his unusual documentaries. The idea behind them was to scour from people their secret hopes, fears, tragedies: their reactions to disaster and distress. (There were few subjects of a humorous nature.) He had invented a technique for procuring these secrets, which I will come to later. At the time of my interview, only a few of the films had been shown, and had caused much interest in the press; there had been some criticism, but mostly critics were astonished by the subjects' confessions on camera – homosexuality, infidelity, dishonesty, life in prison and so on. At that time, too, there were no women reporters in television, apart from the iconic Joan Bakewell in the studio on *Late Night Line-Up*. Certainly there were none 'on the road'. Desmond liked the idea of finding the first serious woman reporter to scour the land for news-making stories.

Desmond was a vain man. Always attentive to his appearance, he wore peach-coloured shirts before his time, and brightly patterned ties. He strutted, rather than walked, conveying an inner feeling of importance. Once he took me for a drink at the Royal Garden Hotel.

'It's like being in a goldfish bowl, for me, going out,' he said. 'I'm recognised all the time.' We pushed our way through the crowds to the bar: never a glance in our direction. On the occasions he joined one of the teams on a story, and ran into a pregnant woman, his reaction was always the same. Without permission he would pat the large belly and give a confident laugh.

'You're going to call him Desie, I imagine?'

He was undaunted if the answer was no, which it usually was: he simply declared that since the popularity of *Man Alive*, a great many boys had been christened Desie.

Desmond had many foibles, for which he was much teased – I had a good time getting at him about his bright pigskin driving gloves with holes punctured on the knuckles – but he was a most loyal boss. His team of reporters and researchers on *Man Alive* were, I believe, the best in television, and a very merry lot besides. Desmond was also courageous in his choice of subjects, daring to make films about situations that were rarely shown on television. He was the second employer to whom I'm eternally grateful. Like Jocelyn Stevens, he gave me a job, knowing I had no experience, beyond a few panel games and a short period as a researcher in television. And although I could not approve of all his methods of interviewing, and hated his style of commentary writing, working on *Man Alive* was a good education.

At my first interview with Desmond, I confessed I had failed several dozen auditions. This did not faze him.

'You can't judge a reporter by auditions,' he said. 'You have to go out and make a film.' He then suggested I should be the reporter on a documentary that was being researched about health farms – not a subject close to my heart, but of course I accepted. I saw he was scrutinising my engagement diary, in which I was writing a suggested date, with particular interest.

'Where did you get that?' he asked.

'Ah,' I said, quickly judging it better not to tell him. His gaze then fell upon my coat.

'And where did you get *that*?'

'Italy. My husband bought it for me.'

I waited for questions about exam results, my education, experience as a writer. None came, though when I mentioned I had worked on *Queen* magazine, he gave me the same sort of look he had given my engagement diary. Half an hour later it was agreed I should start work on health farms very shortly. The payment was to be considerably more than I had ever been paid, and if a couple of films were successful, then I would be given a two-year contract.

'But you realise you won't be famous, working for my team,'

he said, standing, puffing out his peach-shirted chest – 'it's all back to camera with us. The reporter is only important in that he asks the right questions. There's no need for him to be seen.'

I agreed that this was an admirable principle; I had no ambitions either to be famous or to be seen. Over the years I have often thought more reporters should heed that advice rather than hogging the picture. A reporter should have some humility.

On one occasion I did have to face the camera in very tricky circumstances. I was making a programme about lesbians. There had been just one television film about gay men, but never about lesbians. Desmond, with a quick eye for a hot subject, insisted I was the reporter. I was sent to the Gateways, the lesbian club in Chelsea, where I had to dance with a French au pair in a pinstripe suit: the charming director blanched as I passed him by in a reluctant clinch. I had to go all over the place talking to mostly melancholy, bewildered gay women. The wonderful researcher had found some pathetically sad cases. The most shocking was the girl who had been living with a mannish lesbian for a year, but still had not discovered she was a woman. Meantime she had got pregnant, and the murder of her mother weighed heavily on her. No wonder she was reluctant to talk about all this facing the camera. So Desmond insisted it was my job to sit there, impenetrable face never moving. That was not an easy job. It was one of the few *Man Alive* films not to have been junked by the BBC in one of their library clear-outs. When I showed it to my children some years ago, it was hard not to laugh – at my taut, rigid, blank expression, not the subject. *Man Alive* provided a good deal of black humour.

Once I had made two films in England, Desmond decided I should go to America and make two more there. He had thought up what he considered a provocative title: 'Some of My Best Friends Are Black'. This inspiration caused deep concern in the BBC hierarchy. A meeting was called – the head of BBC2 and other senior decision-makers. Was it safe, they wondered, to send a young white girl to the States to interview *black men*? It was only when they heard who my subjects were to be that they relented: one was Gordon Parks, the world-famous photographer: the other was the vice president of Coca-Cola.

I much enjoyed the two years I worked for *Man Alive*. There were crises, dramas, rows, disagreements and a great deal of laughter. I learnt a lot about interviewing, and loved it. Working with some brilliant directors and cameramen was illuminating and inspiring. Brian Tufano was the star among the cameramen. Decades later he was to film *Billy Elliot*, and was employed by many major film companies. I enormously enjoyed going to places I would never have been to, had it not been for the purpose of making a film: prisons, schools, people's houses of every kind, storing my observations somewhere in my subconscious, thinking they would be useful one day when it came to writing a novel.

Moving around filming, in 1967, was not the easy process it is today. There was always a crew of six or seven, taxing many a living room. And as being 'on the telly' was a far more rare occurrence than it is today, should a television crew turn up in a street there was great excitement, crowds gathered round front gates. There was also considerable naïvety about how it all worked. On one occasion I was making a film about 'long

230

engagements' in Yorkshire. I was interviewing a sweet young girl who had had a ring on her finger for several years. Her parents insisted she should wait to marry for several more years. She and I talked in the kitchen – her parents were persuaded into another room as she did not want them to hear what she was going to say. In a whisper she told me that her plan was to get married in three months' time, and would I keep her secret, not tell anyone?

'But when the film appears on television your parents and everyone else will know your plan,' I said. This had not occurred to her. She burst into tears. I wanted to assure her that the private part of the interview would be cut. But such editorial decisions were not mine, but Desmond's. It was not cut.

Sometimes Desmond could not resist driving to a location to see how filming was going. He would whizz there in his gold Jaguar (plus pigskin driving gloves) and, if it was a poor part of a city, hide his car a few streets away from where we were working. We would tease him mercilessly about this practice, which he took in good heart. Sometimes I was the one to be teased, mostly by the funny, clever researcher John Pitman.

Once we were filming a gloomy story in a very rundown part of Birmingham. John warned me the flat we were going to was filthy, and I should not wear anything that I did not want spoilt. He was right about the state of the place. The carpet was so wet it made stains on all our shoes. I looked round, wondering on what uncontaminated place I could sit. John noticed my dilemma. He suddenly produced a copy of *Vogue* and laid it on a stool.

'You'll be OK now,' he said. The story of the girl who sat

on *Vogue* in the slums of Birmingham was one that reverberated through the history of *Man Alive* for a long time, joining the story of my question about frights involving rhubarb in the programme about phobias. I enjoyed the teasing.

Desmond coached all his reporters in his special technique for getting subjects to 'open up'. The skill was this: as the wretched man or woman was approaching the delicate part of his story, the reporter kept quiet. No more questions. All he should do would be to nod, oozing sympathy. If the subject's eyes then filled with tears, there should be a lot more nodding and, if possible, reciprocating tears in the questioner's eyes. Desmond often confessed that tears came to his own eyes, faced with a tragic story, very easily. None of the other reporters claimed this facility. But we were all skilful nodders and learnt to ask questions in very quiet, deeply sympathetic voices. It has to be said the method worked. I could not resist, in my second novel, *Virginia Fly Is Drowning*, including a reporter – who bore some resemblance to my old boss – who had to interview Virginia Fly about her virginity.

It was a marvellous job, working with a lively team of hard-working and talented researchers, all of whom were blessed with a sense of humour. In no other job have I ever known so much laughter. But after two years 'on the road', I began to feel that subjects for films were beginning to overlap, thus watering down their impact. For instance, I was the reporter on a tragic story about women in Holloway Prison. A year or so later I made a film about women coming out of prison, and all the problems therein. But it was a much less compelling subject and I began to think it was time to move on. Besides, I was suffering the clichéd agony of mothers who have to abandon their children in order to work. Often I had to be away filming for a week or more. While Candida was well looked after by Quentin, and her nanny, her face each time I left seared me with guilt and I missed her all the time.

But before leaving *Man Alive*, I was offered the job of presenting a live, weekly arts programme called *How It Is*. This was a complete contrast to the quiet filming of mostly sad, poor and lonely people: this involved interviews with rock stars, musicians, writers, artists, poets ... A memorable occasion was the day I had to spend with John Lennon and Yoko Ono as they sat in bed, all day, eating grated carrot and failing to answer my questions with any spirit.

Live television was an alarming challenge for one used to being an unseen reporter, but I enjoyed the warmth of a studio audience, and the slight feeling of danger that never came with filming. If anything went wrong, or I fluffed my lines reading the autocue, there was nothing to be done. But doing the two different programmes a week meant I was away from home far too much. I began to think that although I wanted to continue in television from time to time, such constant jobs, so inter-ruptive of home life, should soon come to an end.

At the same time as I came to this decision, the thought occurred to Q and me that we had had enough of London. We both yearned for the country. It would make our lives more difficult, in many ways, but we thought it would be worth it. We began the long search for a house.

12

Wootton

Wootton House, Bedfordshire, was the house that ended a long search. Bedfordshire was not a county that we had considered – dull land, no views. And the tall chimneys of a nearby brick factory sent out gusts of noxious smells when the wind was in the wrong direction. But there were things in its favour. It was not far from London, and near our friends Cleo Laine, a jazz singer, and her husband John Dankworth, a jazz musician and composer. They had bought a rectory at Woburn, where The Stables became an ever-expanding theatre, scene of countless musical and literary occasions.

Built in the time of William and Mary, Wootton House was irresistible. It had huge, handsome windows typical of its era. There were lawns on two sides, a rose garden and a vegetable garden at the back, and two ponds, one formally round, the other meandering. Swans wandered from one to another, never able to decide which they liked best. Both were guarded by willow trees, while sentinel elms gave shade to the south lawn, and the church's tall spire looked over the boundary wall. The whole place was large. Much too large. But somehow that seemed no deterrent.

We moved there in 1967. A day or two after we were chaotically installed (the massive job of redecorating had scarcely begun), we heard a helicopter overhead. It landed on the lawn. Out got Tommy Sopwith, who owned it and piloted it himself; with him were Princess Margaret and Tony, and Jocelyn and Jane Stevens. They had come to see how we were doing. Within moments they found themselves stripping wallpaper off the drawing-room walls – probably an enjoyable first for all of them. Finding cups in unpacked crates was impossible, so they went without tea.

Help, obviously, was needed in such a large house. We inherited a gardener who lived in the attics, and an affable man called Chris came to be Q's driver and general helper. He was married to a deeply troubled woman, Edgy, a marvellous cook. The great love of her life was her enormous cat. Unfortunately, a week after we moved in, it drowned in a water butt. Such was Edgy's sad hysteria I thought she would leave, rather than be reminded of the tragedy every time she passed the place where it had struck. Q and I dashed off to kennels known for their pedigree Pekinese dogs, and bought her a puppy – it cost roughly the same as a small diamond – which quickly replaced the cat in her affection. Fella was a charmless dog. He never quite died, though he suffered several near-death mishaps, but his role was invaluable.

Having no idea of what sort of wages a cook-housekeeper should be paid, I asked Edgy what she would consider fair. Six pounds a week, she said. Even in 1967 that was a ridiculously scant amount. I argued with her, but she would not hear of a penny more. As for housekeeping money, eight pounds a week was all she said she needed. Out of that she bought all the food and household stuff, and still managed to put aside enough for various machines for the kitchen. She refused to take a day off more than about once every six months, and worked from early in the morning till late at night. The job was her life, which perhaps made up for her lack of life with Chris, whose agreeableness to us did not extend to his wife. There was an occasion when he chased her with a carving knife.

The great asset of Edgy's job was the new kitchen. This Terence Conran — whom we knew, but not well — agreed to design; not something he normally did, but I think he liked the idea of being given *carte blanche*. It was dazzling white, ultra modern, with — my only contribution — cerulean blue Italian tiles on the walls. It was not at all the sort of kitchen that is fashionable today — quarry tiles, muted paint and Belfast sink: none of that. But it was ultra-practical. The sun poured in and many an hour was spent at one end of the table eating best-ever ginger cake, while at the other Edgy beat up mysterious ingredients for the next lunch or dinner.

She was prone to grumbling, Edgy, about everything from muddy footprints to the government, but the kitchen stumped her. Never a grumble. Her disapprobation centred on the fact that we did not have enough people to stay. What gave her more pleasure than anything was cooking for at least twelve people every weekend. We promised we would do our best to become more regular hosts once the decorating was finished. We also employed a saintly lady from the village who had been cleaning the house for twenty-seven years, and gave extra help when, eventually, we sometimes entertained in the style of which Edgy approved. It was mad, mad. We were living beyond our dottiest dreams but, on the occasions we could cast aside the financial worries, we loved it.

I was still away filming for *Man Alive*, so seemed constantly to be on the M1 driving to and from locations, and at the same time trying to think about carpets and curtains. Q was writing a weekly column for a Sunday paper, which meant he had to go to London at least once a week. Candida was looked after by a quiet young nanny, and spent a lot of time with Q on the days he was home. I was there as much as I could be – though not enough – and loved taking her to dancing classes at Woburn. They seemed not to have changed at all since my own dancing days at EBH: the silk socks and bronze pumps, the Joyce Grenfell singsong voice urging pupils to *skip*, knees held high; the giggling as small girls clustered together as far away as possible from the few small boys. What was fascinating, watching these classes, was the way it was possible to see, even in a group of three year olds, what they might become: there were the perky, enthusiastic ones; the slow, the sullen, the uncomprehending, and the plainly talented who were bored by the pace of the whole thing. Talent, it seems, is recognisable at a very young age, as is character.

Wootton was the second house in my life that I loved completely. I loved its huge windows, through which the sun seemed so often to flare. I loved the large hallway with its two handsome arches: one led to the staircase, one to my study – the most peaceful of rooms, with my father's desk in the window, and the rose garden outside. At Christmas we put a tree in the hall that reached to the ceiling. Once Candida and I had covered it with pale lights, and those glass balls that play tricks with perspectives, the flagstone floor danced with watery shadows, while the lively wood fire made more serious reflections on the pale stone. We loved preparing for Christmas. There were too few years of that.

There was a lift in Q's study which took him up to our bathroom. It was in his study that he and I would have supper when we were on our own. We talked about myriad things – there was always much laughing and teasing. I would be chided for not wanting to explore the world.

He was the most wonderful company, bursting with ideas (some not remotely practical). There was the time he thought up a scheme to recover treasure from a shipwreck off the Dominican Republic. On one of his travels, Q had met a sailor who swore the ship – *El Concepción* – was there, broken up on the sea bed. Q became enthused by the idea of all the fun, and of course the money, that finding the wreck filled with gold would be. He was endlessly on the telephone gathering together a group of people who called themselves The Gentlemen Adventurers. He commanded my old dancing partner, Antony Snow, to 'find the money', which Antony managed to do from various eager, boyish adventurers. The whole project took up a great deal of time, hours of earnest discussion by men who could not be said to be professionals in the world of treasure hunting. And oh, the meetings: Q loved them. Edgy was in her element, having to provide food for the men who turned up in extravagant cars and solemnly spent many hours envisaging the prospect of gold. There were both moments of hope, and moments of pessimistic gloom. In the end the Gentlemen, having failed to bring up tons of gold coins and other precious things from the wreck, disbanded. A group from Chicago were able to spend huge money on the project and, years later, succeeded in securing a valuable hoard. The Adventurers were sanguine about their loss. They may not have won, but they had certainly enjoyed the project.

There were those who thought Wootton was haunted. Edgy complained many times she had seen 'a presence' outside our bedroom on the staircase that went up to the attic. In one of the spare rooms, several people claimed they had heard or seen 'something' in the night – such 'somethings' were maddeningly unspecific – and my old friend Philippa Wallop declared she could never come and stay again, such was the indescribable terror that assailed her one night.

I'd always been alarmed by the very thought of ghosts, having experienced the uneasy feelings at EBH, but never saw or heard a thing at Wootton, either downstairs or on the first floor. Nor did Q. Though once, when I went up to some attic rooms to decide what should be done to them, there was definitely a feeling of not wanting to linger there too long. Nothing distinct. Just a keenness to return back downstairs.

Once the house was finished, we heeded Edgy's chiding and began to have people to stay for frequent weekends. I would hurry back from Cardiff or Manchester, or wherever I had been filming, and dash to the garden to pick huge bunches of roses before people arrived – I had no idea what kind of roses they were, in those days, and regret not having learnt more about gardening at that time. We would never have had so many people to stay if I had had to cook: I was no good at it, and resented every moment it was necessary to be at the stove (a feeling that persists). So the relief of having Edgy was enormous. She did it magnificently and enjoyed doing it.

One weekend, when the Snowdons were staying, John and Cleo Dankworth came over bringing Dudley Moore. He was dressed in a handsome dark green jacket with silver buttons. Not unreasonably, Candida thought he was the postman. After dinner there was music and carousing: Dudley played the piano in his extraordinary fashion, and hilariously imitated various singers. John played his clarinet, Cleo's singing swerved from melancholy to cheerful jazz, Princess Margaret sang numbers from *Guys and Dolls* – she knew every word by heart. Suddenly, we noticed sun in the drawing room: it was 7 a.m. We had eggs and bacon in the kitchen (I could manage that) before we finally went to bed.

Q, most gregarious of men, loved all that sort of entertainment. He enjoyed his role as a host and took great care in choosing the right people together. He was over a decade older than me, and several of his friends were considerably older than him – Osbert Lancaster, for instance, and his wife Anne Scott-James, who came to stay at the same time as John Betjeman and his long-standing friend Elizabeth Cavendish. John would persuade the quartet to go church-seeing: on one occasion they managed to visit twenty-seven churches in a day. John was triumphant, the others were exhausted.

John was always the first down to breakfast. He made sure the door of the dining room was ajar so that he could cock his ear towards the hall, waiting for a signal. Then suddenly he would give a tremor of sheer delight: he had heard Elizabeth's step on the stairs.

'Ah! I know that step! That's my Feeble.' (His nickname for

Elizabeth.) 'Hello, Feeble!' Once she was settled near him at the table the door could be shut again: he was at peace.

John had a wonderfully unpredictable sense of humour. The things that caused him gusts of laughter were often surprising. For instance, once, in some irrelevant context, I mentioned a *cocktail* dress, and he doubled up with laughter. *A cocktail dress from Etam* he found even more hilarious. I saw the acute humour in such a thing, but I'm not sure everyone did likewise. John and I often retreated into corners to have our private laughs about cocktail dresses.

Ken Tynan was an old friend of Q's, and often came for weekends with his wife, Kathleen, for whom I gave a eulogy at her funeral in 1995. I was somewhat alarmed by Ken: he was severe, tense, often funny but often cutting. His admiration for Q was immense: they spent hours playing backgammon together, Ken's perennial cigarette hovering between the third and fourth finger of his left hand. He was scornful, I felt, of my lack of university education and took little notice of me, but I finally won him over in an unlikely way. To test a group of guests, he suddenly presented us with what he called a difficult challenge.

'Who can tell me the word which includes the consecutive letters mkh? I'll give a fiver to anyone who gets it.'

I looked round. Silence among all the clever faces. Then suddenly my childhood riding days snapped into place.

'Gymkhana!' I shrieked.

Totally amazed, Ken handed over the money. It was an odd way to win his respect, but after that he was much more friendly, warm, easy to get on with.

Q loved taking an active part in the village. He was made

chairman of the Evergreen Club, and much enjoyed going to their meetings and giving talks about his trips across the world. We gave many a tea in the rose garden to pensioners who ate quantities of Edgy's cakes and sandwiches. There was an annual fete in the garden in the summer, carol singers crowded into the hall for mince pies and wine before Christmas. Candida's annual delight was to be in the school Nativity play. Her part, she assured us, was the angel's mother.

The rhythm of the Wootton seasons became comfortingly familiar. Always putting to one side financial worries, we imagined we might be there for ever.

Before I finally left *Man Alive*, I was in the Shepherd's Bush office of the BBC one day when I got a call from the care home where my father was not improving. I had seen him in the morning: nothing untoward. Forever the actor, he had struggled to keep up an air of normality, and declared he felt fine, just tired. But at lunchtime a woman visiting the man in the next bed had noticed Dad seemed to be ailing, and rang me. Terrified – of seeing him dead, as much as his dying – I sped to the home at Park Royal. There were screens round the bed. I asked a monk how he was. No answer: so I parted the curtains and went in.

Dad was lying back on built-up pillows, his eyes shut – untroubled, it seemed. His pyjama top was open. Lying on his chest was a small gold cross on a chain that he had worn most of his life. It had a dent in the middle, caused by a bullet shot at him when he was fighting in the First World War. At least, that was his story. I always believed it and, despite a quiver of doubt, still do.

I asked if he knew I was there. He squeezed my hand. My guilt about my horror of death had never been so strong. Surely I should overcome it for the love of my father? In honesty my chief concern was to be gone before death overtook him, and I was not sure I would know when that was, or what I would do once I judged that his last breath had been taken. His hand was warm; the squeeze had been gentle but definite. We remained in silence: for a while I re-consigned every detail of his face to my memory. I knew each line and fold of skin, and the deep, purpureal hollows where his handsome, hooded eyes abided: I knew them all by heart. His strong hand, burnished by old age, did not move again. I was afraid this was my last chance of seeing rather than remembering.

What do you say to a dying father who you love more than anyone? I had a strange sensation of looking down on the scene: dying old man in the bed, distraught but speechless daughter at his side. I felt – and even at the time I was ashamed of this feeling – it was imperative not to come up with some cliché farewell. After a while, both guilty and fearful, I stood and kissed his forehead and told him I was going to start writing my first novel – I knew that news would please him if he heard it. But I will never know whether I declared this while he was still alive, or after he had stopped breathing. Then I slipped back between the curtains and sat on an upright chair.

Eventually – so few helpers for so many bedridden – the monk returned and went back through the curtains, drawing them behind him. He quickly returned.

'Is he dead?' I asked.

'He is.' He looked a bit shocked by my terse enquiry, and

went away. But quickly he came back with a trolley of nameless things that are required for packing up the dead. He suggested I sat in the corridor, which I did with relief. I had no wish to watch his shadow going back and forth as he made arrangements to my father's deceased body. When he had finished he came to ask whether, now that Dad was 'made ready', I would like to see him.

'Certainly not,' I said – too sharply, I know. This time he looked really shocked. Perhaps not many of the inmates he looked after had relations with no desire to see the people they loved turned into corpses. A moment later a trolley was pushed past me, the searingly familiar outlines of Dad's body smudged under a sheet. I was given his gold cross. It was still warm.

The afternoon my father died, my mother did something so out of character it was hard to believe. She prided herself on never, ever going to the theatre. But a friend of hers had insisted she came to *Fiddler on the Roof*, in the hope it might give her a break, cheer her up. Mum had been to see my father every day since he had been admitted to the home – a long journey from central London, but she never missed a day. So her not being there when he died, because she was watching a musical she did not want to see, was deeply ironic.

For four hours I had tried and failed to get through to the theatre. There was nothing I could do but return to the chair in the long, echoing passage that smelt of aged men, and wait for her: she had arranged to come to see him at nine that night.

Eventually I heard far-off footsteps – her usual stomping walk. She reached me, puzzled. I stood up. I quickly said Dad had died four hours earlier. She broke down completely, as sickened by her own uncharacteristic act of going to a theatre and her ironic absence, I think, as she was devastated by Dad's dying.

'What on earth was I doing?' she asked. 'I never go to …' She wanted to know why I was not crying. I said I did not feel like it: Dad's dying was too much to cry for, and I was never able to cry for him in all the years I have thought of him constantly, constantly. His voice is always in my head. To have had him for a father was one of the great blessings of my life.

Shortly after my father's death, my stint on *Man Alive* came to an end, as did presenting *How It Is*. In later years I worked spasmodically in television, both as a reporter and writing plays, and I also did a number of literary programmes on the radio and wrote disparate articles for various magazines and newspapers.

But once the two major jobs were over, I wanted to concentrate on being at Wootton: on Candida, Q, the garden. Also, I had to carry out my promise to my father.

I began writing my first novel, *Nowhere Girl*. There had been a long wait to get started. So many people had said to me, 'You can't write a book before you're thirty. You haven't lived enough.' I regarded that view as bunkum, and still do. You don't need to live in order to write. You need to imagine, to evoke, constantly to observe. Most important of all is to feel the strong urge to put down whatever it is that is crowding your mind. I had been feeling that urge since I was a child. But my various jobs, essential to my bank account, had left scant time for attempting to write a novel.

I approached it with some trepidation, acutely aware of not having a degree in English. From time to time I had read advice from those experts who give you rules, most of which I could not agree with. I don't believe you can be taught to write. Either it's within you, or it's not. As for rules: you make a plan, advise many tutors. Write a synopsis. Work out your chapters, work out your characters. If I had ever tried doing any of that I would have been so bored that by the time I came to writing the novel I would have abandoned it very quickly. It would have died before it ever lived. Apart from that, I'm incapable of thinking in advance. I usually have a rough first page in my head, and I vaguely know how the whole thing ends. But how I travel from one to the other is a mystery: I just have to see what appears. Advisers – and there are so many of them, many without a book to their name – seem to think you can 'learn' to write dialogue. I do not think that is possible. The voices are either in your head, and you follow them, or they are not. For me it would be impossible to think up what a character might say. I can never claim that my writing is a good example of my own methods, but I am incapable of any other way.

I began writing *Nowhere Girl* in 1969 and devised for myself a routine which I have kept to ever since. I would go to my study straight after breakfast, and write for four or five hours. I have never been able to write after lunch – that post-prandial sleepiness plays havoc with a clear mind, and the afternoons have to be kept for practicalities, meetings, friends, children, visitations. Q, in his study next door, a little later than me, would be writing too: we would meet for lunch. It was a happy arrangement that continued for all too short a time.

When I began writing the novel, all I knew was that it

should include an aged character. I was in my twenties but always had a penchant for writing about the old – their dignity, their language, their stalwart way of looking at the world. I also wanted to include Norfolk – a place that has subsequently been in most of my books – and music: that challenge had to wait for many years till a book called *Easy Silence*. My general aim was to try to convey things exactly: I'm fierce about trying to avoid clichés, and overall lazy descriptions. To be precise, specific, I think, is essential. The objectives I collected for myself are things that many writers might not agree with, but they seemed important to me when I was starting out, and they still do. Above all, I wanted to avoid earnestness, something I abhor. I wanted to retain an element of humour even in the most serious of passages.

As soon as I began writing, the magic began. I had only the first sentence and the last in mind – no idea how to get from the one to the other. But pages just appeared: once done, they could be improved, but the extraordinary thing was they just kept appearing. Never for a moment was I stuck about the next paragraph. Writing – and it is different for all of those who do it – is a mysterious business, and also a drug. Once started, I could not stop.

I sent the book to my old friend Diana Crawford – who had become an agent of exceptional talent – as soon as it was finished, never expecting that anyone would want it. But Diana lit on exactly the right publisher, Collins, for whom she guessed it was best suited. Surprising things began to happen. Adrian House, who was to become my editor for several books, accepted it at once: a £250 advance (pretty good, we thought) and immediate lunch at The Ivy.

Next, there was lunch at The Ritz with the head of publicity. (Publishing was a glamorous business in those days.) 'I'm going to devise a huge campaign for you,' he said, and he did: brochures went to hundreds of bookshops; there were advertising campaigns ... And our old friend Peter Sellers, an enthusiastic and conscientious photographer, though not a natural composer of his subjects, asked to take the author photograph. He was thrilled to be able to do this: it was the first time he had had a photograph published and paid for. It was all hard to believe. But there was more.

Diana rang to say Rex Harrison had read the book and wanted to buy the film rights outright: the whole deal was done very fast in a telephone conversation from California where Rex was filming. For 1969, the sum for the book was amazing, and a measure of luck I could never have envisaged. Rex wanted to meet me, to talk about casting.

When he next came to England he invited me to lunch at The Connaught, where he was staying. I was shown into the sitting room of his suite. His secretary was there to entertain me while we waited for him to arrive. She had plainly read the book.

'I was wondering,' she said, 'what Clare, the heroine, was doing between chapters two and three ...'

'Oh?' This was not a matter to which I had given any thought.

'And I imagined,' she went on, 'that she was working in an antique shop. Could I be right?'

I thought hard and fast. Eventually I explained, as politely as I could, that if I had known what Clare was up to between those two chapters, I would have put it in.

Rex was charming, enthusiastic, full of plans for the film, and asked no difficult questions about what might have been going on between chapters. He wanted Shirley MacLaine to play the lead. I could not imagine anyone more inappropriate to play a quiet English girl, but naturally did not quibble. In the event, after much negotiation, he and Shirley fell out. Rex lost heart about the whole project, and the film was never made. But I was able to afford to buy a cottage under the Downs in Wiltshire, the perfect place to carry on writing.

Meantime the book was taken by many publishers abroad, including one in America. And here, David Frost was once again wonderfully helpful. At the time he had a coast-to-coast chat show in the States.

'Terrific you're here,' he said. 'Come on my show.'

I was driven to a stadium the size of Wembley where his programme took place. There I was guided onto a stage so dazzlingly lit I could not see the audience of 3,000. David dashed up to me, gave me several rib-cracking hugs and 'pleased-to-see-yous'. We sat down. He held up the book, waved it about, introduced me. He then asked a couple of dull questions: plainly he had not read a word of it. An idea came to me. I decided to take a chance.

'David', I said, 'would it be better if instead of talking about the book I told the audience about you?' He looked thrilled, relieved.

'Go ahead,' he said.

So I started on some of the stories I had gathered over my years of knowing him. The audience laughed a lot. All too soon it was time for the commercial break. David summoned the floor manager.

'Could you arrange to postpone the next act,' I heard him say, 'so that Angela can carry on telling these stories?'

When they came to an end and I'd had several more hugs I made my way to the stage door. To my amazement there was a crowd of about two hundred people waving the book and wanting my autograph. This, as my publisher explained, was not because it was the first novel by an unknown English author, but because it was by the girl who seemed able to tell appealing stories about David Frost.

So to him I owe my surprising sales in America ...

By the time *Nowhere Girl* was published, Q had moved back to London and Wootton was up for sale. We had been there for just four years. I sent him the first copy of the book that I received: it was dedicated to him in coded language. He sent me the most generous and loving letter in return.

But divorce was upon us: very reluctant divorce, but it had crept up on us and was overtaking us. We engaged no lawyers, made no financial arrangements. Leaving Wootton was traumatic for both of us. Even worse was the fact that we had to share our daughter. When it came to the actual departure, she was the strong one, aged six. She simply patted an outside wall by the kitchen, and said, 'Goodbye, house.'

Q, who scorned sentimentality, drove away with no backward glance. I returned inside to walk round the empty rooms – skeleton plans of all the old arrangements made by marks on walls and carpets – and wrote several charged poems of the kind that great sadness inspires. That evening there was one telephone call: Q to say that he and Candida were missing home.

I was equally missing them. But it was too late to change direction. There was nothing for it but to begin our separate lives.

13

Change

The divorce was technically easy. We agreed on the sharing of Candida, I asked for no money, we saw no need to employ a solicitor. I moved reluctantly to London and look back, now, with some scorn for the foolish mistake I made.

What fortunately never disappeared was work. My first novel complete and published, I took a very unlikely step into shopkeeping. This came about because when making a couple of documentaries in New York, and slipping round the magical stores of Fifth Avenue whenever I had a chance, I noticed the irresistible nightwear, all of it cotton. In England at the time, Marks & Spencer was the chief supplier of dressing gowns, nightdresses and pyjamas, and they were horrible – mostly made of slimy nylon. Why not sell the American stuff in England, I thought?

I appealed to my brother-in-law, Colin Crewe, always one to be both helpful and enthusiastic. In a trice he had found backers, and I found a charming shop in the Fulham Road which I called Night Owls. He and I went to New York for a week and spent long days visiting manufacturers in Seventh Avenue. There we came upon enormous quantities of the kind of irresistible stuff that didn't exist at home. My only problem was restraint. I could easily have spent thousands of dollars, but had to stick to our budget.

Seventh Avenue garment manufacturers, who have been in the business all their lives, live in a curious world full of unusual dialogue and ideas. Their notion of what is cute, for instance, I found puzzling. One of the friendliest sellers asked me to lunch one day. Her plan was to describe the interior of her house in the hope of persuading me to supper there one evening.

'Do you know, Angela, in our dining room the lampshades are the exact colour of a poached pear dessert I make! People notice that ...'

Night Owls had huge publicity and did amazingly well. On our first trip we spent $10,000 and reckoned the stock would last three months. It sold out in three weeks.

I did a biannual buying trip to New York for five years, then felt I had had enough of the retail world. Once Seventh Avenue had become familiar, it became boring. Besides, we were being copied. Someone came in one day and bought dozens of nightdresses: the following year they were all in the major high street shops. I left with no regrets and was paid a small farewell sum – still, I had had ten free trips to America and a lot of entertainment. And I'm pleased to see that the shop, though in very different form, is still there.

It may have been this dipping into a completely different world from writing and television that caused me to look, as I shopped, with a critical eye at supermarkets. I suggested to

Queen magazine that I should write a monthly review about them, and treat them as if they were theatre. I enjoyed that enormously. Determined not just to blast them completely, I made suggestions for improvements. Such was my attack on Sainsbury's delicatessen (they were in a period of lurid green false parsley) that John Sainsbury, then chairman, invited me to design some new pâtés. I spent a morning in a large London branch with three directors with notebooks, all solemnly nodding at my suggestions. One of the pâtés I had made I called Covent Garden – John was chairman at the time of the Royal Opera House. That went down well and I realised how interesting it was to dip into other people's business that had nothing in common with my own work.

After writing about Marks & Spencer, I was invited to lunch with the board of directors where they, too, all politely wrote down my ideas – no more plastic belts or buttons, for instance – and put many of them into practice. Boots approached me about sleepwear for babies after I had berated them for not putting press studs on the legs of babygrows. The difficulty of getting a leg out of the garment, in those days, was ridiculous, but they hadn't thought of that. Still, today, I find myself writing various journalist pieces that I like to think are more helpful than solemn, and enjoy the scrutinising which seems to come naturally.

I could never like living in London, though I was lucky enough to find the perfect small flat under the eaves of a huge house in Holland Park. The estate agent who met me there had brought a torch. Its beam was needed. The place was pitch dark. There was no electricity. Nor was there a window in the bedroom.

'You can see why most people didn't want it,' he said.

But its imperfections seemed trivial to me, and because of them the asking price was extraordinarily exiguous, even then: £6,000. Today it would be hard to buy for £600,000.

I moved in with Candida, whose school was a ten-minute walk away. Sometimes she went to stay with Quentin, in his London flat, or his farmhouse in Staffordshire. I began to write my second novel, *Virginia Fly Is Drowning,* which I later adapted for television: my childhood friend Anna Massey had the lead. I had also started writing plays for television, including the commissioned *Special Co-respondent* for Granada TV, starring Maureen Lipman.

Not long after that, Terence Brady, actor, writer and pro-ducer, commissioned me to write for a series he was producing of plays about holidays. I agreed instantly but then, sitting down to write it, realised I simply did not have an idea. This was one of the very few times that something has not come to me almost instantly, and there was a deadline. In despair, I rang my friend Marika Hanbury-Tenison, the cookery writer, who fancied writing fiction and always assured me she had many ideas. She kindly gave me one. I tried – first time ever using someone else's idea. The end result was adequate but not inspired. In some dread I sent it to the BBC.

Very quickly came a call from Terence, who invited me to lunch. It was a very generous lunch over which he gently explained 'not this time, not quite what we were looking for'. It wasn't quite what I'd been looking for, either. I drove slowly away from the Television Centre, devastated. 'Don't give up,' Terence had suggested as I left him.

At the Shepherd's Bush roundabout an idea came to me.

There it was, whole and sparkling in my mind. I rushed to my desk, typed for two days and nights and sent the finished play back to Terence in a taxi. Again, there was an immediate call. He had been about to commission another writer, but as my new effort had arrived just in time, and he liked it, he would go ahead with it. Constance Cummings agreed to play the lead.

In the Seventies I went quite frequently to New York, both for Night Owls and for fun. *Beyond the Fringe* was playing triumphantly. I sent a message to Dudley Moore and very quickly found myself having lunches with him and Peter Cook, one or the other, or both of them. Peter was without doubt the funniest man I have ever met. Dudley did not make the same rib-aching jokes, or go off into brilliant, extraordinary riffs. But he was extremely funny too, despite the agonising complications in his love life about which he requested endless advice.

One evening I joined them and the Dankworths, who were doing a concert, for dinner at the St Regis Hotel. Peter suggested we dance. He was not a natural dancer, but a brilliant imitator of others' dancing. He had in mind that we should execute a few turns in the manner of the elaborate contenders in the television programme, *Come Dancing*, as popular in those days as *Strictly* is today. I merely followed him, head on one side, as we sashayed through reverse turns, dips and spins. All that was lacking was a vast sparkling dress for me, and a white tie and tails for Peter. Such was his dipping and swaying and spinning, with a ramrod back and never a hint of a smile, that the other dancers quickly left the floor, the better to watch. Our caricature dance, I know, was unforgivable showing off, but I told myself that because Peter was giving such a funny performance, I did not need to feel guilty.

In New York, too, I used to meet the two of them separately for lunch. Sometimes I had dinner with the two of them, when they would behave like a querulous old married couple – squabbling, arguing, banging fists on the table. But in the end laughter always took over.

On most Night Owls trips to New York, David Frost and I managed a meeting. Like Dudley, he seemed to want advice about his hectic love life. He would send his Cadillac round to the Algonquin to collect me. His handsome black chauffeur wore beautiful white jodhpurs. As he opened the car door I could see David lying on something that resembled a leather bed rather than the back seat of a Cadillac, his legs stretched in front of him the better for me to admire his pink tweed trousers. He wore a lot of pink tweed, David, in those days. I often wished he had asked for my sartorial advice rather than advice about girls: I would have been better able to help him. I did my best. His stories and worries were long and complicated, but he managed to be funny, and we had delicious, extravagant dinners in wildly expensive restaurants.

On one memorable evening he suggested I came back to The Plaza with him to look at 'the marvellous view of Central Park' from his sitting room. It did not occur to me that this might involve the sort of suggestions he had never made before: I agreed. When we arrived at the hotel and got out of the car, I saw him whisper to the chauffeur, whose understanding of the situation appeared to be immediate. Presumably he was used to a variety of instructions.

In David's vast suite we had a glass of champagne and, yes, went to the window to admire Central Park and the myriad lights. He put a tentative hand on my shoulder and asked if I would like to stay. I declined the invitation, and he immediately took a gentlemanly step back, laughing.

'I thought that might be the answer,' he said, 'so I told the chauffeur to hang on a bit till you made your decision. You'll find him at the door.'

We had several more happy dinners but no more Suggestions, and he said he sometimes wished more girls said No. Always obliging, he said, could tire a man out.

I grew to like my flat, if not London itself. Luckily I seemed to have had constant work. However, the financial relief did not stop the yearning to be in the country.

Warily, I began to look. Surprisingly soon I tracked down the perfect cottage between Marlborough and Pewsey, said to be 'going for a song'. This was because it was a total wreck. But I'm always attracted to wrecks with potential, imagining how they could be. It stood in one of Wiltshire's enchanting corners, looking on to fields and cows, while behind it was a gathering of magnificent elms guarding the Downs.

I took my sister and then brother-in-law, a property expert, to see it.

'Don't know about this,' said Richard. 'Lot to do.'

But I had not a single doubt. It was instant love. I could see it all.

We sat on the scraggy patch of grass, which would one day be a lawn, pondering our different opinions. Suddenly, next to us, a huge balloon of ladybirds rose into the air.

'It's Ladybird Cottage,' said Candida, aged nine, who had come with us. And so it became.

People said I was crazy. 'It's so remote,' they observed. But I've never been afraid of remote: I like it. Besides, it wasn't that remote, set on the edge of friends' land, and half a mile from a small hamlet on the lower slopes of the Downs. Only fifteen minutes from Marlborough – an appealing and unspoilt country town, then, before it became overrun with tourists on day trips. In those days, there were saddlery shops, and shops that sold tin buckets and lengths of rope. There was Edith who made thousands of pots of jam and chutney and irresistible cakes. There was the best-ever butcher, all long gone: even the weekly market is half the size it was. I feel no guilt for my nostalgia for such English country towns, now blighted by dozens of boutiques, estate agents and building societies. The ubiquitous sameness of thousands of high streets is dispiriting, though weekenders, whose chief concern seems merely to be near delicatessen exotica, appear to be less saddened than permanent country dwellers.

Ladybird Cottage, which was in fact two cottages knocked together, cost £10,000 and took nearly a year to restore. Courtesy of Rex Harrison I was able to do everything I wanted, even put in a small swimming pool. The day I moved in I was aware of the sort of exhilaration I used to feel in Florence. Total happiness, the warmth of solitude. I lighted the fires in the kitchen and the sitting room and the smell of blueberry candles, which I had found years before in New York, was a kind of private, welcoming balm. Within days, as things became familiar, I felt as if I had lived there for ever. The quarry tiles on the kitchen floor caught stray flares of light from the windows at different times of day, their shapes changing according to the mood of the sky. The latch on the kitchen door had a distinctive voice, I noticed on that first day, that still lives in my head. Ladybird was light after darkness, peace after turmoil. I intended to live there, on my own, for ever.

It's hard to remember those early 1970s days when the sophisticated electronic communication of today did not exist: I had but a landline telephone, and an old portable typewriter, so the daily silence was only broken by an occasional tractor stuttering down the nearby lane. Every day at lunchtime there was a call from Candida, at school first near Salisbury, then at Calne. She sounded mournful. My guilt at sending her to boarding school was strong, but there was little alternative unless we returned to London. I often had to be away for work – by now, writing television plays, I was needed on location – so I could not have managed a daily school run and absolute assurance of being home in the evening. She came home most weekends, bringing a group of friends, all in their Laura Ashley pinafore frocks, and with huge appetites for roast lamb and Guards Pudding. Sunday evenings were the bad time. I would drive her back to school, then return to find a forgotten pen, or a single sock on the floor. The missing, the knowing I was sacrificing too much of her childhood in order to work, was searing.

But I was haunted by having to earn the school fees: Quentin, with a new family to support on his farm, could not afford to contribute and I would not have wanted to ask him to do so. It was alarming, but possible if I worked hard – something I had always enjoyed doing.

Inevitably, friends speculated about how long I would last

'stuck out in the fields', as they saw it. To me, this was one of its many charms. Absolute peace was all I wanted. I had no thoughts of marrying again. Ladybird Cottage provided the perfect balance between solitude and visitations. For visitors there definitely were, from time to time. They came in different categories. There were dozens of old friends, there was Candida and her friends and, yes, a few men who seemed happy to visit the cottage from time to time. I liked to think they felt safe from the designs of a predatory woman because they knew I most definitely was not in search of either a husband or a live-in lover.

Michael Holroyd, not a 100 per cent countryman, was the first man to restore my faith in the appeal of men. He was wonderfully clever, self-deprecating in a very funny way, and unusually thoughtful and kind. Whenever I invited single women to meet him, they left eulogising his perfection. They all found many good reasons to contact him. Michael's visits to the cottage provided me with some valuable bits for various novels. There was the day he went for a walk on the Downs and came back pitifully rubbing his shoulder. He had 'pulled a muscle blackberrying', a phrase I used more than once in fictional stories. It denoted an especial kind of character.

Due to the success of his biography of Shaw, Michael had to spend a few years in Ireland for financial reasons. Never the most practical of men, the thought of arriving alone in Dublin and finding and furnishing a house appalled him. Would I go with him and help, he asked tentatively?

As part of me is an estate agent/interior designer, naturally I said yes. I had no idea how much work it was going to be. We met in a hotel in Dublin for a delicious lunch. When it was over he looked at his watch and said, ' Do you think you could find me something by tea time?'

I managed it. There were two possibilities, one obviously right. He agreed, and set about the transaction with unusual speed. But there were still requirements: furniture, carpets and curtains, china and kitchen stuff, and what about the walls? I returned to England, spent two weeks whirling round Wiltshire antique shops and Peter Jones, and sent him everything from beds to teaspoons. He seemed to be pleased and lived in the house for some years until he was allowed back in England.

My four years in Ladybird Cottage were a mixture of quiet, orderly, solitary working in the week and quantities of visitors at the weekend. The friends who lived nearby were not weekenders, but permanent country folk. Candida Lycett Green lived a few miles away in one direction, and Sukie Paravicini in the other. We would get together to swap problems, exchange news, and laugh. Perhaps it is one of Time's tricks, but I do remember so much laughter – mostly at our own mistakes – in the sun.

Once, Bernard Levin requested a visit, and wanted to bring his then girlfriend Arianna Stassinopoulos. I was worried about their happiness in a cottage ... but agreed. They came for a three-night weekend. Bernard, who had no idea how to dress in the country, wore his usual smart suits and ties. Arianna came down to breakfast in variations on a cocktail dress (of the sort that would have caused John Betjeman much hilarity). She also wore abundant blue eyeshadow and far too much tuberose scent. It took six weeks finally to rid every room of its potent, cloying smell.

The cottage was definitely not a natural habitat for Bernard and his girlfriend, but they declared they enjoyed it, and spent many hours drinking champagne (which, generous as always, Bernard had brought).

A memorable occasion was when the novelist Iris Murdoch and her husband John Bayley came over for lunch one Sunday. They had driven from Oxford in their Mini Traveller. Its seatless back was carpeted with old Turkish rugs and cushions. They arrived very late.

'So sorry, Angie,' John said, 'but we stopped to admire the view, bit of fun … you know?' Nudge nudge. That was the year I was a Booker judge and Iris won, though at the time of the lunch it had not been announced. Candida, aged fourteen, had come over for the day, thrilled at the thought of meeting Iris.

'I hear you have a novel in for the Booker Prize,' she began, in a reverential voice I had never heard her use before.

'Well, yes …'

'And I hear you're on the shortlist.'

'I am, yes.'

'I do hope you do well.'

'Thank you.'

'I'm sure you will.'

Candida was teased about this prim encounter for many years – but how right she was in her judgement.

Occasionally I went to London, usually for some kind of work meeting, or for a party. One rainy evening in 1976 I went to a book launch party for Piers Paul Read's book *Alive*. There, among a lively literary crowd, I spotted an extraordinarily handsome back view. Back views have always been as important to me as front views. I made my way round … and found huge melancholy eyes in an astonishingly good-looking face.

Our introduction was almost a disaster. James Howard-Johnston, as he was called, thought my name was Hooth: a name he could not fancy. But later we had a conversation about avocado pears and he took my telephone number, although he judged that Wiltshire was a place too distant to ring. And too far to ask me to come to London for a drink. An invitation to dinner did not occur to him because he never liked to sit 'eyeball to eyeball' with a girl. Luckily, we had a great mutual friend who always gave a party on New Year's Eve. Six weeks after our first meeting, during which time we subtly tried to find out about each other through mutual friends in Oxford, we re-met on New Year's Eve. James was preoccupied by one or more slight girlfriends and scarcely gave me a glance. By 3 a.m. I decided there was no point in waiting any longer. I waved to him from the door.

A moment later we were dancing, and at my postponed departure he promised to come round to my flat for a drink on New Year's Day. He did, and we've been together ever since.

James was and is a Fellow of Corpus Christi College, a university lecturer in Byzantine Studies. He was also, when we met, a Labour councillor, and worked extremely hard in both parts of his life. He lived in college in Oxford and had just bought a London flat. It was little used after our meeting as I persuaded him to spend most weekends at Ladybird Cottage. He definitely did not love it in the way that I did: he found it hostile

– the neighbouring cows, he said, glowered at him, ready to charge, when he went for walks. He gallantly appeared, none-theless, and seemed to enjoy the many gatherings.

A year after our meeting the possibility of some kind of permanency seemed to hang in the air, but no plan was mentioned. But in November 1977 we went to see the film *Jaws*, and on our return, no hint of warning, he proposed. The next morning I asked him if I could tell people the good news.

'No, certainly not,' he roared, and would not say when that time might come. I worried away, wondering if he was going to change his mind, so tried not to mention the subject of marriage again.

In the spring of 1978 we went skiing with a large party of old friends. James was a natural and excellent skier, I was not. But I did my best to follow him down fairly unfrightening slopes. He was encouraging. Then came a day of low and fierce grey sky, cold, wind – not a day to inspire keenness to be out. But I thought I'd better have my usual practice. I got on the ski lift, no other passenger at my side, and as it grunted upwards I realised that I had not pulled down the protective bar. My hands were too frozen to move. Below was a 300-foot-deep ravine. The wind was strong enough to tilt the lift chair back and forth alarmingly, and suddenly I saw all too clearly my bones at the bottom of the ravine … For fifteen minutes I sat contemplating my demise, and wondering what James would do, and how long it would take him to replace me. Mercifully, the ascent then restarted and eventually the summit was reached. My object was to pay the ski instructor, but he had arrived ahead of me and in a trice had disappeared into a wall of damp fog.

Somehow I got down that bloody mountain, falling many times in my hurry just to get back to the chalet. I arrived shivering and speechless with cold. James opened the door. There was a cry of amazement from within. No one had been worrying about me, or indeed wondering where I had been – presumably upstairs reading, they thought. They had all been indoors all afternoon playing cards. Although they were all experienced skiers, they had judged that the weather was far too horrible to go out.

Sometime in the next hour, as I concentrated on defrosting, James gave me the news that I could now tell people we were going to get married.

In August 1978 we had a small wedding in St James's Church, Pont Street. The night before, Sally had organised an extremely merry evening in her house off Ladbroke Grove. James slipped out of dinner early – he had heard of a tradition that the groom should not lay eyes on the bride until she arrived at the church. At breakfast next morning he rang to say he had one more paper to mark ... universities do not heed plans for real life. But at least he was ready: with any luck he would not be late.

At the church, poised by the altar, was my floral dream come to life – a Leaning Tower of Pisa of magically entwined flowers over twelve feet high. On the way to the reception I asked James what he had thought of the unusual arrangement – he said he hadn't noticed any flowers. But, I imagined, so as not to disappoint his new wife, on the way to catch the plane he agreed to go back to the church and take a look.

Next day we flew to Majorca, where a friend had lent us her magnificent house. There was no question of travelling light:

as a Booker judge I had to take with me some twenty or so of the hundred books on the list to be read. James took several of his scholarly tomes – as he always does on holiday – to read, in addition to long lists of Bulgarian vocabulary so that he could carry on learning one of the many languages he teaches himself. One day, on a walk, he confessed he had planned to write twelve books. 'Would you like to hear about them?' he asked.

As I knew nothing about Byzantine history, I explained that his telling, however inspired, might be wasted on me. He understood this. And when, 35 years later, the first of these brilliant tomes was published, and indeed won a major prize, I did read a good deal of it, marvelling at both his erudition and the way he wrote. Goldsmith's words about the schoolmaster in *The Deserted Village* came back to me. Only slightly changed, I've thought of them on so many occasions:

> *And still I gaze, and still the wonder grows*
> *That one small head can carry all James knows …*

On our return, James commuted by car to Oxford, while I stayed in Ladybird Cottage knowing that time was running out. Sadly, for me, we had come to the conclusion that we should move to Oxford. With no train from Wiltshire and the slowness of the A34, commuting could not be considered.

We looked only at one house, Pullens End, Headington. Six large houses had been built in the late nineteenth century in what had once been a rural lane. Pullens End was one of the only two left standing. A delightful elderly widow had lived there for many years and loved it. Inside, it reminded me of an old sewing basket: low-key sad colours, gloomy carpets, grim curtains. But it had potential, and huge windows with shutters. Outside, rare in Oxford, was an orchard of old fruit trees, and guarding it all a magnificent beech tree, said to be the largest in Oxford, which I grew to love in all its moods and colours. I set about renovations.

14

Pullens End

I was dreading moving to the city. The Ladybird Cottage corner of Wiltshire had always been my idea of happiness. Despite its renowned beauty, I had never liked Oxford. Too many hideous shops and buildings are squeezed between the colleges. Vast clumps of sightseers take over the pavements. Parking is almost impossible. I admit the interiors of some of the colleges are magnificent, though the way many of the common rooms are decorated is grim. One of these is lighted by 1970s bald lamps, of the kind chosen by many a station waiting room, while the black leather sofas are built on steel frames whose corners jab every passing leg. Handsome windows are shamed by dull, sad curtains. Whoever has the job of decorating these communal rooms, however academically talented, has no idea of comfort, colour or furniture.

Pullens End was hidden from view down a lane at the top of Headington Hill. Built in 1883, the house was far from the handsome William and Mary house of Wootton – its *jolie-laide* architecture was not the sort of thing I had ever imagined liking. But there was something endearing about it, and there always seemed to be light, if not actual sun, coming through the tall windows. As one who is happiest under huge skies, I missed that life-enhancing element. There was very little sky above our garden at Pullens End, but a bonus for me was that once you turned into the drive you would not know the city itself was only a mile away.

We settled down to thirty fleeting, happy years. Very quickly we grew to love our Victorian house, the garden, the orchard. All that was needed was a child to climb the trees, explore the attics, and watch the foxes at play under the quince tree. Our priority, once settled, was to have a baby. I was by now forty.

Our son Jedediah was born in 1979. He was a Down's baby, and also had a hole in his heart and other internal problems. He was infinitely brave, but died at nine months old. There followed two miscarriages, and instructions not to try any more for a while. But nature was in charge. A much easier pregnancy followed and in 1981 our daughter Eugenie was born.

During the long spell of pregnancies I had been contemplating writing a stage play – something I had always determined to do. My ex-sister-in-law Sally Crewe suggested I go to her barn in Norfolk, where so many happy occasions had taken place. I spent a winter week there, writing. I had made no plans, thought up no plots, though once again I was drawn to the idea of elderly characters. Planning everything in advance has never been my way of working: I simply listen to voices in my head, and add real places and landscapes. I wrote all day for five days, only giving myself an hour to walk along the empty beach where the greys of sky, sea and sand joined in a winter reunion. I returned home with a finished play that came to be *The Understanding*.

I then heard about a play competition organised by the Salisbury Playhouse and, laughing at my own foolishness, sent it off. It won. The excitement of all this, together with Eugenie's birth, meant the chronology of events is jumbled in retrospect: I am no longer sure of how the play got into the hands of the successful producer Michael White, whom I knew slightly. He liked it, and made a deal with the Salisbury Playhouse. This was an occasion when timing was wondrously right: he had been looking for a new play for five years. This was it, he said. Unbelievable. 'We're going to aim high,' he then said, and went off to telephone Ralph Richardson.

The next day Michael rang me to say Ralph, who especially liked the fact that there was a red car that roared off-stage in the play, had taken just two hours to accept the part. Shortly after that, after many discussions about who would play the leading lady, Ralph managed to persuade Celia Johnson to take it. Margaretta Scott and Margaret Rawlings joined the cast – a fine trio of old ladies – while Sylvestra Le Touzel became the young girl with whom Ralph merrily flirted in an orchard of paper trees.

Michael took me to meet Ralph at lunch in Claridge's. He turned up in striped trousers, waistcoat with fob watch, black jacket – to me, wonderfully appealing men's clothes. We got off to an easy start: he had known and worked with my father. There was a lot of talk about painting – Ralph was a pretty good watercolourist. Little talk about the play. Ralph merely said he was looking forward to it all, and agreed with me his character should wear a red cardigan to echo the fictional car. There was a surprising end to the lunch. When the coffee came, Ralph simply poured his into his saucer, and drank it from that.

There followed a couple of months of glorious rehearsal. I found it hard to believe my words were being spoken by such distinguished actors. The rehearsal room was somewhere near Paddington Station. Ralph would drive right into it on his yellow motorbike that matched his yellow socks and yellow helmet. Sometimes his parrot would be sitting on his shoulder. Celia would appear with a string bag full of Brussels sprouts in preparation for the weekend.

'Oh dear,' she would sigh, 'I'm having dinner at Royal Lodge on Saturday and Queen Elizabeth wants me to read some poems. I've got to find something ...' She tapped the old anthology she had brought with her, her mind far more deeply entrenched in sprouts and poems than the play. I was intrigued by her and Ralph's belief that there was not much need for discussion of the text. When the moment came they simply cast off the string bag and yellow helmet, moved to the set and played the scene as if they had been rehearsing for weeks. 'Don't really need to go into it all, duckie,' Ralph would say to anyone who demanded to know what it all meant.

Rehearsals had their good and bad moments. The director, who had previously directed Nell Dunn's *Steaming*, had made copious notes and worked out for himself all sorts of meanings (which had not occurred to me) in the text. He wanted to explain them to the cast. But it seemed all he could do was to give very mild suggestions to the three less famous actors. The set designer had also worked on *Steaming* and had done well. But she was not acquainted with drawing rooms and *The Understanding* was set in an old-fashioned drawing room. 'What does one look like?' she asked. I tried to be helpful and steer her away from the hotel lounge look she had gone for. Meantime, foolishly, the director told her to produce the clothes. When the distinguished actresses turned up to show Ralph what they had been given, he snorted in disbelief.

'They look like a lot of cooks,' he roared. 'Tell them to go to Hardy Amies and get decently dressed.'

Ralph was frequently in touch on the telephone. He spent a great deal of time in his study, overlooking Regent's Park, talking. Once he rang me at 2 a.m.

'I say, duckie, I've just finished a painting I thought would make a good cover for the programme. Come and see it.'

It was a charming picture, but sadly not used.

The play opened in Richmond to rewarding reviews and packed houses. It ran for two weeks before moving on to Brighton where, again, it was hard to get a ticket. It was then to go to The Strand Theatre in London. The Falklands War was raging and audiences had thinned everywhere: we just hoped.

The Sunday before the opening, I had a call from Celia's son-in-law Johnny Grimond. He told me Celia had died that afternoon while playing bridge.

As well as the shock and sadness, this meant a crisis for Michael White: he was frantic. Ralph categorically refused to act with the understudy. The Strand Theatre was dark until

Joan Greenwood magnanimously came to our rescue. Once again the director seemed not able to help her – she relied on Ralph, she told me, for directions.

The play opened the night after the sinking of the *Belgrano*, when even comedies were deserted. Joan had bronchitis and could hardly be heard in the vast auditorium, which was far from full. Ralph, more traumatised by events than he would admit, often left out several pages of his words, but would then say to the audience 'Oh, I should have said ...' and returned to the part he had missed. It was sometimes confusing, but the audience loved him whatever he did.

The Understanding petered out, came to an end after eight weeks. To my amazement the distinguished critic Harold Hobson gave it a marvellous review: but it was too late. Some time later it went round Germany for a year, and I adapted it for television: Rachel Kempson took Celia's part.

I did not see Ralph again for some years. Then we were invited to an Oxfordshire lunch where Queen Elizabeth the Queen Mother was to be. She was in high spirits and promised to start reading William Trevor, whom I had recommended. After lunch we drove in a convoy of very grand cars to Sir John Gielgud's house, one of the wings of the Soane house at Wootton (now owned by Tony Blair). Ralph and his wife were staying there: we were to join them all for tea.

We walked across a lawn towards the house. Coming to meet us, arms outstretched, were the two spry old knights, both in beautiful tweed suits and racing to get to Queen Elizabeth first. Ralph, I remember, was the winner. We all moved on to the house. At the bottom of the steps leading to the drawing room was a wire cage, home to a couple of tortoises. They appeared to be sunbathing.

'Oh, Ralph, do you think they can talk?' Queen Elizabeth asked Ralph.

'Not sure, ma'am,' he said. But he was keen to oblige with an answer. 'I'll find out.' He bent low over the cage. The netting buckled under his weight as he aimed his ear to the ground, the better to catch tortoise conversation. The exquisite tweed of his suit was strained almost to splitting. His friend Sir John looked on anxiously, and eventually heaved Ralph up. He gave another bow to Queen Elizabeth.

'Still not quite sure, ma'am,' he said.

John led us into the drawing room – a very long and elegant room decorated with an extravagance of gold. Despite the brightness of high summer outside, there was a strange feeling of New Year's Eve within, as if the room had been decorated for a party and no one had remembered to take down the decorations. A handsome man, John's partner – wearing a navy blazer with gold buttons, the kind of blazer that is ubiquitous at regattas – was carrying a tray of blinis in tall glasses. We took them into the room where we were to have tea – a long and narrow room almost entirely filled by a table of matching shape. It must have taken half a dozen helpers from the village a whole day to transform it into something resembling a scene from a ballet. The food had been arranged in peaks balanced on exquisite porcelain plates – strawberries, raspberries, éclairs, ten kinds of different miniature sandwiches, small cakes, large cakes … Enough for fifty people, and we were but ten.

Ralph's wife sat at one end of the table to pour tea from two vast silver pots. Queen Elizabeth took her place between the two old knights, who brilliantly flirted with her. She sat there enchanted, her feathery hat flying between them as they amused her with hilarious stories. It was the tea of a lifetime.

When we left, John and Ralph came out to wave goodbye. Ralph was planning to revisit the tortoises to have another try at conversation. It was the last time I saw him.

My worry, after Eugenie's birth, was how was I going to manage both to work and look after her. Luckily we found Jenny Hey, sixty, and 'needing a small job'. She came every morning at nine o'clock and remained part of our lives till she died.

James stayed at home till lunchtime, thus leaving me four uninterrupted hours every day. I took over in the afternoon, and James was a wonderfully hands-on father at weekends. He was determined that Eugenie should go to a state school. I was not in any way averse to this, provided we could find a good one. I looked at six. They were not impressive. Eugenie, at five, and thanks to Mrs Hey, was a fluent reader. I explained this to various teachers and asked if reading, at five, was on the curriculum. It definitely was not.

'If she's a *reader*,' sneered one of them, ' she can sit at the back of the class and entertain herself.' She was the same teacher who explained that the children playing in a sandpit were doing 'Geography'.

I reported nervously back to James, who was in the Labour Group on the county council. He tried to change my mind. He even summoned the chief primary adviser of Oxfordshire to win me round. When that failed, he agreed that Eugenie could go to the local private school, which in the event was not much of an improvement. But some time after these early disasters, I brought out an anthology of poems for children especially written by some fifty contemporary poets. I was then asked to the Christmas Fair at the Dragon School to sign the books, and the registrar enquired whether my daughter would be coming to the school. I explained there was no hope – we had not put her down at birth.

'Never mind,' she said, 'if you let me know by Monday morning if you would like her to come here, there will be a place for her next term.'

The incident could not be described as politically correct, and would doubtless not happen today. But James was delighted Eugenie was to go to The Dragon. He had already resigned from the council when she went to the local private school, although Labour colleagues were unanimous in pressing him to stay. They regarded a man's yielding to the will of a woman as trumping the educational argument. For some reason his resignation made a good many headlines in the papers, and for a while freelance photographers were constantly sneaking up our drive and hiding in the bushes.

The Oxford years were a combination of hard work and entertainment.

There were several gregarious hosts among heads of colleges, all of whom gave frequent and spirited parties. Harvey McGregor (New College) had an idea that undergraduates should meet well-known people from whom they could learn something about real life. With this in mind he used to give lunch parties for some twenty undergraduates and half a dozen distinguished folk who had made a name for themselves. I was invited to some of these lunches to 'help' with the undergraduates, though was never quite sure what I was meant to be doing. On one occasion I sat next to a third-year history student. Iris Murdoch was on his other side. I asked him if he had read any of her books.

'Who?' he said.

'Iris Murdoch. She's on your other side.' He gave her a shifty look.

'Never heard of her,' he said, which seemed to indicate that a love of reading was not ubiquitous among Oxford undergraduates.

Bernard Levin was one of the distinguished guests on that occasion. He did not look well and plainly was not feeling well. But after lunch he agreed to move to Harvey's drawing room and talk to the undergraduates. Suddenly he perked up and for an hour gave a mesmerising performance, shifting from politics to literature to philosophy. His audience – though several of them had not heard of him, either – was delighted. But within moments of finishing he had sunk back into a kind of puzzled stupor and found it hard getting downstairs. I drove him to the station and offered to come with him to London, but he insisted he was fine. I rang him later, relieved to find he had arrived safely. Soon after that a long, grim period of illness overtook him. It was the last time I was to see him.

James and I did a certain amount of entertaining, too, in our Oxford years. We had many a weekend when friends stayed, and others joined for lunches and dinners. Princess Margaret came frequently (often from 2.30 p.m. on Friday till 2.30 p.m. on Monday). She was an avid sightseer and loved academics, so was easy to entertain. On one occasion we took her to Magdalen for a drink with the historian Angus Macintyre.

There had been a Commem Ball the night before, and Angus' room was awash with dirty glasses, and plates encrusted with dried scrambled egg.

'Let's just get all this tidied up,' Princess Margaret smiled at Angus, 'and then you can give me a tutorial.'

She pulled her weight in the clear-up, and then sat down in front of him, intrigued by the thoughts of her eminent new tutor. On Monday morning it would all be recollected in her diary. She was extremely well informed on a number of subjects, always keen to learn, and her memory was excellent. Once she asked a historian from Oriel College if he could remember every Pope who had ever headed the Catholic Church. As he went through the list, by heart, she wrote down their names. He only missed out one, which a don from Somerville supplied. She loved that evening.

She also loved less academic occasions, particularly those that were musical.

John Dankworth and Cleo sometimes came over from Wavendon. John would play the piano while the princess and Cleo sang the whole way through *Guys and Dolls,* which had become their party piece.

The princess was well known for her enjoyment of late nights, but she never presented us with that problem. At approximately 11.30 p.m. James would give a faintly fierce look at his watch. She would jump up at once and agree it was bedtime. Aware that Pullens End was no stately home with a lot of staff, and that we had a certain amount to do in the morning, she always wanted to be helpful. Her particular job was the fire. In our house, and many others, she made it her duty to keep it going with constant logs.

A frequent guest, she was also a frequent host. I often stayed in Kensington Palace, after a theatre or ballet, while James slipped back to Oxford. She liked taking us on what she called her 'treats'. These were memorable occasions she devised for the pleasure of her friends. She took twenty of us to a candlelit Westminster Abbey at 9 p.m. one night. While the organ softly played, we were given a unique tour of the abbey's treasures. As the princess got older and her health declined, I frequently went alone to stay with her. We would go to the ballet, or for a swim at Buckingham Palace, and I would suggest novels I thought she might like. She was a copious reader, always keen for recommendations.

I was often asked to write about her, but never did. Then, not long before she died, the *Daily Telegraph* said they would like a piece about her by an old friend. Would I be willing? I hesitated, but agreed to do it if she gave her permission. It would give me a chance, I thought, to scotch the many disagreeable views of her that had been published over so many years. It would give me a chance to show what a good friend she was. I wrote a very long article and took it round to the nursing home she was in at the time. She declared she was delighted, and said I had only one thing wrong: she wasn't as keen on short stories as I had made out.

Very shortly after that, I went round for tea with her at Kensington Palace. She came downstairs, but was in her dressing gown. As one who rarely ate very much, she enjoyed all the delicious cakes and biscuits that had, unusually, been put out. As always we swapped news of what books we were reading, talked about plays she was planning to see, laughed at all the sort of things that always made us laugh. She was plainly tired, though. When would we meet again, we wondered? We were both vague about this, concealing our secret suspicions as we kept smiling and laughing until the last cakes and biscuits had gone. Then I hurried away, leaving her alone in the dining room, knowing that her faithful butler, John, would be with her as soon as I had left.

She died a few days later.

Living in Oxford, I found it imperative to get out of the city as often as possible. We spent every holiday at Oxnead Mill House in Norfolk. My friend Felicity's parents, meanwhile, rented a cottage in Brancaster, where we stayed on many an occasion. We spent our days on the dunes and the beach, picnicking, swimming, cogitating. Most evenings Felicity and I would go to the marsh and make ourselves reasonably comfortable on huge concrete blocks, left from the war, which only disappeared in the 1970s. At this time – we were both just twelve – we would confess our hopes (lipstick and boys), argue about poetry, and giggle as we contemplated the horizon. Sometimes, after supper with our sisters, we would turn the cottage kitchen into a 'nightclub', dress up in demure scarves belonging to Felicity's mother, and dance on the kitchen table. It was an innocent time.

Since then Brancaster has changed dramatically, with more and more new houses stretch out in every direction. Many of the most expensive ones are left empty much of the year, presumably while their owners wait for their value to go up even further. The village shop, with its cosy past of Bisto, custard powder, boiled sweets and shoe polish, shut down long ago. Now, for food and newspapers people have to drive further along the coast to a garage-cum-charmless-supermarket. Brancaster, despite its myriad new houses, gives the distinct impression of a deserted village, even in high summer.

But the saddest change is in the local small town of Burnham Market — now, understandably, referred to as Chelsea on Sea. Fifty years ago it was a delightful village of unpretentious shops and places to eat. Now, it's clogged with enormously tall, fat cars whose owners come to shop in the overpriced boutiques. Their voices rend the air as they clamour among the gift shops that have replaced the more modest shops of old. The baker, who for over fifty years had been making the best bread on the east coast, finally exhausted by rising at 4 a.m. every morning, closed down in 2014. His appealing old shop is now, inevitably, another boutique … Why, I wonder, are so many boutiques, selling so many of the same things, needed – indeed, wanted? It's an horrible vulgar money,

My ex-brother- and -sister-in-law, Colin and Sally Crewe, did not know Norfolk in the early 1970s, when I first persuaded them to go there. Such was their enchantment that they determined to find a house, and were lucky enough to come upon an old barn in Brancaster which faced the marsh, distant dunes and sea. They bought it. Sally, who has a way with transforming places, turned it into the place myriad families and children will remember for the rest of their lives. We spent some thirty summers there and I would often stay there alone in the winter to write. Both my daughters first went to Norfolk in carrycots, as did their own children. The barn was an annual reunion place for family and friends, brought together by a shared love of it, but it no longer exists. Sold a few years ago, it has now undergone 'boutique-ing' and is unrecognisable. Luckily, the cottage in which we danced on the kitchen table in the 1950s is still there, and is for rent. So that is our summer place now, very un-smart, comfortable, large garden, mature sofas partnered by ailing armchairs ... Since the summer rush to Norfolk is now considerable, we are very lucky still to be able to have our holidays there.

Norfolk is the place I most want to be when I'm not at home. I find myself describing much-loved corners in almost every novel I write. And I paint there – rather feeble watercolours of dun-coloured distances and wavering skies. I have learnt, by going from place to place with my paints, that Norfolk is not as flat as it is generally thought to be. There are rises and falls in the huge wheat fields, long sloping views down to the sea. The hedges, very dark against the crops, are like broken necklaces, full of gaps. And, not far inland from the coast, the trees are magnificent, vast and dark; while those on the coast are wispier, wind-tossed.

When I met James, in 1976, he knew nothing of Norfolk, had never been there. He came to the barn, where various friends were staying. I took him for a walk, that first evening, along the dunes. There was a high tide and, very close to where we were standing to take in the huge panorama of the fading sea, a seal was swimming. I had never seen a seal at Brancaster before, and never have since. We moved on. It kept abreast of us. James was enchanted. Instantly, it seemed, love of Norfolk came upon him. Before long he had bought a small boat and returned to his old love of sailing. Sometimes, long after summer holidays are over, he returns to catch a high tide, and gets together with his many sailing friends. He is an adventurous traveller, goes all over the world both lecturing and exploring, but Norfolk seems to hold an especial place in his heart.

From time to time we paid duty visits to James's mother, Xandra, who was married to Lord Dacre (Hugh Trevor-Roper). They lived in a charming but deeply gloomy house near Melrose, once owned by Walter Scott. Hugh loved Scotland, the house, the garden, the walks. Xandra did not share these passions. Accustomed to a grand pre-war life, it did not occur to her to try to make the house less gloomy, and certainly she had never experienced the inclination to learn to cook. We suffered some of the most inedible meals I can ever remember – in particular her cottage pie. Her method was to boil mince for a very long time and smear it with equally watery mashed potatoes. For supper we had 'soup': i.e. the water the mince had been cooked in. Neither Xandra nor Hugh was at ease with children, and their feelings were not hidden. Both Candida and Eugenie had grim times there. On one occasion Eugenie, very hungry, stretched out for an apple in the fruit bowl on the dining-room table.

'No!' shrieked Xandra, 'You can't eat that! It's wax.'

Luckily, Xandra's brother Dawyck Haig lived close by in a magical, rather spooky old house, Bemersyde, given to his father after the First World War. James had spent much of his childhood there and was devoted to his uncle, who taught him to shoot, and to fish on the Tweed, which ran through a deep valley beneath the house. On visits to Scotland we would spend as much time as we could at Bemersyde.

While Hugh loved their Scottish life, for Xandra it was all

too much hard work, so she was delighted when he was made Master of Peterhouse, and they left for Cambridge. All dreary chores would be taken from her: all she had to do was invite people to dinner and look glamorous. Which she did, for she loved clothes and took great trouble over her appearance. I included her in a book called *The English Woman's Wardrobe.* Four pages of photographs in some of her most beautiful suits and dresses. She was thrilled by that. It caused the ever-hovering chill between daughter-in-law and mother-in-law slightly to thaw.

James, as was Quentin, is a keen traveller, taking many trips to far-off countries to explore ancient sites. Sometimes he went alone, sometimes with his friend Nigel Ryan, one-time head of ITN, a delightfully funny and knowledgeable man, and wonderful travelling companion. They wrote a book together called *The Scholar and the Gipsy.* James, naturally, was not the gipsy. I rarely went abroad with him unless it was to Italy, for which I have a kind of Keats/Shelley passion, or America. I dislike going to countries where I can't speak the language, which obviously leaves me with little choice. (James reads and understands a lot of languages.) I'm always extremely happy to stay at home, or make short excursions to somewhere in the British Isles.

Once Eugenie was at The Dragon, and then Cheltenham Ladies' College, I had a luxurious amount of time in which to work. I wrote a second stage play, *The Trouble with Old Lovers,* which over the years did three long tours, though never came to London. I compiled anthologies (poems for children, eulogies) wrote three collections of short stories and fifteen novels.

One of them was *Land Girls*, about whom I knew nothing, but remembered pictures in my childhood of girls in dungarees, tight jumpers and fetching hats. I was halfway through another novel at the time, not racing along, and the idea about the land girls persisted. As is always my way, I avoided research: I knew enough about country life, the changing of the seasons and the rotation of crops to feel safe with that side of things; all I had to do was find the characters. I wrote chapter one, then decided to write the next one actually in the country somewhere. I borrowed a freezing cottage in Dorset. Rain and fog concealed most of the landscape, but, magically, various characters revealed themselves and I came home with the book at full sail.

It's never easy to define why one book takes off, and another does not. My second novel, *Virginia Fly is Drowning,* I adapted for television, as I did the third one, *Sun Child*. They both did well, but nothing like *Land Girls* which, I suppose, nostalgically conjured a time that a great many of my elderly readers remembered with great affection. I took it to a friend at the BBC, Ruth Jackson, with whom I had made *The English Woman's Wardrobe* documentary starring Mrs Thatcher. Ruth was one of those rare people who make up their minds in a trice. Yes, she said: feature film.

Then there was all the fun of shooting in Devon, with Anna Friel, Rachel Weisz and Catherine McCormack. The slight hitch was that the director had not read the book, and did not want to. He had lived on a farm as a child and I imagine he thought he could simply transpose his experience into my story. Naturally some important bits were left out, and some weird bits put in, but it looked glorious.

I took Eugenie to the shoot one day, having persuaded the producer to allow her to be an extra – a land girl on a tractor. I was keen to make a small appearance myself for the sake of tradition – my father always managed to get himself so minuscule a part in his own films that my mother never noticed. It was suggested I had a non-speaking part as a councillor. I was ordered merely to *look* like a councillor … The morning of the shoot, Eugenie was fetched at 6 a.m. by a chauffeur in a Mercedes. Sometime later I was told to walk to the village. There, in a huge building, was the film wardrobe. With some difficulty I chose some pretty unattractive 1940s clothes, then joined the crowds that lined the small main street. I looked up to see, on the first tractor, my land-girl daughter doing the full actor bit, waving like crazy. As they passed me I yelled to Eugenie. I heard her response to the girl next to her. 'Who on earth is the old bat shouting my name?' she asked. Plainly I was unrecognisable.

A novel that is turned into a feature film can obviously make a huge difference to book sales. *Land Girls* sold in many countries, providing me with foreign publishers. The one I was most pleased about was the French publisher, La Table Ronde: it has published every book since, and almost my whole backlist. I discovered that French publishers have far more respect for writers than do English publishers: they treat them with extraordinary awe and give them a good time. It's a help if the writers speak French: that is much appreciated. At one large book signing in Paris, books all paid for, the customers sat about making no move to leave. 'What do you want?' I eventually asked. 'Please just speak to us,' they said. 'Tell us about your life.'

I had made no notes, given my life no thought, but began to speak and was still speaking an hour later. Then the listeners all got up and bought more copies of the book as well as several copies of previous books. But there was an even stranger time: my editor took me to the Gallimard bookshop where I was introduced to the formidable woman who ran it. When she heard my name, she dropped into a deep curtsey ... For some unfathomable reason I'm much better received in France than I am here.

Quentin, with whom I always remained close, discovered that living in India was not what he had imagined, so after a year he returned to England. I found him a very agreeable flat in the old converted wool mill at Chipping Norton, where he happily spent the last few years of his life. So close to Oxford, we were able to visit him regularly and he often came to Pullens End. He and James held many views in common and joined in teasing me, and he loved Eugenie and her adventurous spirit. Sadly he died before her gap year: her adventures would have appealed to him greatly.

Both my mother and my mother-in-law moved to care homes, so there was much visiting of the elderly. And the rewarding thing was that Hugh became more benign, and seemingly happy, despite his afflictions: he had Charles Bonnet Syndrome − a disease of the eyes that renders someone not only near blind, but also haunted and confused by images of nonexistent things. But he was determined to remain independent. This meant he had some alarming near misses. On one occasion, at Didcot Station, he asked a porter, 'What time does this train leave?' and walked towards the edge of the platform. There was no train. On another occasion, sitting beside me in the drawing room, which looked on to a cherry tree in full bloom, I asked him what he could see. 'A large graveyard,' he said. 'The gravestones are all bending about in the wind.'

One of the pleasures of Oxford was a return to dancing. Ever since a couple of glorious moments of tap-dancing with Cleo Laine, on live television in 1967, I had longed to get back to it. I found classes in Cowley, run by the council, and signed up. Once a week seemed not frequent enough for me, so I arranged private lessons with the inspiring teacher. She persuaded me to take part in what was an annual show for the Cowley workers. She and I did a number to one of my favourite songs, 'We're a Couple of Swells', made famous by Judy Garland. After many rehearsals I could manage the steps: it was remembering the long routine (four minutes) that was hard. (Perhaps, I remember thinking, this was the beginning of old age.) Eugenie was the only member of the family who came to support me in the audience of 300 who turned up. The others perhaps guessed it would be too embarrassing. For me, the top hat, the cane, that music, that slinky tapping: it was a thrilling occasion. Now, I still dance in private along our stone passages, and still hope that one day I can find more lessons.

I could never grow to like Oxford, but we were lucky in our life there. Candida and her husband came to live in Park Town, so the three grandsons spent much time with us. And once Eugenie's gap year was over (a year covering a great deal of the world, doing charitable work), she came up to Oxford to read Classics at New College. For us that meant four years of the happy swish of undergraduates through the house and garden, the summer sipping of white wine under the beech tree. My regret of never having been to Oxford myself flared occasionally, but the vicarious life was very enjoyable. From time to time I mentioned to James how good it would be to leave the city for the country. Once Eugenie had left home to teach in London, and his retirement drew nearer, he finally agreed.

15

Forty Years On

To recognise, instantaneously, whether a house is for you is a form of falling in love that some people are blessed with – and is certainly a help when looking for somewhere new. It happened for me with Wootton, Ladybird Cottage and Pullens End, but it did not happen sixty-seven times when we decided to leave Oxford. Often the estate agents had failed to mention a piggery next to the garden, or a vast building jammed up against the house, so I did not bother to get out of the car and look inside. But I did enjoy some of the 'strongly recommended' interior decorations: such as the bathroom, in a sixteenth-century cottage, that 'boasted' an ultra-modern shallow basin swinging from an aged beam.

Then, one day in 2006, beginning to despair, I looked on the internet and found a very handsome Georgian farmhouse in Warwickshire. I rang the agents and said I imagined it was no longer on the market as it was just the sort of house that attracts people wanting to live in the country. The estate agent laughed. Not many people had been after it, she explained, on account of the CV (Coventry) postcode. 'People from London want GL,' (Gloucestershire) she assured me. 'They wouldn't consider a CV.' Not being of that ilk myself, I arranged a viewing.

In the two years I had been looking at houses I learnt much about estate agents and what a rum bunch they are. The women are often dressed as if for a part in a James Bond film, and turn up in a snarling sports car. What they have not taken into account is the fact that their stilettos are not up to a tour of the garden, so the prospective buyer stands no chance of being guided to the roses. (A relief, in fact.) They share an annoying habit of constantly pointing out things you can see for yourself. 'Just look out of the window,' one of them said, giving me a bossy nudge – 'look at that tree.'

The woman who greeted me at the sixty-eight house was dressed as if she was going to a race meeting and wanted to make her mark in the paddock. Her white stilettos nearly tripped her up several times as she tried to cross the gravel courtyard. She knew nothing about the history of the house, but had her own ideas. I followed her down dangerous steps to an extremely damp cellar. 'I expect this is where you'll want to put the children,' she cooed in an attempt, I daresay, to bond with her client.

I seethed with fury at her incompetence, but did not really care because this was the house I knew we had to have. It had everything I longed for: a courtyard, large south-facing windows and infinite possibilities. It also had a cottage, a barn, stables and eight acres – not quite the downsizing we had intended, but irresistible. Added to that there had been little work on it for forty years: things needed doing.

Pullens End, meantime, had been sold to the Bishop of Oxford, so at least we knew we could pay for a new house. But on Christmas Eve 2006, he and his advisers pulled out: panic ensued. Luckily someone else stepped in, and such were my enthusiastic descriptions of Temple House that, although James had not seen it, he agreed we should make an offer. We did so at once – it was accepted immediately. Then came the moment James had to see what I assured him was the perfect house.

He had lived in Oxford for much of his life and did not want to move to the country, though agreed that as his retirement was coming up it was my turn to choose the new house.

He was appalled – above all because it made the prospect of moving all too real. As he examined the rooms he looked sadder and sadder – leaving his much-loved Oxford house, I could see him thinking, for this. I tried to describe what it would be like when walls were ripped down, bookshelves put up, new fireplaces ... but he couldn't see it. Most people find it hard to envisage change. It was up to me to make him fall in love just as I had done. So the agreement was he would not return till at least most of the work was finished.

It took some eight months before we were able to move in, though builders carried on for a long time. We saved a great deal of money by not employing an architect. I would simply draw plans, and details of shelves and cupboards, thereby avoiding tedious discussions as well as saving thousands of pounds. There was still the barn to be renovated, and the major job of restoring the cottage for future tenants, and the garden ... But once we were in, the miracle happened. James, too, became devoted to the house. No matter how late a night we have in

London or Oxford, he wants to return home and wake up there. His study is on the top floor, overlooking a gentle English landscape of fields, horses, sheep, trees: he loves it as much as I do. My study, two floors down, has the same view.

We have lived in Temple House for ten years, now, and have settled into a tranquil life that we hope we may never have to leave. One of the delights of old age, to many, is the planning of retirement, the joy of giving up the work and routine that has ruled so many years. James and I have never entertained such thoughts. Life without work does not exist in our plans, although James' job as a don officially came to an end in 2009. There was a farewell dinner given for him in Corpus, where many lively tributes were made about his talent as a teacher, and his qualities as a historian. The dinner went on very late, but the next morning he was up at his usual early hour. I asked where he was going. 'To my office,' he said. I reminded him that last night he had officially retired, a fact that plainly had not made the slightest difference to his plans. There has scarcely been a day since that he has not gone into Oxford to teach, to do research, to prepare a lecture or join colleagues several times a week in lessons of ancient languages (Ethiopic, Syriac and Arabic among others), and recently he announced that he had found three more scholars who, like him, could not resist the idea of learning Chinese. But Chinese characters proved too much for him.

The job James had so determinedly clung to after the retirement party is not exactly as it was. He no longer teaches undergraduates: his pupils, most coming informally, are now all graduates. That leaves him with more time for his own work – time to finish his second major tome. The first one, *Witnesses to a World Crisis*, which took him some twenty years to write, was published in 2010. Much to his surprise it won the British-Kuwait Friendship Prize from the Mubarak Foundation in Kuwait. When he's not reading work-related books, he goes through quantities of thrillers, history books and novels. There are few free moments in his days, either in Oxford or at home. But he's a crafty Scrabble player, and a keen watcher of football and motor racing. He is also a wonderful grandfather to his two official grandsons, and to his three step-grandsons. He loves them all equally, and the love is mutual.

Like James, I too hope never to retire unless I am forced to by some misfortune of health or circumstance. For most of my life, except for a few years as a journalist and a television reporter, I have kept to a self-imposed routine that I would find very difficult to give up. On holiday I try to keep to at least a measure of that routine in the mornings, because I find it hard to imagine beginning the day not at my desk. I get up at 6.30 a.m., and switch on the computer at 8.30. I write until lunchtime then, every day, eat oats with honey, yoghurt and blueberries, so there is no need to ponder on anything else – making decisions about food is one of my least favourite occupations. I deal with admin and go for a walk, gauging the seasons by the magnificent trees that long ago replaced the famous Warwickshire elms. I try to think about what, if anything, I should write next. My dread is that one day the ideas stop coming …

To date, I have always started a new novel or short story when a first sentence has appeared in my mind. Occasionally I have to wait a while for a character to have a name, and once that has arrived I can write the first paragraph, which has been clear to me for some time. After that, it's free fall. I write from 8.30 a.m. till 1 p.m. – almost never in the afternoon. I avoid all research if possible: on occasions this, I shamefully confess, has led to risible mistakes, such as the time I declared Inverness was on the wrong coast of Scotland. Very rarely do I just stop writing – although, occasionally, for a few worrying moments, not a single word appears. Once when this happened I looked out of my Oxford study window and saw a cat stalking a pigeon. It leapt, killed: feathers ballooned in heart-breaking clumps. This small incident became the next paragraph in *Invitation to the Married Life*, and I was on my way again.

Many people have suggested that leading a relatively unexciting life in the country must be boring after all the dazzle of Oxford. I completely disagree. In the country you are always aware of the profoundly gratifying rhythm of the seasons, whereas in cities it's often not possible to tell what time of year it is. One of the pleasures of the quiet life in the country is the daily lack of large excitements: the routines that gently tumble on, unremarked. James fills the dishwasher, I empty it. He puts out the rubbish, I order plants for the garden.

We rarely go to London, except to the occasional theatre or exhibition, but are lucky to be very well culturally provided for here: Warwick Arts Centre, Birmingham, Oxford and Stratford. At weekends there's some to-ing and fro-ing between Warwickshire friends' houses, but as we're all slightly more tired than of old, and very busy, that form of entertainment is much less frequent than it used to be. Our life now is a quiet one, though punctuated with gregarious moments.

295

With time running out there are just a few goals left to chide us: James the traveller longs to go to Peru and return to India. I want a new floor in the barn so that I can organise more tap lessons.

We are lucky in that the children and grandchildren live near enough for frequent visits. Candida and her husband were divorced in 2008, but Candida stayed on in Oxford with her three endearingly spirited boys – an actor (19) training to be a chef, a computer programmer (17) of extraordinary talent – already global jobs are beckoning – and a Polo-playing architect (15). The boys' father, Donnie, taught them to shoot rabbits and pigeons in our fields: they seem to love coming here – as happy as they are every summer in Norfolk. Candida is constantly employed as a journalist by several national newspapers, but the job she most loves is teaching university students who want to write better, and helping them to do so.

Eugenie, back from three years in San Francisco, where she had been studying at Berkeley, returned here for our first Christmas in 2007. One William Paul Teasley III, known as Bud, from South Carolina, came with her. They had met at the end of her gap year, kept in touch all through her Oxford years, occasionally crossed oceans for brief meetings. That Christmas they walked over the fields to Chesterton church, a small church on a rise of land a couple of miles away. No electric light, no heating. They sat on a bench outside and Bud proposed. Due to technical regulations they had to have a wedding in America. That took place in California, on the beach where Hitchcock had filmed *The Birds*. Eugenie wore a dress from eBay, and gumboots against the wet sand. The wife of the vicar who married them was their photographer, their two dogs were the only guests. A second marriage took place with Bud's family in South Carolina. Finally they returned to England, and the church where Bud had proposed. The wedding took place by candlelight, conducted by a vicar friend from Norfolk. Bud, who used to be a chef, did a psychology degree at Sussex University, trained to be a maths teacher, and is now teaching at a school near Brighton, where they live. Eugenie started the charity Spark+Mettle, but having set it up and seen it flying, she got to the point where there was not much left to do but keep it running smoothly. By extraordinary good luck she was invited to set up a much larger, well-endowed charity, the Goodall Foundation, which funds educational and character-development programmes in the UK and abroad. This entails a fair amount of travelling, which has taken her so far to Tanzania, the Gulf and India. It's the perfect job for an efficient organiser who has constant good ideas, and who loves travelling. They have two boys, an imagination-fuelled street funk dancer (aged seven) and a running, dancing, mischievous two year old.

I often regret that my parents never came here – indeed my father never saw Pullens End, either. He loved the country, would have wanted to spend a great deal of time here. My mother would have been polite, but impatient to get back to London or Oxford. She was not a natural countrywoman, so her enjoyment of Norfolk was surprising, though she was a strong swimmer, a fierce tennis player and a great dog lover. So long as she was with her dog she would happily walk very fast for a long way. I also much regret that they never saw the two youngest grandchildren, for she was an entertaining grandmother (my father was the imaginative one). She was devoted, noisy and energetic – a far better grandmother than she ever was a mother.

Once you have reached the age of retirement, even if you have no intention of giving up work, you can be aware of the past nudging your memory, often awkwardly. In the 1950s, Sandy Wilson wrote a musical called *Salad Days*. Rich in gentle advice and much merry dancing and singing, it was enormously popular and ran for a very long time.

'I'll remind you to remind me, we said we'd never look back' went one of its most famous songs. But of course part of the fun of old age is looking back, judging where you got things right and where you got it completely wrong.

I have written diaries for some fifty years but, strangely, have scarcely referred to them while writing this memoir. My recall of things in the distant past is pretty clear. I can remember whole conversations from the 1950s, and useless things such as the many clothes in my wardrobe, and on what occasions I wore them. I can remember reams of poetry, thanks to the teaching of the remarkable Miss Dillon-Weston in the 1950s, and am always surprised that contemporary children seem to know so little, and are not much interested in learning things by heart. As for books, remembering detail of plot is not my forte, but remembering how the characters felt, the mental pictures they produce, the colours they induce, is constantly with me.

My worry about writing this book has not been anything to do with the past, but how to convey the more than forty years of extraordinary happiness. Contentment, I learnt, is very hard to describe – unhappiness is much easier. And who, I thought, would be interested in reading about the myriad ordinary, probably dull things that are the ingredients of that happiness? I would never expect people to be fired by stories of my children and grandchildren, the warmth of routine, the occasional triumph of a soufflé, the laughter caused by jokes that don't have to be explained.

Each day feels wonderfully slow while it exists, but the moment it's over, it suddenly joins the other slow days that become time passing with terrifying speed. There is the pleasure of the view from my study window, the constant huge delight of coming home, the joy most evenings, as I'm cooking supper in the kitchen, when I hear the husband's twenty-year-old open-top Peugeot swooping into the courtyard and silently rejoice, knowing there are no plans for the evening.

It's hard to remind myself that, despite such bonuses, time is running out.

Appendix

In the years since leaving Oxford, I've been reflecting how old age has affected me, and come to the conclusion that I have become both fiercely critical and frequently disappointed. Both sensations stem (in my unimportant opinion) from the ubiquitous use of ill-chosen words, which seem constantly to multiply and irritate. (I bet no one said 'shouty' twenty years ago.) I decided to make some of them into a list. People like reading lists, and seem to enjoy agreeing or disagreeing. My intense feeling about these words is no doubt irrational, but doesn't seem to be fading. In its favour, I only have to mention a few of them and a clamour of differing opinions rises to join them.

I'm not going to add Nancy Mitford's list of words, which became so famous in the 1950s, to my own list of weird dislikes. They are still there, familiar, much used, but I see no point in repeating them. But as other people's horror words make for good entertainment and surprise, I thought I would end with a list of some of the words to which I and many others are most allergic. My sister recently confessed her most disliked word was 'sprinkles' – a word I confess I have never heard of used as a noun. She herself finds nothing wrong with poorly: ah, well, the thing is once someone is loyal to a particular word, for whatever reason, it's unlikely he or she is going to change.

MEAL

Other people's use of language accosts us all every day: for irrational reasons many of the words they choose either do not register, or give delight, and many of them cause a distinct shudder. What words should do, and I admit this is my own possibly unreasonable theory, is to produce a picture in the mind. I first came to this conclusion when I heard the constant use of MEAL as a child in the war. I used to take a bucket of mashed-up stuff, the so-called meal, to feed the chickens. That, to me, is the meaning of meal. It has not gone away and I hate it. Equally bad is *hot* MEAL, and when in a restaurant I'm told by a waiter to 'enjoy your meal', I find it difficult to be polite. If someone asks us 'to a meal sometime', I rarely accept until I've found out what the meal is: I want to know if it's breakfast, lunch, tea or dinner, so that I can picture it – and so that it can stamp out the mash in the bucket.

MOIST

This, according to a recent survey reported in *The Times*, is one of the most hated words in the English language. Questioning even a few people seems to confirm this theory. I'm with them absolutely, as it conjures up all sorts of unappealing images. I admit there is not a large choice of similar meaning words with which to swap it – 'clammy' comes to mind, not a happy choice either, but minimally less offensive. What is very strange about MOIST is that various nearby words – joist, hoist – are completely inoffensive.

POORLY
Squirm-making, prissy. Why not 'ill' or 'not well'?

PORTLY
Why not 'fat'? So much less scornful.

CARING
There's something horribly smug about this word, particularly when someone describes themselves as a 'caring person'.

WEALTHY
Why not 'rich' or 'well off'?

DAINTY
Beyond the pale, though admittedly almost extinct. To be fair, when describing an elaborately iced sponge cake in an ironic voice, dainty is probably the right word.

CORRIDOR
A long, darkish, ugly passage – much loved by hospital architects. The sort of place you wouldn't be surprised to find someone carrying a box of …

TABLETS
… which would be far less menacing if they were simply called pills.

EVERSO

I get the impression that this word, rampant in the 1950s and once loved by the elderly, is dying out. Great relief. 'Very' is so much better.

COUNTRYSIDE

Much used by people who live in towns, this came ubiquitously into being after the Countryside March. Before that, country was plain country. And people don't say 'I'm going to the countryside for the weekend.' Let's hope it will return without the '–side'.

HORSEBACK

The kind of back on which someone is riding should only be mentioned if it's *not* a horse – i.e. camel, elephant, donkey. And once you're mounted on a horse, there is no need to say so. 'I'm going horseback riding' is something no one who lives in the country, and rides, ever wants to hear. Of course it's on a horse you're going to ride.

TRAIN STATION

The kind of station should only be mentioned if it's *not* a train – i.e. bus – station.

STYLISH

The most appallingly overused word in the world of fashion. These days I'm overwhelmed with catalogues in the post, all claiming 100 per cent of the often hideous clothes are 'stylish'. Even distinguished fashion editors allow themselves this horrible word – so ubiquitous that all real meaning has long been drained from it. To wear something, or produce something with 'great style', on the other hand, is fine.

ON TREND

Another catalogue phrase also much overused by fashion journalists. People should remember that there are a great many people who are appalled by the idea of being on trend … It's not a compliment but a lazy insult.

LIFESTYLE

It's not just because it includes the word 'style', but because it's completely redundant, put together fairly recently perhaps to denote importance. People who talk about their lifestyle rather than their lives convey an irritating self-importance.

TASTY

Food writers' equivalent of STYLISH. Much overused and lacking in proper description. Presumably it means something tastes good, but it doesn't go on to say what the food tastes OF.

PLEASANT

A cold and cheerless word belonging to an elderly vocabulary. I've never heard anyone under twenty use it. 'Have a pleasant journey' isn't a warming wish, while 'a pleasant view' is only worthy of illustrations in cheap calendars.

PARTNERED WITH

His or her partner is all we need to know.

PURCHASED

Much less pedantic is, simply, 'bought'. 'I purchased a property' is pompous, dreadful. 'Property' is as surely the language of developers as 'Purchased'. We should know precisely what the property is – cottage, barn, castle, whatever.

PRICEY

One of the worst, along with its close relation 'costly'. Expensive is the word.

ROOMY

This gives no idea of *how* big, so is a pretty useless word, besides being ugly. How big is a big room? My big room may be your very small room, so it's an entirely pointless word among descriptions.

SHOUTY

This suddenly went viral very recently. It's strange that some people think if they add a 'y' to the end of a word it will become not only new but important. It won't. It's also a childish word. The grown-ups who use it sound ridiculous.

HANDY

Another of the lazy y-ending words: it's meant to convey usefulness, so why not say, simply, 'useful'.

POP

Visually horrible. 'I'm going to pop out to the shops.' Worse: 'We/they popped into bed.' I see the speakers being shot out of one of those children's small wooden guns that make an explosive noise. POP is not a pretty word.

GRAB

Closely related to POP, but sounds more nefarious – i.e. like a robbery. 'To grab a coffee' does not produce a calm picture of someone handing over £2.80 for a cappuccino.

CHAT

While some people love the whole idea of a chat, others abhor it. I am one of the latter. I want a talk, a conversation, a discussion or a meeting, but never a chat, which implies a squirm-making cosiness.

CONDIMENTS

Where did this prissy word come from? Salt and pepper are all that are needed.

FLORAL TRIBUTES

Floral *on its own* is of course fine. Paired with tributes it is not. And why not just say 'flowers'?

LOVED ONES

I know I'll be in trouble here, but I cannot bring myself to say these now ubiquitous words. 'People I/you love' is the best alternative.

LEAFY

This originally perfectly harmless word has been battered to death by all writers who ever describe the suburbs – LEAFY suburbs apparently exist everywhere and are very desirable. I see LEAFY budding even in the best-written newspapers and magazines. It's lazy as well as ubiquitous: I mean, on what kind of bushes or flowers does this leafiness grow? How should we picture it?

POO
This should be kept for small to medium-small children. It's deeply embarrassing when grown-ups, especially the old, say they want a poo. Or when it's used by doctors, nurses and others whose job it is to enquire about states of health. Possibly it's meant to put people at ease. I think it does the opposite.

PASSED AWAY
A horrible euphemism, presumably used to make death sound less harsh. Much better to go simply for 'died', or 'dead'. Death can't be softened.

GIFT
The word drifted over from America probably in the last war: both prissy and unevocative, reminding one of sterile 'gift shops'. When it's turned into a verb, it's the pits.

TODDLER
Nothing actually wrong with this word, but I just hate it. It's so easy to describe a child by its age. Toddler is patronising, like calling an old and unsteady man or woman a 'wobbler'.

GORGEOUS
One of the very worst of my hated words ... To think it was one of Shakespeare's original beautiful words ('the gorgeous palaces') and now, ubiquitous, it's ruined, utterly cheapened by

its use for everything from a pudding to a ball dress. Often pronounced 'gorguss', it comes very close to MOIST and MEAL …

MINE and YOURS
These are horrible additions to new words by the young, meaning 'my or your house, flat, place, or whatever'. Grim description, no picture of what it actually is, and can lead to disappointment.

PICTURE PERFECT
Another recently popular description, extremely lazy. What does it mean? Millions of pictures are far from perfect. Which picture does the writer have in mind – the *Mona Lisa*? A description of WHY something is perfect would be far more understandable, though I daresay that kind of analysis is too taxing.

PICTURESQUE
Another lazy way of trying to convey something good, but brings no picture to mind beyond sunsets on cheap calendars.

FLAVOUR/FLAVOURSOME
Nothing actually incorrect about either of these words: I just prefer 'taste'.

MUNCHING
This is another recent favourite of food journalists or anyone who writes about food. Millions of people apparently *munch*

everything from chocolates to trendy salads. Millions of crashing jaws come to mind. MUNCHING is the kind of word too many writers think is better than just 'eating'. I can't agree. It's too animal.

PORTION

A PORTION brings instantly to mind those employed by caterers who have been trained in silver service and skilfully hold a spoon above a fork the better to help diners to the food in the silver dishes ... The trouble with the word is that it's impossible to tell whether the PORTION which is to be served is small, medium or large. 'Slice', on the other hand, is very much easier to judge ('a small slice, please'), see, and calculate into your daily tally of food. Life would be simpler if PORTIONS were abandoned (an ugly word, anyhow) and 'slices' – or 'spoonfuls', when appropiate – took over.

COMMENCE

Very pompous way of saying 'start', much used by railway staff who have been trained to give out announcements, and who also use the curious 'train station' as much as possible. If we're passengers on a train, it's obvious the next station we're coming to is for trains, not buses ...

GOWN

A gown to me is either an academic's gown, a dressing gown or a surgeon's gown. Anyone who describes a dress as a GOWN brings up the gloomy picture of one of those long, elaborate, and over-decorated Victorian numbers. Can't think why so many fashion writers have abandoned the simple description 'dress'. Could be it's the same reason as 'pudding' has been replaced by 'dessert'? Whatever that is – faux grandeur, perhaps.

NIBBLES
A particularly horrible word, conjuring pictures of bits of food nibbled by mice.

PERSON
I can't keep a straight face when someone describes themselves as a PERSON – a 'caring person', a 'conscientious person', or some other kind of PERSON: if you're talking to someone then obviously they're a person if they are definitely not an animal ... PERSON seems to have reached the status of a boast. And apart from that, it's an unattractive word. I suggest it should be expunged completely ...